ANGEL MEDICINE

Also by Doreen Virtue, Ph.D.

BOOKS

THE CRYSTAL CHILDREN
ARCHANGELS & ASCENDED MASTERS
EARTH ANGELS
MESSAGES FROM YOUR ANGELS
ANGEL VISIONS II
EATING IN THE LIGHT (with Becky Prelitz, M.F.T., R.D.)
THE CARE AND FEEDING OF INDIGO CHILDREN
HEALING WITH THE FAIRIES
ANGEL VISIONS
DIVINE PRESCRIPTIONS
HEALING WITH THE ANGELS
"I'D CHANGE MY LIFE IF I HAD MORE TIME"
DIVINE GUIDANCE
CHAKRA CLEARING (available in tradepaper, and also as a hardcover book-with-CD)
ANGEL THERAPY
THE LIGHTWORKER'S WAY
CONSTANT CRAVING A–Z
CONSTANT CRAVING
THE YO-YO DIET SYNDROME
LOSING YOUR POUNDS OF PAIN

AUDIO/CD PROGRAMS

ANGEL MEDICINE: A Healing Meditation CD
ANGELS AMONG US (with Michael Toms)
MESSAGES FROM YOUR ANGELS (abridged audio book)
PAST-LIFE REGRESSION WITH THE ANGELS
DIVINE PRESCRIPTIONS
THE ROMANCE ANGELS
CONNECTING WITH YOUR ANGELS
MANIFESTING WITH THE ANGELS
KARMA RELEASING
HEALING YOUR APPETITE, HEALING YOUR LIFE
HEALING WITH THE ANGELS
DIVINE GUIDANCE
CHAKRA CLEARING

ORACLE CARDS (44 divination cards and guidebook)

HEALING WITH THE ANGELS ORACLE CARDS
HEALING WITH THE FAIRIES ORACLE CARDS
MESSAGES FROM YOUR ANGELS ORACLE CARDS (card deck and booklet)
MAGICAL MERMAIDS AND DOLPHINS ORACLE CARDS (card deck and booklet)
ARCHANGEL ORACLE CARDS (card deck and booklet)
GODDESS GUIDANCE ORACLE CARDS (card deck and booklet)
(available July 2004)

All of the above are available at your local
bookstore, or may be ordered by visiting:
Hay House USA: **www.hayhouse.com**
Hay House Australia: **www.hayhouse.com.au**
Hay House UK: **www.hayhouse.co.uk**
Hay House South Africa: **orders@psdprom.co.za**

Doreen's Website: **www.AngelTherapy.com**

AN GEL MEDICINE

HOW TO
HEAL THE
BODY AND
MIND WITH
THE HELP OF
THE ANGELS

DOREEN VIRTUE, PH.D.

HAY HOUSE, INC.
Carlsbad, California
London • Sydney • Johannesburg
Vancouver • Hong Kong

Copyright © 2004 by Doreen Virtue

Published and distributed in the United States by: Hay House, Inc., P.O. Box 5100, Carlsbad, CA 92018-5100 • *Phone:* (760) 431-7695 or (800) 654-5126 • *Fax:* (760) 431-6948 or (800) 650-5115 • www.hayhouse.com • *Published and distributed in Australia by:* Hay House Australia, Ltd., 18/36 Ralph St., Alexandria NSW 2015 • *Phone:* 612-9669-4299 • *Fax:* 612-9669-4144 • www.hayhouse.com.au • *Published and distributed in the United Kingdom by:* Hay House UK, Ltd. • Unit 62, Canalot Studios • 222 Kensal Rd., London W10 5BN • *Phone:* 44-20-8962-1230 • *Fax:* 44-20-8962-1239 • www.hayhouse.co.uk • *Published and distributed in the Republic of South Africa by:* Hay House SA (Pty), Ltd., P.O. Box 990, Witkoppen 2068 • *Phone/Fax:* 2711-7012233 • orders@psdprom.co.za • *Distributed in Canada by:* Raincoast • 9050 Shaughnessy St., Vancouver, B.C. V6P 6E5 • *Phone:* (604) 323-7100 • *Fax:* (604) 323-2600

Editorial supervision: Jill Kramer   *Design:* Tricia Breidenthal

The author of this book does not dispense medical advice or prescribe the use of any technique as a form of treatment for physical or medical problems without the advice of a physician, either directly or indirectly. The intent of the author is only to offer information of a general nature to help you in your quest for emotional and spiritual well-being. In the event you use any of the information in this book for yourself, which is your constitutional right, the author and the publisher assume no responsibility for your actions.

Library of Congress Cataloging-in-Publication Data

Virtue, Doreen.
  Angel medicine : how to heal the body and mind with the help of the angels / Doreen Virtue.
     p. cm.
Includes bibliographical references and index.
  ISBN 1-4019-0234-0 (hard) — ISBN 1-4019-0235-9 (pbk.)
  1. Spiritual healing. 2. Angels—Miscellanea. I. Title.
  BF1999.V585 2004
  615.8'528—dc22

                              2003021972

                    Hardcover ISBN 1-4019-0234-0
                   Tradepaper ISBN 1-4019-0235-9

                    07 06 05 04   4 3 2 1
                   1st printing, September 2004

                      Printed in Finland

Blessings and Gratitude to . . .

. . . Steven Farmer, George Kelaiditis, Charitini Christakou, Konstantinos, Dr. Polichronis ("Chronis") Mada, Andres Kannelopoulos, Reid Tracy, Jill Kramer, Julie Davison, Anne Yvonne Gilbert, Leon Nacson, Kristen McCarthy, Rachelle Charman, Rhett Nacson, Eli Nacson, Robert Nacson, James Van Praagh, Jo Lal, Michelle Pilley, Megan Slyfield, Emma Collins, Bill Christy, Judith Lukomski, Charles Schenk, Grant Schenk, Betsy Brown, Lynnette Brown—and to all of the people who allowed me to reprint their angel-medicine stories in this book.

CONTENTS

PART III: HEALING WITH ANGEL MEDICINE

INTRODUCTION

Angel Medicine

I write this while overlooking the *caldera*, the ocean-kissed volcanic crater of Santorini Island (also known as *Thera*), in Greece, as depicted in the photo on the back of this book. Santorini holds a special significance for me, for the topic of this book, and for you. The reason is that many people believe that Santorini is the remaining land mass of the lost continent of Atlantis. The ruins of one of the many Atlantean healing temples are here, along with all the mystical energies and traditions. What a perfect location to write about healing—a place where I lived eons ago . . . perhaps along with you.

When Atlantis sank in a fiery explosion, much of the advanced knowledge and wisdom of its people also disappeared. In the first part of this book, I'll discuss some of the ancient healing wisdom practiced by the magical Atlanteans and the secrets of healing imparted to me by the angels of Atlantis. In the second and third parts, I'll present stories and methods that you can incorporate into your own life to heal yourself and others. I've also included scientific studies that corroborate this ancient healing knowledge.

THE HEALING ANGELS

Angels are celestial beings with no egos, meaning that they're nonjudgmental and all-loving. Our deceased loved ones can perform angelic functions; however, we technically call them "spirit guides."

Speaking as a lifelong clairvoyant, I know that every person has at least two guardian angels and at least one spirit guide with them. It's obvious that not everyone listens to their angels, or we wouldn't have cruelty or self-destruction in the world. Nonetheless, the angels are there whenever we're ready to talk to and listen to them.

Angels are nondenominational and are as much a part of the lives of skeptics and atheists as they are of believers; they're with cruel people as well as Good Samaritans. Angels are with us to enact God's plan of peace, one person at a time. While we're all still personally responsible for our actions, the angels can help us choose the most effective plan of action.

And while we can grow through pain and struggle, we can grow even faster through peace. Anything that helps us be peaceful—no matter how large or small—is something that the angels are happy to assist us with. However, we've got to ask for their help before they're allowed to intervene because of the "Law of Free Will," through which this Universe operates.

When you work with angels, you can borrow or lean upon their light, as well as their ego-free higher selves. The angels can help you heal your mind-set so that you repel fear, and approach situations with love. Your angels have no time or space restrictions, so you need not worry that you're bothering or overtaxing them.

The word *angel* means "messenger of God." When you pray to the Creator, the angels are sent as message-carriers from the Creator to the created. It's not blasphemous to speak to angels, as any conversation with God results in the angels speaking to you. Angels, after all, are one with God—they're extensions of God. And so are you.

When we team up with the angels, healings occur at miraculous rates and in amazing ways. The angels can help us heal physically, spiritually, emotionally, financially, and intellectually. They assist us with our careers, health issues, love lives, families, homes, and anything else that's important to our peace of mind.

So whether you desire healing for yourself, for a loved one, or for a client, you'll be tapping in to a mighty channel of healing energy by enlisting the angels' assistance.

ABOUT THIS BOOK

This is a three-part book. If you enjoy reading true spiritual adventure stories, then begin with Part I. However, if you're more interested in reading solely about angel-medicine steps and related stories, then Part II is a stand-alone section that you can read first if you choose. Part III is a reference section with angelic healing methods that have been touched on in the first two parts of the book.

Part I of *Angel Medicine* is another chapter in my story of spiritual discovery and adventure, which began with my book *The Lightworker's Way* and continued with its sequel, *Healing with the Fairies*. However, it's not necessary to read those books in order to get what you need out of this one.

PART I

The Angels
of Atlantis
and the Secrets
of the Healing Temple

CHAPTER I

Journey to Atlantis

I never planned to go to Santorini, but after my travel itinerary was set by my Grecian publisher, as well as by my husband and traveling companion, Steven Farmer, I began to understand why the trip was necessary. As part of my European book tour, Steven set up a relaxing holiday for us at Santorini Island. Little did we know how intense the holiday would turn out to be.

From the moment our flight to Santorini was booked, the Universe gave me signs of confirmation. It seemed that every Southern California magazine or newspaper I opened had a travel piece about the island, and each one mentioned the connection between Santorini and Atlantis. The kicker happened one morning when I woke up earlier than normal and knew that I needed to call my friend James Van Praagh, the famous spiritual medium and author.

"This is amazing!" James exclaimed when I called him. "I also 'got' a message to call you this morning."

When we met for breakfast an hour later, I mentioned my forthcoming trip to Europe.

"Honey, there's one place that you absolutely *must* go," he said.

"Okay," I replied, open to hearing James's suggestion. After all, in addition to being a phenomenal and caring psychic, James is also an experienced world traveler.

"You have to go to Santorini Island. It's one of my very favorite places in the world!" he said with enthusiasm. He leaned forward, looked into my eyes, and whispered, "And you know that it's Atlantis."

I drank in his words and replied, "James, this is uncanny, because Steven and I are already booked to visit Santorini Island. A few weeks ago I'd never even heard of the place, and now the Universe is bombarding me with messages to go there. And so much research seems to point to Santorini being one of the locations of Atlantis. I'll send you an e-mail when I get there!"

SANTORINI ISLAND

As Steven and I descended onto the island in our tiny aircraft, I was reminded of the Daryl Hannah movie *Summer Lovers,* which was filmed on this tiny Greek island. The clear bright sky and ocean blended together like a giant blue screen, with hundreds of stark white stucco cottages dotting the foreground.

The 50-or-so passengers walked down the steps of the aircraft onto the tarmac and were greeted by hot, steamy air reflected from the smoldering runway. By the time we retrieved our bags, all the taxis had been taken. Since the airport was in a remote area, our only other transportation choice was a rental car. Our Suzuki Alto was so small that it reminded me of a motorcycle with a car covering, yet all of the island cars had the diminutive look of toy automobiles. Suzuki, Hyundai, Fiat, and Peugeot seemed to be the top brands for the compact cars.

The clerks at the car-rental agency told us that we'd find our hotel by looking for a tourist office on the right and then turning in to the first dirt parking lot on the left. With these not-very-specific directions, we drove to the town of Imerovigli. The dirt parking lot was easy enough to find, but where was our hotel? The wall facing the parking lot sported a dozen hotel names, including our own, but there were no arrows directing us. A pathway from the parking lot went in two directions, and we figured that our hotel was toward the end of the peninsula, so we carted our luggage and walked that way.

I soon discovered that my two-inch wedge heels and the thousands of stairs on the island didn't mix. I stopped, knelt down to open my luggage, and changed into a pair of flat sandals. I wore those sandals (and also running shoes) for the remainder of our holiday, despite my pre-trip fantasies of dressing in long, flowing Grecian gowns with heels.

It was hot and dusty, and we were tired after flying from Los Angeles—with stops to change aircraft in London and Athens. So, struggling with heavy suitcases on uneven steps and pathways wasn't our ideal beginning to a Grecian vacation. And we still weren't sure that we were going in the right direction!

Steven finally said, "Wait here with the luggage while I check to see if we're in the right place." He returned in five minutes with a smiling dark-haired man who silently grabbed all of our luggage and motioned for us to follow him. In answer to my puzzled expression, Steven explained that he'd found our hotel's office and that they were expecting us. This was the bellman, who, I suspected, wore a few different hats on the job. I thought this because he was like a four-wheel-drive vehicle that climbed up and down the stairs effortlessly, all the while carrying our heavy suitcases. We struggled to keep up as he led us through a maze of outdoor stairways, and finally to our hotel.

Our room was built into the side of a cliff, with a large rock about the size of a piano protruding into it. We were told that this was normal among cliffside hotels. The rock's energy was profoundly alive. As we settled into the room, it felt as if a third person was in the room with us. We were visiting the rock's room, and we were its guests.

Since water is trucked and pumped into Santorini Island, the bathrooms and showers are quite different from standard hotels. They basically consist of a corner of a bathroom and a drain. To take a shower, you first have to heat the water by pushing a button about 20 minutes before hopping in, in order to activate the solar-heating system. Then you pull back a curtain to separate the rest of the bathroom from the shower, and turn on a hand-held shower wand.

After showering and changing into walking clothes and shoes, Steven and I set out to explore the countryside. We paid close attention to the location of our hotel so that so we could identify it upon our return. At first glance, the hotels and villas on the island all looked very much alike.

The first thing we noticed was that Santorini Island was filled with wandering short-haired cats of all colors. The cats looked lean, as if subsisting on handouts from visiting tourists. They were quite friendly and affectionate, and had undoubtedly learned that rubbing against a tourist's legs was a sure way to be petted and fed. As we passed by the shops lining the street, we noticed several calendars for sale entitled "Cats of Santorini," featuring cute photographs of the cats sitting next to white villas and cottages.

REMEMBERING THE LIGHT

The time-zone change, the fresh air and sunshine, and the previous months of hard work all combined to make Steven and me feel quite tired. We'd been going nonstop and suddenly realized that we were exhausted. The first day in Santorini marked the beginning of a relaxing pattern of taking long, leisurely afternoon naps.

The first day, I awoke from my two-hour rest with visions of bright colors and lights in my mind. I was aware that I'd been visited by angels in my naptime dream, and that the angels had given me messages about the healing power of light and color. Although I couldn't remember what they'd said, I trusted that the information was stored safely in my unconscious mind.

That night we met with three men who'd been referred to us by our Grecian publisher: Janis Renieris, who owned the hotel where we were staying; Polichronis ("Chronis") Mada, a local holistic medical doctor; and Andres Kannelopoulos, who'd recently returned from several years of studying with an Indian avatar (an avatar is a living person who's learned how to perform and manifest miracles).

As we watched the rainbow-colored sunset, Janis told us a remarkable story about his son's healing: On June 9, 2002,

19-year-old Manolis had been deep-sea diving when his spear discharged and pierced his head. Now as a former seafarer himself, Janis had always felt protected by asking St. Nicholas for help. As a result, he was inspired to send this saint to watch over his children. So when Janis got the call about his son's diving accident, he prayed and then rushed to the hospital. His son was lucky to be alive, said the doctors.

"How did you ever manage to get out of the water?" Janis asked his son.

"I went to the light, Dad," replied Manolis from his hospital bed, "and St. Nicholas was with me the entire time."

The doctors said that Manolis would be blind and paralyzed for life, but Janis refused to see his son as "broken." He held a vision of Manolis as being whole and healthy, and within one year, Manolis was completely healed! His miraculous healing renewed the faith of everyone in his town, including Manolis's formerly skeptical classmates.

Chronis and Andres smiled as they listened to Janis's story, for they were already men of deep faith. Chronis functioned as Santorini island's chief medical doctor, virtually being on-call around-the-clock to treat ailing people in their home or at his office.

Chronis looked more like a male model than a medical doctor, with his sinewy figure and youthful face. He reminded me of a darker version of Mark McGrath, the lead singer of the band Sugar Ray. He talked about how he blended spirituality, natural methods, and medicine.

"Angels aren't far away in some distant Heaven," he said. "They're here on Earth, and their purpose is to help us manage our thoughts. These days, karma is instant, and our thoughts are manifested instantly. Whatever you give out comes back to you magnified ten times greater, instantly. It's the same with dark thoughts: They come back to you immediately. Previously, your karma would meet you in your next lifetime. Now it's in this life."

Chronis was a traditional M.D., but he'd started to feel that there must be more to healing than prescribing medications and ordering tests. He'd noticed that his ill patients were all shallow breathers, so he studied ways to help people learn to breathe deeply and fully as a path to wellness. This led to Chronis becoming a licensed chiropractor so that he could maneuver his patients' bodies to be more open to receiving oxygen.

Chronis also observed that people who drank a lot of water healed the fastest, so he began prescribing increased water intake to his patients. He then studied the chakras (energy wheels within the body that push along life-force energy) and became a Reiki master as well, which gave him a framework to do energy work with his patients.

He also noticed that his patients who harbored guilt became ill and stayed sick for longer periods than those with a clear conscience. "Guilt is killing us, angering us, and saddening us," Chronis said. "I tell my patients to either stop feeling guilty, or stop doing the behavior that *makes* them feel guilty in the first place." But the greatest healing agent that Chronis came upon was love. When he sent loving energy to his patients and also helped them focus on love, they always healed rapidly.

Chronis used a blend of the esoteric, holistic, and medical sciences in his healing work. As a result, his services were very much in demand, and our two meetings with him were wedged in between patient appointments.

Chronis's roommate, business associate, and longtime friend was Andres. He had an air of quiet, understated wisdom to him. Andres was the type of person who didn't talk much, but when he did, you were blown away by the profundity of his words.

As I mentioned, Andres had just returned from India, where he'd studied and lived with a renowned avatar and his devotees for seven years. It's been recorded that this avatar has manifested objects from thin air, has bilocated, has made his body disappear, and has levitated, among other feats (which include miracle healings). During his years with the avatar, Andres learned a great deal about the nature of healing.

"The avatar taught me that certain colors heal specific illnesses," said Andres. "You visualize these colors around the person you're healing—or yourself if you're in need of healing. You can also invoke the colors by requesting that they surround the person's body."

Andres told us that the avatar also taught him that:

- purple light can heal cancer and kill viruses;

- white light closes wounds in the physical and
  aural body;

- pale blue light cleanses and detoxifies the body like
  water; and

- golden light opens the third eye and keeps the body
  open (after it's been cleansed with purple, white,
  and pale blue light).

I remarked that these colors were so angelic. Purple light is associated with Archangel Michael, who carries away fear from our bodies and mind. White light is the essence of all angels. Pale blue is connected to Archangel Raguel, who brings harmony and faith to our lives. And golden light is associated with the Holy Spirit and Christ energy.

Andres's words about golden light opening the third eye reminded me of my readings of the original, unedited pages of *A Course in Miracles*. The term *spiritual sight* was used liberally in the original text, but was later replaced with *Holy Spirit* when books were edited for bookstore use. So, even the *Course* associated Holy Spirit (which is the golden light) with spiritual sight, or clairvoyance.

"It should come as no surprise to us that visualizing light can heal the body," said Andres. "After all, doesn't enlightenment mean that you're immersed in light?"

"I've learned that light plus love equals healing," Chronis added.

"Light plus love equals healing," I repeated, with a feeling of déjà vu from that day's naptime angel visitation. Chronis's phrase sounded eerily similar to the messages that the angels had related to me in my sleep.

Our evening with Chronis, Andres, and Janis wound down with discussions about life in general, and Steven and I slept especially well that night.

EXPLORING THE ISLAND

The next day, Steven and I woke to a glorious sunrise shimmering over the caldera bay. We decided to walk to a little neighborhood market that sold freshly baked bread, vine-ripened tomatoes, and kalamata olive spread. The morning hike up and down the hundreds of steps spread throughout Santorini Island helped us work up a sweat and an appetite.

Rita, the owner of the shop, greeted us with "Kalimera!" which we'd learn meant "Good morning" in Greek—except that people said "Kalimera" until sunset, so we figured the phrase had the dual meaning of "Good afternoon," too. And then, once the sun began setting, you'd say "Kalispera," or "Good evening." I also learned that "Thank you" in Greek, "Efharisto," sounded remarkably close to the phrase "a fairy store," so I'd say that to people and they'd smile pleasantly at me.

Rita was beautiful in a homespun way. Her graying hair was neatly spiraled in an upsweep, and her matronly figure was flattered by layered clothing. Her smile would melt butter, it was so warm and genuine.

Steven and I enjoyed making sandwiches consisting of still-warm-from-the-bakery bread, sliced tomatoes, and olive spread. Since all the ingredients had more flavor than we'd ever tasted, we never tired of these sandwiches during our trip. For dinner, I'd eat grilled Grecian mushrooms, called *plevrotus.* Similar to oyster mushrooms, they're basted and sautéed in balsamic vinegar, oil, and seasoning until well done. No matter which restaurant we frequented, the mushrooms always had the same flavor and texture, like grilled steak. And with all our stair-climbing, we didn't even gain weight from the olive oil.

In fact, we learned that the Mediterranean diet (vegetables, fruit, fish, and olive oil) is associated with longevity. A 1994 study published in the British medical journal *Lancet* found that those people with myocardial infarctions who switched to a Mediterranean diet reduced their coronary problems by 73 percent! In June of 2003, *The New England Journal of Medicine* published results of a study of more than 22,000 people who had been on a Mediterranean diet: Those who ate traditional Mediterranean food lived the longest. The study's authors concluded: "Greater adherence to the traditional Mediterranean diet is associated with a significant reduction in total mortality."

Many scientists believe that the alpha-linolenic acids in olives and olive oil are responsible for this heart-healthy effect. Alpha-linolenic acid helps regulate blood pressure, heart rate, and blood vessel dilation. No wonder then—even though so many Greeks seem to smoke cigarettes—that the life expectancy for Greek men is among the highest in the world—between 72 and 74.5 years of age.

Steven and I decided to walk off our Mediterranean breakfast and explore the area north of our villa by foot. As we turned onto the main trail, we were joined by a large dog with curly blonde fur. She sidled up next to us as if we'd known her for years. I began calling her Molly for some reason, and she responded to the name. We hiked to the end of the trail, where a beautiful church stood in a wooded area. A priest walked out of the church in dark robes, and our new friend began barking furiously at him. Since Molly hadn't made a sound up till then, Steven and I decided to take her cue and go back down the mountain.

Santorini is famous for its hundreds of little white adobe churches with bright blue enameled dome roofs. The churches reflect the sunlight brightly, and provide a stark contrast to the backdrop of ocean that's visible wherever you are on the island. Although only 10,000 people reside on Santorini, it has 250 churches of the Greek Orthodox faith. Many of the churches are so small that only ten or fewer people can fit inside them at one time. And some churches are built on nearly unreachable sides of cliffs.

What's going on here? Steven and I wondered. Villagers explained that sailors whose lives had been saved while at sea built churches in honor of their patron saints to repay them. They believed that if they built a church, it would please the saint in whose name the church was built. This saint would then continue to protect the sailor and his family.

Since marble was mined abundantly in Grecian mountains, most Santorini villas had marble exterior porches and landings. Even dilapidated shacks had exquisite marble outdoor entryways. Since we were accustomed to only seeing fine marble floors in the interiors of upscale buildings, Steven and I marveled at the liberal outdoor use of marble throughout the island.

Soon enough, we reached the perimeter of our hotel and bid Molly farewell. Fortunately, throughout our trip, we got to see (and feed) our new friend daily.

We returned to our villa as the sun reached its noon apex. The sunlight seemed different in Greece. It had a definite golden cast to it, coloring everything in a flattering candlelight-hued glow. Everyone's skin reflected the golden light on their tanned bodies.

CHAPTER 2

Inside the Healing Temple

The sunlight and the walk had made Steven and me very tired, and we happily fell asleep for our afternoon nap. I slept deeply, but was simultaneously aware of another visitation from the angels. This time I remembered them telling me about the healing power of the golden sunlight. *"Put your hands into the sunlight and absorb its light,"* they said. *"Then, place your hands upon your heart to energize and awaken your heart-chakra energy."*

When I awoke from the nap, I went outside on the porch and cupped my hands under the sunlight. I visualized the golden rays pouring into my hands, and I felt my hand tingle with new life. I then placed my warmed hands upon my heart and felt an ecstatic rush surge through me as my heart opened wide with blissful love.

That evening, just before sunset, Steven and I hiked to a small mountain called Skaros that jutted into the ocean. Skaros hooks to Santorini Island via a small peninsula trail. It seemed like the perfect place to watch the sunset. As we began walking down the trail, we passed several American tourists coming toward us. Red-faced, perspiring, and panting, they warned us that the hike to Skaros was an ordeal. Steven and I looked at each other, momentarily considered an alternative to the hike, and then went anyway. After all, our daily two-mile jogs had given us a fitness level to sustain a challenging hike. And the mountain was so pretty—dotted with beautiful wildflowers, long grass, and flat stones. We *had* to make the trek!

As we got closer, we realized that the mountain wasn't really a mound of dirt after all—it was an ancient fortress on a hill, overgrown with moss and covered with soil! Steven climbed closer to the structure: A double-Capricorn, he could walk surefootedly along the piles of rocks leading to the castle entrance, while I watched from my comfortable seat upon a smooth, flat stone.

I laid back, and the stone radiated heat from the day's sunshine, which felt wonderful in contrast to the cool evening air. As the sun descended toward the ocean's edge, Steven joined me. The orange, pink, and yellow sunset rays illuminated the castle and surrounding hillsides. At that moment, it was easy to believe that this magical setting had once been ancient Atlantis.

The earliest recorded references to Atlantis were in Plato's two dialogues: *Critias*, written in 370 B.C., and *Timaeus*, written in 360 B.C. Plato received his information about Atlantis from Critias the Younger, the grandson of a Greek ruler named Solon, who learned about Atlantis while visiting Egypt in 590 B.C.

Plato wrote in *Timaeus*:

> Now in this island of Atlantis there was a great and wonderful empire which had rule over the whole island and several others, and over parts of the continent, and, furthermore, the men of Atlantis had subjected the parts of Libya within the columns of Heracules as far as Egypt, and of Europe as far as Tyrrhenia. This vast power, gathered into one, endeavoured to subdue at a blow our country and yours and the whole of the region within the straits; and then, Solon, your country shone forth, in the excellence of her virtue and strength, among all mankind. She was pre-eminent in courage and military skill, and was the leader of the Hellenes. And when the rest fell off from her, being compelled to stand alone, after having undergone the very

extremity of danger, she defeated and triumphed over the invaders, and preserved from slavery those who were not yet subjugated, and generously liberated all the rest of us who dwell within the pillars.

But afterwards there occurred violent earthquakes and floods; and in a single day and night of misfortune all your war-like men in a body sank into the earth, and the island of Atlantis in like manner disappeared in the depths of the sea. For which reason the sea in those parts is impassable and impenetrable, because there is a shoal of mud in the way; and this was caused by the subsidence of the island.

And in *Critias,* Plato wrote:

Of the combatants on the one side, the city of Athens was reported to have been the leader and to have fought out the war; the combatants on the other side were commanded by the kings of Atlantis, which, as was saying, was *an island greater in extent than Libya and Asia,* and when afterwards *sunk by an earthquake,* became an impassable barrier of mud to voyagers sailing from hence to any part of the ocean. [Emphasis mine]

Plato's references to Athens and Libya placed Atlantis in the Mediterranean or Middle-Eastern regions. I had strong visions of a land mass extending from Greece, Turkey, and Italy to Egypt and Northern Africa. Could this be the area that now encompassed Santorini, Crete, and the other Greek islands? Could this, in fact, be Atlantis?

Atlantis's location was definitely controversial. Among scholars and spirituality students who accepted the premise of Atlantis's reality, the theories about its location were split among those who thought it was in Santorini; and those who placed it in Indonesia, Bimini (in the Bahamas), the Bermuda Triangle, the British Isles, and Mexico. There was evidence to support each theory, if one dissected the words of Plato; or modern mystics such as Edgar Cayce, Ruth Montgomery, and Dolores Cannon.

Plato's description of Atlantis certainly matched Santorini: "One kind of stone was white, another black, and a third red," which perfectly described the colors of the island's dirt and cliffs. Plato also described the island of Atlantis as a circular island with hot and cold natural springs, which again described Santorini to a T. Some people believe that the word *Atlantis* was derived from the Atlantic Ocean, but in truth, the name actually comes from Greek mythology. Poseidon gave the island to his son, Atlas, and named it after him. *This is one more connection that Greece had with Atlantis,* I thought, as I sat on my sun-warmed stone.

REMEMBERING ATLANTIS

Through past-life regressions and spontaneous memories, many of us have recalled Atlantis as a very advanced society—one in which modes of transportation, lighting, and healing operated from the power of focused thought amplified by crystals. Atlantean healers worked with the energies and cycles of nature—coupled with positive expectations and partnership with angels and other Divine beings—to effect miraculous results.

"This is a perfect time for a past-life regression," I said to Steven.

"You're right, it is!" he agreed. As a psychotherapist and meta-physician, Steven is experienced in regressing people to their prior lifetimes. Ever since landing in Santorini, I'd been itching to recall my Atlantean past life in greater detail. I knew that a regression would bypass my conscious mind and excavate ancient memories.

As Steven counted me down into a hypnotic state, I held the intention of returning to Atlantis to recover information about physical healing. Intentions we hold at the outset of hypnosis are like a road map helping the unconscious choose among the millions of memories it stores. Because of my deep trust for Steven, I easily went into a heavy state of relaxation.

I saw my long, dark brown hair and my thin young arms and hands. I was one of several female attendants at the healing temple. All of us knew, with certainty, that perfect faith was the key to all healing.

We women sang prayerful chants to keep from being demoralized or distracted. And I began singing a foreign language in a sweet melodic voice that wasn't my own.

Two male high-priests often demoralized and distracted us female workers from our healing efforts. The men were loud and had harsh energy. Their coarse ways dissipated the sacred atmosphere of the healing temple. Our songs kept us centered and helped patients stay calm and relaxed.

The healing temple had a clear, crystal pyramid in its center, about two to three feet high, with a holographic image of a large, all-seeing blue eye projected in its center. The eye and pyramid collected and magnified sunlight that streamed down through a round hole in the ceiling above the pyramid.

We workers poured olive oil on our hands and then held our hands to the light. This effectively cleared our hand chakras. Bread, water, olives, apples, and other fruit were on an altar near the pyramid, where they'd absorb the light. Consuming these items helped patients ingest light.

Steven asked my name, and I replied without hesitation: *Domya* (although I'm unsure of its spelling). Steven asked where the pyramid and eye originated from, and I instantly said, *"From Hermes."* Although I had some limited knowledge of Hermes, I had no idea until I conducted research later that Hermes is closely associated with both Greece and Atlantis. Some writers say that Hermes is one and the same as the Egyptian god, Thoth, the inventor of writing and an important figure in alchemy.

I'd written about Thoth in my book *Archangels & Ascended Masters,* and I vowed to do some digging on the connection between Hermes and Thoth when I returned to my home office. But these were thoughts that I had after the regression. During the session, I was Domya, and I was fully present at the time of Atlantis, helping patients at the healing temple.

Our patients climbed into a bed made of quartz crystal that was shaped in a concave, shallow U shape. Seven of us female workers would take turns holding a large crystal point above the patients' chakras. Each worker was responsible for sending the color correlated with that chakra, so we'd concentrate upon that solo color. When we were done saturating the patient with the chakra color, the next worker would begin working on the chakra above it. We'd start at the root chakra and work upward. I was frequently assigned to work on the heart chakra, the throat chakra, and the third eye. My favorite was the heart chakra, because in addition to its main focal color of green, I'd see so much pink intermingled and swirling among the green—like a beautiful rose with leaves.

A buzzing, whirling sound came out of the main crystal pyramid, like a generator sending sparks through the crystal points we held above the patients' chakras. I'm not quite sure how the sparks leapt to our crystals, but it was all orchestrated perfectly.

Our patients spent quite a bit of their time with us strolling through the gardens, napping in the sunshine on long chairs, breathing fresh air, and mostly getting away from the cares and concerns of the world. Our healing temple was a safe haven, one that all armies respected as a cocoon for the gods and goddesses. Its very location stood at the base of a mighty mountain that seemed like a guardian overseeing and protecting us. The mountain cast afternoon shadows upon the temple before we were prepared to accept the oncoming darkness.

Most of our healing work occurred during the daylight hours. It was only during the times of the full moon that we all descended into the darkness. On full-moon evenings, we female workers would stand in a circle mimicking the moon's roundness. We'd count our blessings silently, capture the moon's energy within our circle collectively, and afterward, say kind and supportive words to one another. I suppose you could call it our support group. It certainly recharged our batteries, and I always noticed that the days following full moons were our best days of all in terms of patient care. The crystals seemed alive and charged with full properties. I couldn't help but wonder if our recharged batteries did most of this extra-effective work.

We workers slept in a separate building slightly up the hill from the temple. We all shared one large room that had several beds and a common closet area. Since we all wore the same sheath garments, no one cared whose clothing belonged to whom. We operated in a cooperative manner most of the time, with only the occasional crankiness causing friction among us.

The men were our chief source of irritation. The two priests dressed in dark robes, and they seemed to have too much time on their hands. Out of boredom, perhaps, the men made distracting bodily noises without seeming to feel shame or guilt at all! The two men would talk much too loudly, and they strutted about like they were guards overseeing us. Of course, they did pitch in whenever a heavyset patient needed boosting onto the crystal bed or needed to be carried somewhere. At those moments, I forgave the men for their previous irritations.

I loved going to the gardens with the patients, and I'd often volunteer for this task. I'd hold the hand of the patient, and we'd sit in silence, absorbing the bird songs, flower fragrances, and sunlight rays playing through the tree leaves.

Our patients progressed into wellness if they were motivated to become well again. Occasionally, a patient would relapse into dark despair, and it was always clear that the patients who expired were the ones who had given up on living. They were tired and wanted an excuse to go Home, to put it bluntly. But it was clear to me! I could always tell who was "giving up the ghost." Their gray complexions spoke of a lifeless attitude that soon resulted in a lifeless body. I always thought that it was the patients' right to decide if living was what they wanted, so I never tried to persuade anyone to live who was ready to leave.

I reluctantly left Atlantis as the night air chilled my body, drawing me out of my hypnotic trance. "Your face has changed," Steven remarked as I stretched to stand up. Apparently I'd shape-shifted during the regression since I'd so deeply taken on my previous persona.

On the walk back to our villa, I felt like I was floating. As soon as we entered our room, I began writing down my recollections of the regression. Since Steven had interviewed me during the hypnotic session and I'd answered his questions, he clued me in on details that I didn't consciously remember.

THE ANGELS OF ATLANTIS

That evening, Atlantis haunted my thoughts with recollections of the healing wisdom I'd possessed during that time. It was an everyday wisdom that most people of Atlantis—especially those of us who were healers—knew as facts of life. I remembered knowing the following:

The health of the human body reflects the human's outlook—which we call the soul or personality. The spirit is always bright, but the soul can get weighed down with cares and worries. It is then less able to reflect the Divine light, so it appears darkened, like a dusty lightbulb. Invoking the angels means calling upon the light. The angels' light magnifies our own, which helps us get back on course, much like a driving instructor temporarily takes over the wheel until we can make our own steering corrections.

On Atlantis, the healing temples had crystal points that faced in the direction of the person receiving the healing. Various colored crystals were used for each type of situation, and clear quartz crystal directed sunlight prisms for general healing. This same type of energy is encapsulated in Reiki healing today, which has rainbow-colored energy associated with it. One can also think of sending or receiving a shower of a certain color of light, which will generate the same effect.

Low energy and hopelessness can lead to illness and injury, and the cure is to cleanse the dark attitude and low energy with an infusion of cleansing light. Calling upon angels to enter your body and flush out low energy is akin to calling upon chimney sweeps to clean away ashes, or a plumber to flush away blocks. Focusing on love brings light into our consciousness. And when our consciousness is lit, our body follows suit.

The next day I still reeled from the past-life regression. Although I was no longer in a hypnotic trance, the memories continued to flood my mind. It was as if I'd opened the vaults of an ancient memory bank. The angels, particularly Archangel Michael, talked to me during my nap that day about recapturing the healing ideals of Atlantis. *Of course!* I realized, *Michael was there during the time of Atlantis!* Michael and the other angels of Atlantis talked to me emphatically about light and its role in mental and physical health. Their words made me focus more than normal upon light.

I'd noticed that in areas of the world with a lot of strong sunlight, people dressed in bright colors. In colder climates (and also in the fall and winter), people usually dressed in dark, muted colors. When Steven and I vacationed in sunny locales, we tended to dress in brighter colors than when taking a holiday in the north. The implication was clear: Sunshine sparked sunny dispositions and bright moods, which was reflected in the clothing we chose to wear.

I was concerned: *Were we out of touch with natural light?* My question triggered a memory of a time when all worship and spiritual ceremony was held outdoors. We would dance, sing, and pray while surrounded by greenery, fresh breezes, and all types of weather. We were oblivious to the rain or heat, since we accepted nature's changing temperaments as part of the holy design. When the ground was muddy, we'd go barefoot. And when the ground was steaming hot on summer days, we'd stand on newly cut greenery. There was never any thought about sheltering or shielding ourselves from the environment.

The introduction of formal religion changed all that. Our old ways were labeled "pagan," and anything remotely resembling paganism was strictly forbidden. Campaigns were waged to convince people that paganism meant worshiping the devil in order to discourage its practice. Worship became formalized and fear- and guilt-based, and was moved into cold, damp buildings with small windows that blocked out most light.

That night, Steven and I joined hundreds of Santorini residents and visitors outside as we all enjoyed the sunset. This nightly ritual was a testament to the Greeks' appreciation of the splendorous colors washing across the sky. The sunsets on Santorini had to be among the most colorful in the world.

As we watched the sun dip into the ocean's horizon; and the clouds burst into fiery oranges, pinks, and reds, the angels told me: *"Colorful sunsets evoke feelings of beauty. The colors in the sunset, especially orange, correlate with the second sacral chakra, and they set the body into motion for a good night's sleep. Watching sunsets is vital, because the colors clear out the day's residue in the second sacral chakra so that the body can sleep soundly."*

That makes so much sense! I thought. When we humans stay indoors and miss the sunset, our chakras remain clogged with the day's accumulated energy. Using artificial lighting, we attempt to keep the daylight hours going well past the sunset hour. Insomnia can result from missing sunsets, leading us to turn to other sleep aids, such as medications or alcohol.

The angels told me that the invention of the lightbulb marked the onset of new diseases in the human race. Artificial lighting spurred us to extend our waking hours, as we tried to create an endless period of daylight. Lightbulbs allowed us to bypass our natural circadian rhythms of waking and sleeping with the sunrise and sunset.

The problem of staying indoors under artificial lighting was also compounded by sun and moonlight being filtered through glass windows. The angels said, *"Being outside beneath the rays of the sun, stars, and moonlight is infinitely different from staring at them through a filtered lens. Your mind and body absorb the light's pure essence and full spectrum only when you experience them directly."*

MY PRIOR LIFETIME AND EXPERIENCES WITH MOONLIGHT

The angels' words about the moonlight triggered the memory of the past-life regression with Dolores Cannon that I'd had about a year before. (Dolores is the author of numerous books on past-life regression, including *Conversations with Nostradamus* and *Keepers of the Garden*. She does historical research through her past-life regressions, and I was fortunate to have gone through a session with her, which I'll recount below.)

After Dolores counted me down into a hypnotic trance, I found myself in ancient Babylon . . .

I was a male astronomer/priest—one of many. Our temple was on a high hill, and most of our time was spent tracking the stars' movements.

Nightly, we made marks on a tablet indicating the stars' positions, relative to the pillars that formed the front of the temple. The pillars functioned like vertical lines on a graph, allowing us to record which constellations were positioned next to each pillar. The temple had no roof, just a large triangular shape connecting the tops of all the pillars in the temple's front. The main reason we recorded star movement was to tell village farmers when to till, sew, and harvest their crops.

During the day, I'd function in my priest role, visiting families and offering spiritual counseling and conversation. I wasn't evangelical or judgmental—I was more like a spiritually minded uncle who would drop in for supper and uplifting conversation with the townsfolk. I was well liked and respected, and fairly happy in my life.

I was also clairvoyant, as were all of the astronomer/priests. We used a powdery topical substance to boost our clairvoyance, which we rubbed on our third eye, and also rubbed on our patients as a healing balm. The substance consisted of slate stone ground into a powder, mixed with mercury, and infused with moonlight. The powder-and-mercury mixture was a gift given to our chief teacher from an unknown source.

Our teacher would go off into the secluded woods and glens and would be given the substance. We all suspected that the mixture had an extraterrestrial origin, and I believed that it was from the Pleiades. We were taught to take the substance and charge it up on the evening prior to the full moon. This was the night when the moon would act like a mother's breast and give the milk of her magical healing energy to whomever or whatever her light would touch. This was a night when magical manifestations could also occur.

Our temple had statues of goddesses in each corner. I called one of the statues the goddess Diana. A round carving with the face of our political leader was on the triangle on the front of our building, above the pillars. Stairs led down to the side of the mountain and into the village.

I was confronted one day for teaching farmers how to read and write, and warned not to do so again. Toward the end of my life, the villagers began rioting in protest of the class divisions. In an illogical act of self-destruction, they began setting their own village on fire. I tried to stop the rioting, but things were too out of control for anyone to intervene single-handedly. A few weeks later, two soldiers stopped me in the street because I'd continued to teach the townsfolk how to read. The young, brash soldiers took justice into their own hands and killed me. I died in the street.

The regression had a profound impact on me, since it opened my eyes to the healing power of moonlight. The day after the regression, I began researching Babylon, since I hadn't known much about it before. Imagine my surprise when I learned that Babylon was considered the place where astronomy was first introduced, and that the astronomers had also been priests! I read about our mapping of the stars, and even saw photographs of the tablets on which we drew the location of constellations, using shorthand symbols to identify each star cluster.

During the regression, Dolores had somehow managed to get me to draw the symbols of the tablets while I was still under hypnotic trance. The symbols I'd drawn were identical to the archaeological photographs depicting ancient Babylonian astronomy figures!

Later, while researching my book *Archangels & Ascended Masters,* I came upon some startling material about Babylon. It turned out that the Babylonians worked with Archangel Haniel to create a healing substance called "astral light," which sounded miraculously similar to the powdery mixture I'd recalled in my regression.

After reading this information back then, I decided to create a similar substance. Since mercury was considered dangerously toxic, I concentrated on the powder and the nearly full moon. After praying for guidance from Archangel Haniel, I chose to grind up clear quartz crystal and mix it with ground slate stone, since, in the regression, the base of the powder had been slate stone. The powder of my regression was shimmery and sparkly, probably from the mercury. I thought that I could attain the same properties from clear quartz crystal.

After grinding the powder into a fine substance, I placed it into a silver bowl that had an airtight sealable lid. I then set the open bowl with the powder on my balcony in Southern California, on the evening of the night prior to the full moon. I looked at the moonlight and saw the bluish white light covering me and everything around me. I pointed the bowl to face the moon directly, and throughout the evening I moved the bowl to access the maximum amount of moonlight.

I decided to take the substance to an upcoming reunion meeting of certified Angel Therapy Practitioners—people who had taken my six-day psychic-development course. Without offering too many details about the ingredients of the substance to my former students, I rubbed the substance on the third-eye area of willing participants. I also rubbed it onto any areas of their bodies where they were experiencing pain (but no open wounds).

I then asked the volunteers to give me their honest feedback about the substance. Nearly everyone found that their clairvoyant abilities were boosted and that their pain was alleviated. The mixture seemed to retain its power without needing a recharge, since I kept the container with its closed lid on my altar. It seemed self-charging and self-regenerating, once it had been initially charged and boosted by the nearly full moon. Of course, I believe that the substance would be charged even more if it were again placed outdoors to receive this degree of moonlight.

The moon is very powerful, and for centuries, civilizations have created ceremonies in celebration of its cycles. Most spiritual traditions consider the time of the full moon one in which to release old patterns and negativity, and the new moon (no moon) as the time to manifest and reap the harvest.

Although scientific studies are inconsistent about whether full moons really do create lunacy in terms of increased crime and accidents, we do know that the moon definitely affects our bodies. This makes perfect sense, given that the moon regulates ocean tides, and our bodies are mostly water.

In January 1986, the prestigious *New England Journal of Medicine* reported a study that stated that a significant number of women had their menstrual periods during the new moon, while a lesser percentage had theirs during the full moon. Researchers concluded that there was a significant relationship between menstrual and lunar cycles.

CHAPTER 3

A Link with the Past

On Tuesday of our Santorini holiday, we decided to visit the town of Akrotiri. Dr. Chronis had told us about excavations of ancient ruins there that many believed were part of Atlantis.

I laughed as I watched Steven back our tiny rental out of the parking lot—he looked like he was driving a toy car! For some reason, the island seemed to have a disproportionate number of large trucks that sped through the town straddling both of the narrow lanes. Our car shuddered as trucks skimmed by, and more than once, Steven had to pull to the side of the road to avoid being plowed over.

On the way to Akrotiri, we stopped in the island's main town of Fira. Many people spoke perfect English there. This was probably because the huge cruise ships were moored nearby, allowing tourists to disembark, shop, and eat. We parked in a small dirt lot and walked through Fira's shopping area to purchase an electrical converter for our laptop computers. As we walked past a restaurant called "Mama's," a large matronly woman in an apron called to us in a booming voice: "Yoo-hoo, babies! Are you hungry? Mama's here!"

As Steven and I politely assured "Mama" that we'd already eaten, she lovingly argued, "Are you sure? You've never eaten food like mine!"

Once out of Mama's sight, we giggled at her exaggerated appearance and voice. We found many people enthusiastically announcing their wares to us and other obvious tourists. "You'll break my heart if you don't stop and look at my jewelry!" a shop owner said to me. "Come inside, classy couple," another shop-keeper pleaded. From the looks of things, business was brisk at most shops. The owners seemed to genuinely enjoy being bark-ers, calling more people inside their shops. We found everyone on the island to be as warm as the weather.

After buying our electrical convertors, we walked past Mama's and hoped that she wouldn't notice us. Fortunately, she didn't! We climbed into our little car and drove through the thick traffic of Fira.

I held the road map as we drove into the countryside. Even though there was only one main road on the island, we would eventually turn onto another street to reach Akrotiri. The middle of the island was oasis-like, with green fields flanked by the blue ocean and azure sky. Remnants of ancient ruins stood silhouet-ted against the sea. As we got closer to Akrotiri, I noticed that the seaside ruins sported carvings of dolphins, mermaids, and mermen.

I'd written about "merpeople" in my book *Healing with the Fairies*, and had recently completed a deck of oracle cards about mermaids and dolphins. My research had revealed that ancient civilizations worldwide had mermaid statues, going back to the time of Babylon. With so many cultures acknowledging this image, some basis in reality was undoubtedly present in the "merperson" archetype.

I recalled the clairvoyant vision I'd had while writing *Healing with the Fairies*. It showed me that mermaids and mermen actu-ally existed at one time and then consciously chose extinction to avoid the pain and suffering imposed on them by cruel mariners. And a mystic had once told me of a vision in which the people of Atlantis had become mermen and mermaids who swam from the land to avoid destruction. The mystic said that the merpeople had become the dolphins of today.

I thought of all the words that contained "mer," such as *mer-chandise, summer, mesmerized, astronomer, shimmer,* and *mer-cury*. I also realized that the surnames of my husband and editor

(Farmer and Kramer, respectively) and the names of the deities, Merlin and Mercury, contained the "mer" suffix. Then I noticed an ancient world map that named the oceans as "Mara."

A search of world language dictionaries showed some interesting root meanings of "mer" and its derivatives "mar," "mara," and "mir." The word for *ocean* and *mother* are related in French ("mère" and "mer"); German ("mutter" and "meer"); Italian ("madre" and "mare"); and Spanish ("madre" and "mar").

The link between *sea* and *mother* seems to be one more reference to our ancient roots to the ocean. Are the merpeople our ancestors? Did we emerge from the depths of the sea after the sinking of Atlantis?

Journey to an Ancient City

We found Akrotiri after only one wrong turn, and pulled our little car up next to two large tourist buses filled with cruise-ship passengers. The excavation site was completely covered with plastic, giving it the appearance of a giant greenhouse.

As Steven and I entered the site, we both began to weep. As I looked at him, I knew that my husband was feeling the same sense of homecoming. Our sentimental feelings were coupled with fond memories of a city now in ruins. It was like visiting your hometown and finding it destroyed, and remembering the joy of that life and the pain of its destruction. Still, a sense of inner wisdom assured us that the end of this civilization had occurred in a peaceful and loving way.

The city was completely intact, although definitely aged by being buried beneath volcanic ash for thousands of years. Archaeologists estimated that the volcanic explosion that sank much of the island occurred around 1625 B.C. The inhabitants of the city knew that destruction was imminent, as not one skeleton was found in the excavation. In addition, fragile items were found, deliberately placed beneath the protective wooden beds. All valuables were missing, although paintings indicated that the women wore elaborate jewelry. The people knew that there was little time left, so they packed up their valuables and fled the city.

Then the volcano exploded, taking most of Santorini with it and creating the caldera crater in the harbor. The volcano exceeded Krakatoa in its impact—in fact, tree rings as far away as Ireland and California showed evidence of a dramatic climate change at the time of this volcanic explosion, indicating that it impacted a great deal of the world.

For 300 years following the earthquake, Santorini was uninhabited. It wasn't until the 1960s that excavation began at the site. The almost perfectly intact city lay 12 feet beneath grape fields, covered and preserved by volcanic ash. At the point when we visited them, archaeologists had only uncovered 3 percent of the entire city.

As we walked along the city street, I felt the surreal sensation of being aware of two moments in time: one was present-day, and the other was when the village was populated. As I walked in a trance, I melded into the town's yesteryears, seeing and feeling it as if it were alive in its heyday.

> *The whole community is filled with swooping angels and goddesses who live side by side with the population. Clear quartz crystal points and lapis lazuli are encrusted everywhere, and the powerful energy of these crystals is palpable. The entire place is imbued with prayer, laughter, and joyful energy—there's such a clear, light, yet powerful energy here. The power of gentleness is well known.*
>
> *Violet lilies and grapevines grow everywhere. People are constantly celebrating and also feasting upon fish, grains, raisins, and honey. There's so much harmony and cooperation here—a peaceful bliss, with everyone caring for one another. We all enjoy basking in the infinite sunshine, and we're very happy. And so many angels here!*

I placed my hand on the cornerstone of a building and felt a current of electricity surge through my body. Was this Atlantis, as everyone was saying? Historically, the volcanic explosion occurred too recently, according to Plato's dialogues. Unless—as some scholars estimate—Plato or his translators had made an error in dates. In *Timaeus* and *Critias,* Plato discussed the end of Atlantis 9,000 years earlier. Yet, if he actually meant *900* years instead, then the time would correlate with Santorini's destruction. Many scholars believed that the Greek ruler Solon, who learned about Atlantis during a trip to Egypt, may have misread the Egyptian symbol for 900 as being 9,000. And since Plato heard Solon's findings secondhand (through his grandson, Critias the Younger), it was easy to imagine the finer details being changed in the retelling of the story.

The excavation, as with the entire island, was composed of red, black, and white stone, as Plato had described. I also noted a stone structure of a bullhorn, and an excavation worker explained that the bull was the sacred animal of the civilization. So, bullhorns were carved on the top of palaces. And Plato had written about the presence of bulls in Atlantis.

There wasn't evidence of buildings of pure crystal as some have speculated, and I didn't see landing pads for flying vehicles. However, I certainly did feel the presence of crystals everywhere. If this wasn't Atlantis, it certainly held a strong connection. And its energy triggered floods of past-life memories of my time there, as well as a more open channel of Divine communication with the angels of Atlantis.

CHAPTER 4

Crystals and Olive Oil

The following day, Steven and I visited the Fira Prehistoric Museum, which displayed the paintings and objects recovered from the Akrotiri excavation site.

Elaborate paintings depicted goddesslike women wearing makeup, and elaborate gold and silver jewelry. As mentioned earlier, no valuables or human remains were found at the excavation site, indicating that the citizens knew of an impending disaster and packed up and left in an orderly fashion. Only very intuitive people could foresee such a volcanic eruption—one more indicator of the Atlantean connection, since Atlantis has always been held as an ideal model of a population with highly developed psychic abilities.

Many of the paintings found on the inner walls of the ruins of Akrotiri corroborated both my visions, and also Plato's descriptions of Atlantis. The paintings showed that the area had been overgrown with lush tropical flowers and plants. Other paintings showed a fleet of ships, with a background mirroring the concentric rings in the cliffs that Plato described.

Most remarkable, though, was a display of crystal beads found at the site. The round beads were polished with a hole for string, just like modern jewelry. And the crystals were the same ones that I felt were there: clear quartz and lapis lazuli. Both crystals are associated with increasing psychic and healing abilities. In addition, amethyst and orange carnelian crystal beads were displayed.

Today, quartz crystal is mined worldwide, and lapis lazuli is prevalent in the Mediterranean. These were the two stones I saw psychically encrusted everywhere in the Akrotiri excavation site. However, amethyst and carnelian aren't currently native to Greece: Amethyst was found in North America, the United Kingdom, South America, India, Russia, and Africa, while carnelian was mined in India, Eastern Europe, Peru, the United Kingdom, and Iceland. How did amethyst and carnelian beads get to Santorini so long ago? Were they imported by boat, or did the land mass extend from mainland Greece to Egypt, allowing travel by foot? Or were they brought from another area of Atlantis?

The round crystal beads were identical to those worn on modern "power bracelets," those consisting of crystal beads strung on elastic. As we stared at the crystals, Steven and I felt a huge presence behind us. We both turned, but no one was visible. However, I certainly felt and heard the presence say, *"Those who wear crystals today are the Atlanteans. It is the sign among yourselves that identifies you to one another."*

That evening we drove to the town of Oia to meet Dr. Chronis and Andres for an after-sunset dinner. Oia had much newer and more plush villas and shops than the other towns of Santorini. It was situated on a point, making it a perfect location for sunset viewing. In fact, all activity in Oia ceased while everyone gathered at the point to witness the intense colors of the sunset's rays. I thought of the angels' message about the importance of watching the sunset to activate the chakras for nighttime and sleep. It was certainly soothing to watch the sun dip into the ocean, leaving the fiery sky, which blended into twilight colors.

When the last trail of orange had been exchanged for deep blue, Steven and I walked to the Oia Café. Like most restaurants on the island, the majority of the café's dining tables were outside on the patio.

Chronis and Andres arrived at the café just as we sat down. After exchanging warm hugs and greetings, they described a patient they'd just seen during a house call. House calls were common for the doctors' practice, depending upon the patient's mobility and the availability of transportation. If a patient couldn't get to their office, Chronis and Andres would visit him or her.

"How do you clear yourself after seeing a patient?" I asked.

"I wash my hands with olive oil," Chronis immediately replied. I gasped to hear him mention a practice that I'd seen in my past-life regression the previous evening. I'd never heard of using olive oil for anything but cooking. And now a medical doctor was describing its usage in exactly the manner I'd seen the other healers and myself use it in the Atlantean healing temple! I remembered the scientific study that associated olive-oil consumption with longevity. Olive oil seems to have magical properties, and perhaps that's one reason why olive branches are associated with peace.

SUNSETS AND SUNSHINE

We enthusiastically described our sunset viewing, and although Chronis and Andres had witnessed thousands of similar sunsets, they happily drank in our words vicariously. It was obvious that Santorinians didn't tire of appreciating nature's wonders.

"The sunlight is not only soothing, but it's also very important for physical and spiritual health," said Andres. "Remember how I told you that golden light opens the third eye? Well, you can invoke the golden light by meditating upon the sunlight, either with visual memory or by sitting in it directly."

I was beginning to accept that my angel messages were being spoken to me during my waking hours so that I'd really pay attention to them. Why else would Andres say the very words that the angels of Atlantis had taught me about cupping the golden light and then placing my hands upon my heart?

I recalled the healing temple of Atlantis that I'd experienced in my regression, where a round hole located above the crystal pyramid directed golden sunlight into the pyramid. The sunlight was amplified by the crystal itself, and the prayerful thought

CHAPTER 5

On To Athens

Too soon, our Santorini holiday was over, and it was time for us to fly to Athens to meet with my Grecian publishers and present my workshop.

As we drove to the beachside Athens hotel, I noticed red spray-painted messages on the highway walls that read, "Killers, go home!" I asked the driver who the message was referring to, and he answered solemnly, "Americans." I gulped. The Iraq war had just begun, despite worldwide protests. In our travels, we'd been asked frequently why the American people "allowed" President Bush to start the war. They didn't realize how many Americans had joined with other countries to protest it. I mentally prayed that the Greek people were forgiving and nonjudgmental toward Americans.

George Kelaiditis and Charitini (pronounced *Har-i-tini*) Christakou, our publishers in Greece, met us in the hotel lobby. (While Hay House was our publisher for English-speaking countries, in other countries, foreign publishers obtained rights and produced the translated books.) Within five minutes, I realized that George and Charitini were both interested in New Age topics—something that's not always the case with publishers. Charitini had been an attorney, and her partner, George, was an engineer. Tired of their mainstream professions, they decided to publish the channeled *Kryon* books by Lee Carroll in Greek. This led them to seek out, translate, and publish a number of similar-themed Hay House books.

Charitini told me that she was writing a book about her past-life memories of Lemuria. "While translating your book *Healing with the Fairies,* I was amazed by what you wrote about the mer-people," she said. "And in your book *Earth Angels,* when you discussed how some people are incarnated mermaids, mermen, merangels, and merfairies, everything suddenly made sense! I believe that the merpeople are the Lemurians, and that we were merged between dolphins and humans."

"And the merangels are merged between dolphins, humans, and angels," I added.

"Yes!" said Charitini. "This is what I'm writing about in my Lemurian book."

"She's also developed a new form of Reiki energy based upon her Lemurian memories of the merpeople," George added. "It's called Mer-Reiki."

"I can feel its watery properties already," I said. Charitini and I instantly bonded, since I too had memories of the ancient tropical land of Lemuria. When I shared my studies about Atlantis with her, she told me that I'd come to the right place.

"We've arranged for a special tour guide to show you the Parthenon and surrounding areas tomorrow," she explained. "This man is a psychic, historian, and author. He'll be the perfect person to tell you about the real spiritual meanings behind the historical monuments in Athens."

COAST-TO-COAST

The next morning I was scheduled to be interviewed on the *Coast to Coast* radio show (hosted by George Noory during the week and Art Bell on weekends) by telephone. I was happy to appear on this popular show, especially since the Grecian time zone meant that my interview would take place at eight in the morning, instead of live from the United States in the middle of the night. The topic to be discussed was my book *The Crystal*

Children, which I wrote about the sensitive and psychic young children who are often misdiagnosed as autistic, when they're actually telepathic.

At 8 o'clock, I was poised by the telephone. I'd meditated, prayed, and was ready for the show. But the phone didn't ring. Accustomed to producers calling at ten minutes past the hour to allow for news broadcasts on the hour, I didn't worry. But when they hadn't called by 20 minutes past eight, I knew that something was wrong.

"Archangel Michael, please undo any errors or mistakes in this situation," I asked. "Please help the radio-show producer get in touch with me." A few minutes later, the telephone rang. It turned out that the Grecian hotel operator, who spoke limited English, couldn't find me on the guest roster, but the tenacious *Coast to Coast* producer had called back continuously until he found me.

Meanwhile, my mother was listening to the show live (my father had fallen asleep by then, as it was one o'clock in the morning in California, where they live). She was horrified when George Noory dramatically said at the beginning of the show, "We can't find our scheduled guest for tonight, Doreen Virtue. All we know is that she's somewhere in Greece, and you know how the Middle East is right now. After all, Greece is right next to Turkey. . . ." My mother was scared to death listening to this, and began praying. Undoubtedly, her prayers and mine helped the Grecian hotel operator finally locate my name and room number.

After the three-hour interview, Steven and I went down to the hotel lobby for our tour of the Parthenon. We happily hugged two friends and Angel Therapy Practitioners from Texas, Jerry and Savroula "Stav" Stefaniak, who were joining us for the Parthenon tour and my angel workshop. I'd met them in 1998 when I spoke at a Universal Lightworkers Conference in Houston. My mother, who had traveled with me, had an instant bond with Jerry because of their shared interest in *A Course in Miracles*. Jerry and Stav, a licensed psychotherapist, taught *Course* classes, and Jerry had authored two books on the topic, including one titled *Compassionate Living*.

Stav was originally from Cyprus, so she spoke fluent Greek. When Stav and I had talked a few months earlier during an Angel Therapy Practitioner course (where she was a staff member) she'd offered to fly to Greece and act as a translator during my workshops. I sensed that her performing this service would not only be good for the audience, but would also be a way for Stav to give back to her native land.

The four of us piled into a taxi headed for the Parthenon. Thirty minutes later, Steven gasped and said, "Oh wow!" loudly.

"What?" I asked, seeing nothing. Then the taxi rounded another corner, and I said the same thing as Steven: "Oh wow!"

There, in front of us, was the Parthenon. Although I'd seen countless photos, illustrations, and videos of the structure, it was breathtaking to see it in person. The sun illuminated its pillars in golden light, and I practically heard the angels singing as we drove closer. We were all hungry for lunch, but we were too excited to stop to get a bite.

The Psychic Historian

As Steven bought a granola bar to tide us over during our tour, I looked at the crowd near the gate. Charitini and George were there to personally introduce us to our tour guide, but he needed no introduction. I could have spotted him in a filled stadium, as his aura and persona glowed so brightly. He also wore a purple shirt that screamed, "I'm a New Ager!"

He first made me swear that I wouldn't use his real name in any written materials, and in honor of my promise, I agreed to call him Nicholas with the hope that someday he'd identify himself publicly. Nicholas feared that the information he was going to impart to me would put him in danger, professionally and personally.

Nicholas was an energetic man who spoke in a high-pitched nasally accent that reminded me of Andy Kaufman's character "Latka" on the television show *Taxi*. His wealth of knowledge about ancient Greek spirituality and history spilled out faster than I could write on my pad of paper. Often, when I couldn't understand his English, he'd take the pad from me and write his words, while emphasizing them verbally.

Nicholas lived near the Parthenon and had spent several years walking the grounds while meditating and receiving psychic messages. He'd also studied ancient texts surrounding its history and legends. In addition, he was the author of several books on ancient Greek personas—with one being about his past life, but which was written as a straight historical text.

Nicholas was passionate about the goddess Athena, for whom the city was named. I'd worked with Athena since writing my book *Archangels & Ascended Masters*, yet that day I embarked on an even deeper relationship with her.

As we walked around the platform below the Parthenon, Nicholas said, "The Parthenon means 'Temple of Virgin,' and it's Athena's temple," he explained. "Most people say Athena's name incorrectly, by emphasizing the 'theen' sound, when it's correctly pronounced 'Athen-AH,' emphasizing the last 'ah' syllable."

I was going to learn a lot from Nicholas. I transcribed his words rapidly, while trying to keep up with his fast walking pace. Steven, Jerry, and Stav trailed behind, unsure of whether to get in the middle of our teaching session or enjoy a more leisurely gait.

Nicholas pointed and said, "See the steak juice?"

"Steak juice?" I asked.

"No—not steak juice!" he said. "*Steak juice!*"

After several more attempts, Stav stepped in and said that Nicholas was telling me about "statues." His thick Greek accent meant that I'd need to pay close attention. I asked my angels for help in hearing him correctly, and very soon, his words sounded normal to me.

Nicholas said, "Athena is the goddess of wisdom. Her symbols are the olive tree and the black pigeon. Most people think that her animal is the owl, since it's equated with wisdom. But it's really the black pigeon." Nicholas pointed to the numerous black pigeons surrounding the Parthenon. "White doves mean peace, but black doves or pigeons are signs of wisdom," he added.

He showed me an ancient carving of black pigeons, etched into a wall below the Parthenon. When I touched the carving, I was transported to another time. The surroundings of the Parthenon turned from brown and dusty to a lush and colorful garden. As if bridging the past and the present, a butterfly briefly landed on my hand.

Then Nicholas pointed to the top of the Parthenon and said, "The ancients built an etheric pyramid over the Parthenon to keep birds from landing on it. The birds sense the energy grid as if it were a solid structure. They called the pyramid an *'aornos petra,'* or a 'no-birds stone,' which meant a place where birds couldn't fly." Sure enough, although I saw dozens of pigeons in the area, none of them were near the Parthenon itself. And not one bird was on top of the Parthenon's roof, something that has helped preserve the aging structure.

THE COSMIC SERPENT

Nicholas motioned to some statues of beautiful women. "Those are the Athenean women who kept the goddess's flame alive, and they were workers at the temple of Erechtheion. Erechtheion was a serpent who tried to make love to Athena. He impregnated her without intercourse, and she gave virgin birth to the god of metal."

The story of the virgin birth and the serpent sounded familiar. Nicholas explained his theory. "The original Atheneans were Serpent People from the Pleiades. Then, in the sixth century B.C., the Olympian gods changed their DNA and made them into upright people. This process was completed in the fifth century B.C."

His words reminded me of the book *The Cosmic Serpent,* by Jeremy Narby, which Steven and I had recently read. Narby, an anthropologist, discovered that all indigenous peoples had myths, paintings, and drawings depicting humanity's origin from serpents. Narby speculated that these ancient beliefs speak of the serpentlike DNA, which may have extraterrestrial origins; and he theorized that the original peoples of the earth may have been serpentlike, and that their bodies may have today's DNA. In other words, our ancestors existed inside our DNA.

As we walked through the museum of artifacts, we saw many statues of serpent-people. "Serpents have been demonized in the Bible and other texts," Nicholas said. "But I believe that they're our origin."

We also saw many statues of mermaidlike people who had serpent bodies; mermaid tails; and human upper torsos, arms, and heads. "The god Poseidon engaged in DNA experiments and created many anomalies such as gargoyles, mermaids, serpents, centaurs, and sea monsters, but Zeus put a stop to this practice," Nicholas said. I remembered the many mermaid and mermen carvings I'd seen in Santorini, as Nicholas added, "The merpeople are called 'Gorgonas' in Greek.

"Three hundred thousand years ago," he continued, "the Pleiadeans, who were also known as 'Anunakis,' which means 'those who came from Heaven to Earth,' came to this planet. The serpent, or the original Pleiadean form, is now our spinal column, DNA, and kundalini energy. The human body is the form from the gods and the angels. So, humans are a marriage of the angel and the serpent, or the higher and lower selves.

"We humans are meant to have twelve strands of DNA, or six pairs. But hostile and controlling invaders engaged in genetic engineering so that we wouldn't have communication with a higher authority, leaving us with our current double strand of DNA," Nicholas explained. "The invaders' curse upon our DNA will be lifted at the end of 300,000 years, which falls on December 21, in the year of 2012. At that time, our five other pairs of DNA will be reconnected."

I thought of the Mayan calendar, which ends in 2012. Many people believe that this signals a coming apocalypse. Yet the angels had always assured me that 2012 was the end of the *measurement* of time . . . not the end of time itself. The angels said that wearing watches and using calendars kept us locked in the third-dimensional illusion of time. When we stopped measuring time mechanically, all seeming limitations would be lifted for us. We'd be able to re-access our naturally miraculous powers.

Nicholas continued, "We don't need to wait until the year 2012 to reconnect our other DNA strands. We can pray to God, Spirit, the Universe, Love—however you call the First Creator. Just be sure that you're praying to the First Creator, because there are other lesser creators who don't appreciate the superiority of the human race. That's why lightworkers came to Earth—to help the humans reconnect with their spiritual gifts.

"Just hold the intention to connect with the First Creator, and it's done. Then, demand to regain the full 12 strands of DNA. You'll regain them fully within three months."

ATHENA'S TOMB

As I absorbed Nicholas's words, we walked along the Parthenon. Then Nicholas stopped. "Athena's tomb is under the statues of the Athenean women," he said, his words startling me. Like most people, I assumed that Athena never had a mortal body. Reading my thoughts, Nicholas said, "Athena was a superperson with a mortal body."

I wondered, *Could Ignatius Donnelly be right?* Donnelly had theorized in his 1882 book, *Atlantis*, that the Atlantean kings and queens and high-priests and high-priestesses left Atlantis before its destruction and went to Greece, Rome, the Celtic lands, and Egypt, where they were deified for their Divine gifts. Donnelly believed that the gods and goddesses of those cultures were actually the high-ranking people of Atlantis.

I was definitely intrigued, and as Nicholas escorted me to the area of Athena's tomb, I noticed barbed wire and construction workers surrounding it. "They're revitalizing the Parthenon for the Olympics," he explained.

I was drawn to the area that Nicholas described as Athena's tomb. He lifted the barbed wire, and I climbed underneath while Steven, Stav, and Jerry watched. I snagged my long dress on the wire, but I didn't mind, as the energy drew me toward the boxlike structure.

"Hey, you're not supposed to be there!" screamed two of the workers. But I was determined, irresistibly drawn to the energy.

"I won't touch anything, and I'll just be a moment," I promised with all the femininity I could muster.

As the men shook their heads and looked away, I mentally called to Athena for a message. I wrote quickly, as her message came:

"Women must learn to exercise control over their many emotions," she said in a sweetly loving voice sprinkled with sage wisdom. *"The emotions are beautiful energies, yet nonetheless, they must be properly contained and channeled for maximum effectiveness in shepherding this earth and her holy inhabitants back to order.*

"The Divine feminine essence is harmonizing and balancing men and women alike. Woman's strength lies in her kindness and nurturing, yet these need to begin with her own holy self."

In other words, we women needed to be as giving toward ourselves as we were to others.

A loud shrieking sound jolted me from my trance. A red-faced, uniformed man blowing a whistle angrily yelled at me, "Get out before I arrest you!"

I scrambled out under the wires, and we hurriedly left the area. Jerry joked, "Time to put on our Harry Potter invisibility cloaks!"

CHAPTER 6

Pythagoras and Hermes

As we walked out of the museum and admired the view from the hill, Nicholas asked me, "Would you like to know how they got all of these stones up on this mountain?" When I nodded, he said, "The ancients annihilated the force of gravity with the power of music. The priests used the vibration of music to levitate the stones.

"And in a battle between the Greeks and the Persians, the Greeks were outnumbered, with very few men and few ships, while thousands of Persian soldiers descended upon them. Yet the Greeks won the battle. How was this possible?" Nicholas asked rhetorically. "The Greeks used music to levitate stones, and they also knew how to create fire with flutes and magic spells. The fire went to the Persian ships only, and defeated them."

"Is this related to Pythagoras's musical theories?" I asked. Just then, as if the Universe were answering me, three butterflies flew by, intertwining themselves in midair. I took this as a sign, since in classical Greek language, the word for *butterfly* and for *soul* is identical: It's the word *psyche*. And ancient wisdom believed that our souls assumed the form of a butterfly while they searched for a new incarnation.

"Pythagoras was an *elohim*," said Nicholas, "a god from Atlantis who took human form."

While the Greek philosopher Pythagoras is famous for his mathematical formula for finding the hypotenuse of a right-angle triangle ($a^2+b^2=c^2$), he brought so much more to the world. A philosopher and spiritual teacher, Pythagoras was born around 580 B.C. on Samos Island. It's said that he was named for the python—another connection to the primordial serpent.

Legend says that Pythagoras learned extensively from travels with his father through Egypt and India. After political uprisings that offended his morals, he left Greece for southern Italy. There, he founded a philosophical and spiritual mystery school. Potential students were investigated and watched for three years before being allowed admittance to his school. The initiates were vegetarians who took vows of silence and also abstained from politics. (His rule, "Refrain from beans," referred to the fact that people voted with beans in those days.) He and his school were attacked by outsiders, and many of his students were executed for their beliefs. It's said that Pythagoras committed suicide as a result of these tragic incidents.

Several years earlier, I'd had a lucid dream in which my Grandma Pearl told me clearly, "Study Pythagoras." I obeyed her advice, and found that the Greek philosopher believed that everything in the Universe was mathematically precise. This included music, and Pythagoras's findings that certain chords and notes were associated with healing specific illnesses led to the introduction of music therapy into the early Grecian hospitals, named for the Greek god of healing, Asclepias. My studies of Pythagoras inspired me to explore sacred numerology, which led me to examine and use the tarot. When I noticed that many of my tarot clients were scared by the pictures on the cards, I knew that I needed to create a deck of angel divination cards without frightening images. And so, my first card deck, the *Healing with the Angels Oracle Cards,* was born.

If that wasn't enough, I discovered two books about pre-Socratic philosophers, both published by Oxford University Press, with a reference to Pythagoras that knocked my socks off: "Heraclides of Pontus says that Pythagoras used to say about himself that he had once been born as Aethalides and was regarded as a son of Hermes." Hermes told Aethalides that he could choose anything he wanted except immortality. Athelides asked to be able to retain, both alive and dead, the memory of things that had happened. He therefore remembered everything during his lifetimes, and when dead, he still preserved the same memories. Later he was born as Euphorbus.

In the books *The First Philosophers* and *The Pre-Socratic Philosophers* was this reference:

> Euphorbus used to say that he had formerly been born as Aethalides and had received the gift from Hermes, and used to tell of the journeying of his soul and all its migrations, recount all the plants and creatures to which it had belonged, and describe everything he had experienced in Hades and the experiences undergone by the rest of the souls there. When Euphorbus died, his soul moved into Hermotimus, who also wanted to prove the point, so he went to Branchidae, entered the sanctuary of Apollo, and pointed out the shield which Menelaus had dedicated there . . .
>
> When Hermotimus died, he became Pyrrhus, the fisherman from Delos, and again remembered everything, how he had formerly been Aethalides, then Euphorbus, then Hermotimus, and then Pyrrhus. And when Pyrrhus died, he became Pythagoras and remembered everything that has just been mentioned.

There was the Hermes connection again!

RETURN TO ASCLEPIAS

"Would you like to go to the site of the Asclepias Hospital and the healing temple?" Nicholas asked.

"You mean it's here?" I replied with urgency and excitement.

"It's right over there," Nicholas told me, pointing to the backside of the Parthenon's hill.

While Nicholas took us on a leisurely and circuitous tour, I couldn't wait to get to the site of the healing temple. He stopped us in front of the side of the hill, where raw dirt and stones mingled with dead weeds. "What do you see here?" he asked me.

I closed my eyes. "I see a second city below the city of Athens, glowing with a yellow-white light. The city's so clean and bright!"

"Exactly!" said Nicholas. "There are tunnels below the Parthenon leading to a city underneath the city. It's forbidden for anyone to speak of it, because the power of this second city could be manipulated and used for destruction."

I'd heard and read about the "Hollow Earth Theory," which says that spiritually powerful beings live deep inside the earth. I'd always written it off as science fiction. But my vision of the second city *was* very real and completely spontaneous, so I vowed to keep an open mind about the topic.

"I'll show you the secret entrances," said Nicholas in hushed tones, "but you must swear to never reveal their locations."

Unsure of what I was getting into, and feeling like a character in a spy novel, I followed Nicholas to a small tunnel in the side of the hill. "The Hollow Earth has many entrances, and this is just one of them. You'll notice tiny churches randomly built around Athens. Many of these churches are smaller than a toilet stall and wouldn't fit more than three people standing shoulder to shoulder. These churches have been deliberately built over the Hollow Earth entrances to prevent people from discovering them."

While his words sounded like some sort of conspiracy theory, I listened with an open mind as Nicholas continued. After all, it was historical fact that Christianity and Catholicism had adopted old Pagan beliefs and ceremonies such as Ostara, which became Easter; and the Winter's Solstice and Yule, which became Christmas. So Nicholas's words were feasible enough to consider.

"Five or six races of beings live in the Hollow Earth, including dwarves, fairies, Atlanteans who possess knowledge of high technology, and aliens who aren't Pleiadeans." *This sounds like something straight from The Lord of the Rings*, I thought, immediately rejecting Nicholas's words. Yet, when I considered it, I realized that perhaps *The Lord of the Rings* had a historical basis. Again, I vowed to stay open to these concepts.

"Those who know about the Hollow Earth have an annual springtime feast called *Kalikantzaroi*, as a show of respect to the beings who reside there. The ceremony honors the elves and other elementals. You could say that Kalikantzaroi is like a little Halloween that shows respect for the dead."

As we stood in front of the tunnel, Nicholas explained that whoever entered it was transformed from a third-dimensional to a fourth-dimensional being. He told me that the tunnels are connected to vortexes and "ley lines," which are energy lines that run across the earth.

As Stav looked at the tunnel, she gasped. "In meditation yesterday, I had a vision of myself going into a tunnel just like that!"

Finally, after what seemed like eons of stopping along Nicholas's tour, we reached the site of the healing temple.

"Take off your shoes," instructed Nicholas. As we stood barefoot on the stones of ancient Atlantis, I felt energy running upward through my feet. I recognized the kundalini energy extending from my root chakra all the way to my crown.

As we walked over to the site of the healing temple, I started to cry. When I stood at the site, which encompassed ruins of stone walls and a foundation, I was transported back in time. The gardens overflowed with morning glories, grapevines, and colorful singing birds. The healing temple was at the base of the mountain, exactly as I'd seen it in my regression at Skaros.

"This is one of the Atlantean healing temple sites," said Nicholas. "The Asclepias Hospital was later built over its site. At the time of Atlantis, virgin priestesses did healings using ceremony, pyramids, light, color, and olive oil."

My body was covered in chills, as Nicholas described the contents of my Atlantean past-life regression exactly. "How did you know this?" I asked him intently.

"I was a high-priest at the healing temple," he replied calmly. I stared at him. No wonder I'd instantly recognized him. And no wonder some of his actions had endeared me and some had irritated me—he *was* the same soul, after all!

"In my life after Atlantis, I was the epic poet Omiros," Nicholas said. "I was blinded by the priests as punishment for betraying the holy secrets in my writings."

Omiros was the ancient Greek name for the poet Homer, who wrote *The Iliad* and *The Odyssey*. These books comprised much of the Grecian philosophy, as well as information about gods and goddesses. This helped me understand Nicholas's desire to stay anonymous while providing esoteric information. His soul remembered the pain of being blinded for teaching spiritual secrets, and on a deep level, he feared that it would happen again.

I told Nicholas and the other members of our group that I needed some time alone, so I walked to a corner of the healing temple garden and sat with my pad of paper. The next thing I knew, I was transported back in time, and I wrote the following:

> *I'm in the healing temple, feeling a profound love coming upward. The essence of healing is grace and compassion for another's suffering and misery. Connect with the ailing person through his or her pain, and then lift him upward. You cannot lift him until you've first connected with him in his own reality. Let him bask in it momentarily, and then lovingly lift him up like a mother embracing, lifting, and comforting a crying child.*

As I wrote, I thought, *There are so many ghosts of my past here!* Then I felt sad, as I realized that the ancient beauty of these grounds had been replaced with dead, brown grass and trees lacking color. Yet, the healing temple prayers were imbedded so deeply within the soil that the true beauty could never be removed. The love imbued in the stones of Atlantis was deep, lasting, and real.

I saw visions of dragons and giant beast-men walking around Atlantis, and I realized that the Sphinx of Egypt was modeled after them. The Atlantean culture extended widely, incorporating Greece, India, Egypt, and possibly Indonesia, South America, and Mexico. As Atlantis sank, its inhabitants migrated to these lands and spread their wisdom, legends, and knowledge.

I saw the Minotaur, the half-bull, half-man of legend. It was real! I recalled the bullhorns carved into the buildings in the Akrotiri ruins, and I also remembered Plato's words about the bulls in the streets of Atlantis, and how they were sacrificed to please and appease the gods.

IN THE LIGHT

When my vision returned to the present day, Stav, Jerry, Nicholas, George, Charitini, and I held hands in a circle around the healing temple site. I asked my friends to join me in the process I'd seen in my past-life regression: We circled around where the crystal pyramid once stood and collectively put our hands into its light. Then we cupped this light and placed our hands on our hearts.

The eye in the middle of the pyramid was an all-loving vortex. It was a multidimensional representation of the higher self's oneness with God. I recalled my past-life regression, where I remembered that the light was from Hermes. I saw that this light of Hermes sprang from a vortex of underground energy. A ley line from beneath the earth was feeding light into the bottom of the pyramid, and the sunlight from above fed downward into the pyramid. These lights met in the middle, where the blue eye stared holographically in all directions.

As we all compared notes on what we'd seen, a common denominator among our visions was that we'd all seen milky-white light in the pyramid. This reminded me of something that Andres had said when we were in Santorini: White light *was* the milk of the Universe. My own experience had been that white light was an intelligent, loving, and living entity. When we surrounded ourselves, our loved ones, or our possessions with white light, we were really invoking angels. Since white light was our own true essence and substance, white light and love were the bases of all life.

Then it occurred to me: If Nicholas's theory about the serpents merging with the angels was true, could the angels represent the love; and the serpents, the light? After all, the serpent was a vibrational being requiring sunlight and heat to exist. And weren't angels pure beings of love? Perhaps our origin—light plus love—was the reason why this formula equated healing. Light plus love was what we were. And what we were was already healed, whole, and perfect in every way. When we called upon light and love, we were actually calling upon our higher selves to come forth and shoo away all illusions of illness or darkness.

Nicholas walked over and sat down next to Steven and me. I told him about my vision of Minotaurs walking around the healing temple. Nicholas said, "On the island of Crete, which was ruled by King Minos, there was a creature known as the Minotaur. The Minoans worshiped the bull as a symbol of the moon goddess, since the bullhorns are shaped like the crescent moon. The Egyptian goddess, Isis, had bullhorns on her headdress, because she too was connected with the half-moon."

I wondered whether there was some secret power to the half-moon—beyond the full and new moons—that I should know? Especially given the fact that I was a Taurean woman astrologically connected to the bull? I later discovered that the half-moon crescent in the U shape of a bull horn is a sign of power. It's the Taurean sign to move forward to meet your goal fearlessly, as a bull would. The bullhorns and crescent moons collect the fruits of manifestations, similar to a forklift scooping up objects.

Nicholas's words reminded me of how symbols of goddesses had been demonized and persecuted. For instance, the 13 moon cycles in a year had resulted in the number 13 being viewed as a symbol of bad luck. Women have 13 menstrual flows a year. Was that why bulls, the symbols of the moon and goddesses, were sacrificed in Atlantis? Was even *that* advanced society afraid of women's power?

As I explained my feelings to Nicholas, he said, "Atlantis had a numeral system that was based on the number 13. Thirteen is the number of the feminine, as you know. There are 13 universes, and Atlantean computers were based on the operation of 13 numbers." So Atlantis was more progressive toward women than our current system, which excludes the 13th floor from hotels!

Nicholas continued, "In the healing temple, you priestesses used to sing in order to energetically open the vortexes." Then he began singing the same song that I'd sung in my Atlantean past-life regression! Steven and I looked at one another, reeling in surprise at receiving one more corroborating piece of evidence pointing to the reality of my regression.

"You mustn't teach the song to anyone who could possibly misuse it," Nicholas warned. "If they knew the song, they could find powers that could possibly harm many beings in several dimensions." Then he smiled and added, "However, singing in general is very healing for all of us, and it definitely increases our healing abilities."

That night as Steven and I watched the sunset from our hotel room, the angels spoke to me. They said: *"Watching sunsets doesn't just evoke pleasant feelings because of the pretty colors. The sunset bathes you in the colored lights that activate your lower chakras, which helps ground you. That is why at early night, humans use lower-chakra activities such as food, drink, and sex to relax your-selves. By bathing in sunset light, you can activate more naturally as a way to ground yourselves. It's very important to watch sunsets and to go outside and bathe in their light, or at least stand next to an open door or window where you can bathe in the sunset light without the filtering effects of glass.*

"Moonlight and starlight activate the late-night chakras in the auric field, including the third-eye and throat chakras, which are part of this field and are useful for healing during dreamtime. This process includes receiving psychic instructions during dreamtime. Sunrise light activates the heart chakra, to awaken the energy lev-els and the psychic senses for daytime intuition. Sunlight during the day keeps your upper and lower chakras in communication and in sync."

Upon hearing the angels' words, I made a mental note to research the healing benefits of sunlight more thoroughly. I won-dered, *Are the health scares about sunlight just more ways to sup-press our power?*

I thought about island living. Steven and I had spent quite a bit of time in the Hawaiian Islands and had found that the small-er islands offered everyone the experience of seeing both the sun-rise and the sunset bounce off the ocean waters. The watery reflection created dramatically colored sunsets, with vividly bright oranges, reds, pinks, purples, and yellows.

Perhaps that's why so many of the young "Crystal Children" (sensitive and psychic toddlers and infants) are so fascinated with the moon, sun, and stars. Countless parents wrote to me during my research for my book *The Crystal Children* to tell me how their youngsters spent hours staring at the moon. One woman even said that her daughter's first word was *moon,* which was spoken when she took her daughter outside during a full moon.

Is being indoors, away from natural light, one more reason why children dislike school? The studies are clear that the average schoolroom's fluorescent lighting flickers at a rate that creates low-level anxiety and concentration problems for most students.

I thought about the Mediumship Mentorship class that I'd recently taught in a new classroom. Whereas I'd previously taught in a hotel ballroom with limited natural light, I'd since moved to the Inn at Laguna Beach in California, where the classroom is completely surrounded by floor-to-ceiling glass overlooking the ocean. Most of the time we opened the doors to allow in fresh air. We kept the lights off, as the sunlight sufficiently lit the room.

The difference in my energy level at the end of a day of teaching in that room was dramatic. Where I'd normally feel tired and drained by day's end, I would now feel energized and refreshed from being in an atmosphere filled with natural light and fresh air.

Tunnels of Light

Steven and I both slept soundly that night. In the morning, we discovered that we'd each had flying dreams, but I'd also had another dream that gave me food for thought.

In the dream, I was with my childhood best friend, Anita, and some other people I couldn't identify. We were all upset because there were some blocks in the drainpipes of our home and city. Anita bravely volunteered to go into the drainpipes and try to clear them.

As she ventured downward, we were all concerned about her. Happily, Anita surfaced a few minutes later with a big smile on her face. She wasn't wet or soiled at all. Instead, she exclaimed, "Oh, there's a whole city down there! It's the most beautiful thing I've ever seen!"

The dream showed me that I needed to pay attention to the symbolism of the tunnels Nicholas had shown me. I thought about the parallels between the tunnels and our conversation about serpents, since the tunnels were serpentlike.

My thoughts returned to a vision I'd had in 1996. I was teaching psychic development, and while the class engaged in giving readings to one another, I closed my eyes and was transported back in time. I saw the earth before humankind's inhabitation. Water was everywhere, and I was aware of floating on the surface of the water. I realized that I was a simple monopod, a tubelike creature. A worm.

"Are you okay?" A student's voice pulled me out of the vision.

"Yes. I was having a past-life memory," I answered.

"Well, it didn't look like a very pleasant one," the student said. "Your face was scrunched like you were in pain."

I'd never forgotten the sights and also the feelings associated with that vision. Sitting on my Athens hotel balcony overlooking the ocean, I thought, *Perhaps snakes and worms weren't Earth's first inhabitants. Perhaps etheric tubes were, like the tunnels experienced during death and near-death experiences. These tunnels bridged the material and spiritual worlds.*

After all, weren't we born through the vaginal tube? At birth, our umbilical-cord tube is severed and replaced by a silver-cord tube that holds our soul connected to our physical body. And much of my spiritual healing work involves cutting etheric cords that are thought-forms of fear.

These etheric tunnels may have calcified eons ago and formed the original essence of what is now our spinal columns, and the trunks of trees and plants—the literal Tree of Life. Perhaps the drainpipe in my dream was a representation of life's origin, just like the tunnels to the Hollow Earth in Athens were representations.

I wondered, *Is our spinal column a tunnel to our own inner city of light? A bridge to the kingdom within—to Heaven? Is this why so many of us experience shooting sensations in our back, known as kundalini energy, during meditation?*

Did this mean that back problems represented spiritual

blockages? I began visualizing sending light through my spinal column, and vowed to continue this practice. Previously, I'd only sent light through the core of my body.

Could the spinal column be the body of the serpent, and its head be our reptilian brain, also known as the *medulla oblongata?* Could the reptilian brain still operate out of our old instincts, including the instinct to protect our body by striking out at predators? And if it were true that our snake-essence merged with a higher angel-essence, did we still need the old instinct to strike out for protection? I recalled the times when I'd behaved aggressively and later regretted it. Was this my "devil" and "angel" conflict, as mythology had portrayed? Was this why it was insulting to be called a "snake" or a "worm"?

I wondered if we could retrain our instincts to habitually turn to our angels when we felt endangered. I recalled the scientific studies performed on Buddhist monks whose physiological vital signs didn't waver when their bodies were under stress. Scientists concluded that the meditative practices of the monks had resulted in a mind-set that was unflappable. Perhaps we could all attain similarly peaceful states through regular meditation.

No Time Worries

My time on Santorini taught me that the Grecian people were relaxed about schedules and time. This was, according to the angels, a healthy attitude, since time measurement held us in third-dimensional limitations.

My Saturday-morning Athens workshop was scheduled to begin at 9:30, at a venue about 15 minutes away. So when George said, "The car will pick you up at 9:30 to take you to the workshop," Steven and I were surprised.

"Greek workshops never start on time," George said, in answer to my unspoken question.

The next morning, Stav, Jerry, Steven, and I waited in the hotel driveway for our car. It arrived at 9:35. Steven was a little uptight about being late, since keeping agreements about appointments was important to him. I always admired his integrity about that. I was more relaxed, though, enjoying the cultural differences in Greece compared to other places where I'd spoken.

On the drive, I noticed countless billboards advertising Nescafé coffee and various brands of cigarettes. Like a lot of Europeans, Grecians seemed to chain-smoke. Sure enough, when we arrived at the venue, the auditorium was empty, and the approximately 300 participants were in the cafeteria smoking cigarettes and drinking coffee.

How am I going to teach psychic development to them if they're buzzed on stimulants? I worried, but then I gave the fear to Archangel Michael to sort out.

George announced that the workshop was going to begin, and he escorted me to an office where I could rest and lay down my personal items. It was now 10:10, and no one had raised an eyebrow about the event starting late.

A man and a woman in a booth above the auditorium translated my words. Their Greek translations were piped into earpieces that three-quarters of the audience, who didn't understand English, wore. The translation was done almost simultaneously with my talk. So I had to talk a little slower than normal, but otherwise could speak nonstop. This was in contrast to my lectures in Germany the previous year where I traveled with a translator named Angelika. We would take turns talking: I would say something in English, stop, and then Angelika would translate my words into German. This method of translation took twice as long, especially since several bilingual people in the audience argued with Angelika about her choice of word translations!

The audience members were lovely people, and they truly opened up their hearts to see and hear the angels' messages during the day. When they paired up and I walked them through the steps of conducting a psychic angel reading, I saw that the joy, faith, and love in their hearts stimulated successful readings.

Stav and Jerry helped with those who had questions, and Stav volunteered to conduct private readings after the workshop for a small fee. Her schedule filled up immediately, and dozens more people still wanted readings. So Jerry—who didn't speak Greek—arranged for a translator to help him give angel readings. Stav and Jerry were booked with angel readings for three days! It was hard work and took a lot of dedication on their part, yet I also sensed that it was important for Stav to give back to her native land in this way. Something deep was healing for her.

Steven and I returned to our hotel in time to sit outside during sunset, to enjoy our last evening in Greece. The next morning we flew to London, where Steven and I were to give more workshops and make bookstore appearances. Steven had brought his didgeridoo along on our trip, which is an Australian wind instrument made of hollowed-out tree branches.

Steven carried the didgeridoo in a black cloth carrying case, and we were always asked by airport security guards about the case's contents. The Athens airport was no different, and when the security officials asked, "What's this?" I gave my usual answer: "It's a flute," which seemed a shortcut way to explain the exotic instrument to those unfamiliar with it. Steven always corrected me by saying, "No, it's a didgeridoo." He seemed to enjoy introducing the indigenous instrument to various cultures. At one airport, the guards asked him to play the didgeridoo to prove that it was a musical instrument, something that Steven was only too happy to oblige.

CHAPTER 7

The Land of Enchantment

A s we landed at Heathrow Airport, I felt excited about spending time in England because it has always seemed like a magical and enchanted land to me. This country reminds me of a fairy-tale picture book, with its castles, swans, weeping willows, acres of rolling greenery, ornate architecture, and beautiful gardens filled with wildflowers. I love tea time, British accents and manners, Stonehenge, the town of Glastonbury, and Harrods department store, among many other things.

The managing director (Megan Slyfield) and marketing director (Jo Lal) of Hay House United Kingdom (UK) greeted us at the airport, which seemed far and away beyond the call of duty for a Sunday morning, when most people are sleeping in. Yet throughout our trip, Megan and Jo would prove how intensely committed they are to the authors they work with. They worked long hours to support Steven and me in spreading the word about our respective books, and they both seemed to genuinely enjoy their work.

On the evening of my first workshop, we met with Megan and Jo, as well as Michelle Pilley (the managing editor) and Emma Collins (the publishing assistant) of Hay House UK. Michelle is a longtime New Age student and investigator. And as I had with Megan and Jo, I felt a special kinship with Michelle and Emma.

I thought, *Everything always feels right when I'm in England.* Then I wondered, *Why is that true in certain places and not others?*

That night I spoke at the St. James Church, a beautiful, old Victorian structure complete with pipe organ and balconies. The event was sponsored by Alternatives, a nonprofit spiritual organization run by three caring men: Steve, Tom, and Richard.

My talk was to begin at 7 o'clock sharp—and since Alternatives only had use of the church until 8:30, the workshop needed to begin promptly. Two minutes before its start, Tom looked at his watch and began the countdown of seconds leading up to the moment he was to introduce me to the audience. What a contrast to the nonchalant attitude about my starting time in Greece!

I wondered if the sunny locale of Greece made a difference in attitudes about punctuality, compared to the relatively darker skies of the UK. I thought about how in Hawaii, appointments are loosely kept according to "island time," which meant that a 3 o'clock appointment might not take place until 4:30. Did sunshine and warm weather create a more relaxed attitude about time? And since the angels said that time measurement created limitations, did this point to the benefits of sunshine, as the angels had been discussing with me?

The workshop began and ended precisely on time, and everyone was happy. During our first week in England, I gave nightly talks and signed books at stores throughout the country. Jo would invariably take the wheel, as she was a strong, confident driver who knew the roads. Often, we'd drive two to four hours to a bookstore, and I was happily entertained by the beautiful scenery. On the way home, we'd munch on the vegetarian foods that Jo had packed for us.

During our second week, Steven and I arranged to visit the magical southern England town of Glastonbury with Michelle and Megan. Michelle was quite familiar with Glastonbury lore and spirituality, so she was our guide for the day. On the drive there, Michelle talked about the ley lines running beneath England. As touched on earlier, ley lines are subterranean energy lines or grids that function like underground spiritual power lines.

"We'll be climbing the Glastonbury Tor today," said Michelle. The Tor was a mountainlike mound in Glastonbury. "There's a powerful ley line extending from St. Michael's Mount on the Land's End Peninsula in Cornwall, to Michael's Church on the top of Glastonbury Tor. All the sacred places dedicated to Archangel Michael run in a straight line, which we call the 'Angel Line.'

"There's a ley line called the Mary ley line that intersects with Michael's ley line beneath the Tor, which adds to its energy," Michelle explained. She went on to say that while the Angel Line was straight, Mary's line had twists and turns and was called a "serpent ley line."

I was stunned to hear the reference coupling angels and serpents again! And the fact that the angels were grouped under a male energy heading, while serpents were paired with feminine energy, was most interesting. It reminded me of the serpent in the Garden of Eden who was the tempter of Eve—who was ultimately blamed for The Fall.

As I discussed these thoughts with Michelle, Megan, and Steven, Michelle added, "In fact, there are two paths leading to Michael's Church on Glastonbury Tor. One is straight and quicker. The other is serpentlike, circling around the Tor. This takes longer, and is usually reserved for women only. It's a wonderful way to have a walking meditation as you climb the Tor."

The traffic slowed to a crawl because of a car wreck. As ambulances and tow trucks arrived, traffic stopped completely. "Look!" said Steven. "There's Stonehenge!" Our diverted and slow drive had taken us in front of the ancient circle of standing stones. We all agreed that there was a reason for our slow drive— so we could admire and absorb Stonehenge's beauty.

"Stonehenge is on the Michael ley line," explained Michelle, as I wrote down these words in the journal I'd kept since Santorini. I was very grateful for the information she was imparting.

THE ISLE OF AVALON

As we drove into Glastonbury, my breath quickened. Noticing this, Michelle commented, "Glastonbury is called the 'heart chakra' of the world for good reason, don't you agree?" It certainly was a magical land, which was one reason why Steven and I returned to it annually. An old church, partly in ruins, known as the Abbey, had markers on two gravesites, indicating that King Arthur and Queen Guinevere were buried there side by side.

The romantically mystical qualities of Glastonbury, and its many charming shops and natural wonders, made it easy to envision King Arthur, Merlin the Magician, and Archangel Michael. Legend said that the Isle of Avalon, made famous by King Arthur stories and the book *The Mists of Avalon,* was located in Glastonbury, just behind the Abbey.

"Yes, it certainly opens the heart to be in Glastonbury," I agreed as we pulled into the parking lot of Chalice Wells, a botanical garden with natural healing water wells. Jesus' uncle, Joseph of Arimathea, brought the Holy Grail to the Isle of Avalon. When he reached Glastonbury, he planted his wooden walking staff into the ground. The staff took root at the location of Chalice Wells and grew into a blossoming thorn tree that blooms at Christmastime each year. The breed of tree (*Crateagus Monogyna Praecox)* was normally only found in the Middle East. Next to the Holy Thorn Tree, two wells sprang: one with red iron-filled water and one with clear white water. Travelers drank water from the wells, which was reputed to have healing powers.

We were amazed to be the only people in Chalice Wells, which was normally a busy location for both tourists and locals. We spent the time meditating; and enjoying the beauty of the springs, flowers, and energy. And we ceremoniously drank from the healing waters of both the red and white wells.

The sky began to darken with threatening clouds, so we decided to visit the Tor before night or rainfall set in. Since it was starting to sprinkle, we opted to take the straight trail up the hill. Construction workers had covered St. Michael's church with scaffolding as they cleaned and repaired the church. The scaffolding marred the visual appearance of the church, yet its energy was still enormously appealing as we made the climb.

On top of the Tor, cold winds pushed us toward the church. A sole female construction worker worked high on the scaffolding inside. Michelle and I peeked inside. "Sorry, no one's allowed in here," the woman said. I noticed her feminine face and curly hair beneath her hard hat and overalls.

"Couldn't she pop inside for just a moment?" Michelle asked on my behalf. "This is an American author who's researching the Tor for her new book."

Michelle's energy and sincerity melted the construction woman's resolve, and she motioned for me to come inside. "Just for a minute, though," she cautioned.

The first thing I noticed were carvings of Archangel Michael and the Celtic goddess Bridget. I'd worked with Bridget since meeting her on my first visit to Ireland. Bridget was a fiery and passionate protector goddess who had been briefly adopted and sainted by the Catholic church. I always told people that Bridget was the female equivalent of Michael, in that her energy was so hot that it made people perspire when she was around. Bridget also mirrored Michael's ability to boost confidence and courage, and to protect those who called upon her.

I'd always associated Bridget with Ireland, and yet, here on the Michael-and-Mary ley-line intersection, it was appropriate to acknowledge both the feminine and masculine aspects of the Divine.

I exited the church after a moment, out of respect for the construction worker, whose energy was definitely goddesslike. There, under that hard hat and overalls, was a goddess keeper of the temple.

As I walked outside, the wind whipped up my hair and journal pages. I felt Archangel Michael's strong, loving presence around me, so I walked to an edge of the church that blocked the wind and began writing his words:

"This church, which is named in my honor, is built over the energy of Avalon, over the former location of the Healing Palace of Avalon. I bridge both worlds, bringing the ancient healing

traditions into Christianity and other organized religions—with one foot in the old dimension that is just beneath the organized religions' foundation—supporting it patiently without judgment. One foot in the old world and one foot in the new, as a bridge.

"Your Avalon healing circle energies are still infused into the crust of the earth here, and the energy has been transferred to the healing stone circles called Avebury and Stonehenge. These stones were transferred from the vibrational dimension of Avalon to their current locations. Their molecules were vibrated to transport them through the high-vibrational thought processes.

"Just as the chapels in Greece cover the vortexes of Atlantis, so does the Tor church capitalize upon ancient energies. It is not a conspiracy; it is archaic angelic direction of the masons who built this church for us to ensure the continuation of prayers upon the site, which are carried into the bloodstream of the earth.

"Ley lines are the connecting arteries of the earth's chakras, like the kundalini serpent connecting your body's chakras."

I barely had time to absorb Michael's words as rain began to fall, and we hurriedly made our way down the hill. I held my journal tightly inside my jacket to protect it from the rain.

ENERGY VIBRATIONS

The following week, Steven and I arranged for a private, up-close tour of Stonehenge, which allowed us to touch the stones and sit by them. Steven brought his didgeridoo to play a sunset ceremonial song, while I brought my journal and several pens to write down messages and insights.

Our guide for Stonehenge, Phillip, was quite knowledgeable about both mainstream and esoteric information. He explained that Stonehenge originally had 56 wooden poles surrounding the stones. This number was significant, as it was 28 doubled, mirroring the 28 days in a lunar cycle. Phillip said, "Historians estimate that the posts were 30 feet high and made of oak, and that they were used to measure moon cycles for farming."

This reminded me of my Babylonian past life as an astronomer/priest, where we tracked constellation movement against the pillars of our temple. Our guide continued, "Thirteen different ley lines intersect at Stonehenge, which is significant since there are 13 full moons in a year." Once again, the goddess's lunar energy was apparent!

Phillip showed us how a large heel stone marked the celestial position of the summer solstice, and two smaller stones marked the autumn and spring equinoxes.

"There's so much speculation about how the stones arrived at Stonehenge," said Phillip. "One legend says that Merlin flew the stones in from Ireland. The blue stones of Stonehenge are only found in Wales and Ireland, at least 250 miles away. There's no smooth path to pull the stones to Stonehenge, as there are many mountains and rivers between Wales and Salisbury, the location of Stonehenge."

A painting of hundreds of men struggling to pull the large stones with ropes was on the wall of the entrance to Stonehenge. All the speculation about Stonehenge and the Egyptian pyramids seemed based on humankind's current knowledge of material objects. Scientists didn't seem to take into account our possible metaphysical knowledge about bypassing earthly physical "laws."

I recalled Archangel Michael's message to me at Glastonbury Tor about the placement of the stones: *These stones were transferred from the vibrational dimension of Avalon to their current locations. Their molecules were vibrated to transport them through the high-vibrational thought processes.*

While it sounded like something straight out of *Star Trek,* wasn't it possible to train our thoughts to affect material items? After all, scientific studies had shown that psychokinesis—thoughts affecting material objects—was real. I'd read countless studies where subjects' thoughts affected pinball machines, computers, random-number generators, and such. Why couldn't people who studied metaphysics—without modern time interruptions such as television sets or office jobs—and who put all of their efforts in that direction have catapulted this power into the ability to dematerialize and rematerialize stones?

I also remembered what Nicholas had told me in Greece: "The ancients annihilated the force of gravity with the power of music. The priests used the vibration of music to levitate the stones." It made sense that music vibrated at a higher vibration than dense stones. And if scientists agreed that all material objects were truly composed of energy at the atomic level, why couldn't we rearrange atoms through vibrational influences such as music or thought?

While writing my book *The Crystal Children,* two families had told me that their children had successfully levitated their toys. The new Crystal Children, who are highly sensitive and psychic, have such uncompromising faith that their pure belief allows them to perform miracles such as levitation, instant spiritual healing of loved ones, and falling from high places without getting hurt.

These children's crystal-clear intentions and unwavering faith undoubtedly create these miracles. This ancient wisdom harkens to the Master Teacher, Jesus, saying repeatedly, "As is your faith, so is it done unto you." The new Crystal Children are way-showers of what is possible, helping us recall abilities we had in the days of Atlantis and Avalon.

HEALING MESSAGES FROM STONEHENGE

As I stood in the middle of the Stonehenge circle, I took off my shoes and wriggled my toes into the dark, mossy soil. The sun was beginning to set, and I could feel thousands of angels and ancient wise ones surrounding me with great love. A pleasant vortex energy emanated from the circle, and I heard the stones sing a low-pitched mantra song.

The stones spoke to me of much pain and suffering being endured at Stonehenge. The stones had absorbed this pain. I could clearly see the eyes, noses, and mouths within the stones, the features of the stone people—the confidants of priests and priestesses who'd come and told them about their troubles.

The stones sang to me about the ancient astronomers who recorded the movements of the stars on the stones' vertical templates. The astronomers were also telepathically aware of the plight of people everywhere. They knew about poverty, begging, hysteria, and humankind's waste of precious natural resources.

The secrets of Stonehenge were passed down through the generations of service workers who were posted at the stone circle. There was even a mass slaughter of Druid priests who were called "heathens" for their paganism, yet the souls of these highly evolved priests were able to immediately return to Earth life by walking into other people's bodies in a soul-exchange program, based on free will and not on possession.

As Steven's didgeridoo music echoed through the sunset-lit stones, I sat down and posed questions to the stones:

"What is the relationship of Stonehenge to healing?"

The stones immediately answered: *"The healing energy emitted by the ancient peoples continues to envelop this land [England], making it a healing sanctuary. That's why you and so many people love and adore England for her nurturing maternal energy.*

"Archangel Haniel was here and still exists on several planes of existence. She is a moonlight angel who was worshiped here by the names of Diana and Demeter. You were involved with Haniel and her goddess aspects many times in our history as well."

Their words made me stop and recall my past-life memories of Babylon. One of the goddess statues at the temple looked just like Diana. And my research had connected Archangel Haniel with Babylon and the astral-light powdery substance we'd used. Now the standing stones were telling me that Haniel and Diana were one and the same! Of course—they were both moon goddesses! And the connection to Demeter, the Greek goddess of abundant crops, was also an aspect of Haniel. Well, I knew that Haniel helped us manifest abundance, so this also made sense.

I wondered, *Were the archangels present at Atlantis, and were they also aspects of the gods, goddesses, and deities of the world's cultures and religions?*

While I pondered that question, I queried the stones about their origination and how they'd arrived in Salisbury.

They answered: *"You were already given that information whilst you were in Glastonbury. We stones arrived perfectly intact through the portal of Avalon and Atlantis, which were simultaneous civilizations. Avalon and Atlantis held the thought patterns of evolving mankind in check as they began to discover and create weapons and other means of cruelty and destruction.*

"We stones were disintegrated into particles of thought-forms, and reconfigured on this vortex intersection, which runs through Glastonbury and Jerusalem."

I asked, "How could Atlantis and Avalon have simultaneously existed? Wasn't Atlantis well before the time of Jesus, and wasn't Avalon *after* the time of Jesus?"

The stones replied: *"This is a lesson in simultaneous realities, as there are many parallels and overlaps. Avalon is an ancient land, with definite boundaries that overlapped Atlantis, both geographically and in time frame. After Atlantis fell, the geography of Avalon was altered significantly, but its essence continued into what you consider 'Arthurian times.' The ancient energy of Avalon was transferred into us [the stones] to ensure its continuation for eternity. We are indestructible couriers of the light that has always been with us, a light that was condensed and concentrated into our packaging."*

I asked, "So you're similar to the Ark of the Covenant, in which the eternal flame was carried in a finite object?"

The stones answered: *"Finite isn't the best term to describe either the Ark or our structure; however, we share certain qualities and similarities, definitely."*

Just then, Steven came over to me and said that our guide, Phillip, had shown him a carving in one of the stones of a dagger with Grecian markings. He told me, "The dagger itself is affiliated with Greece."

Very interesting! I asked the stones, "Is Stonehenge also connected with Athens?

They replied: *"The introduction of healing wells coincided with that in Asclepias hospitals—that of blessing the water and then pouring it over sick patients."*

Next I asked, "What about healing with light, crystals, and colors?"

"We are monuments to the power of nature," answered the stones, *"which definitely includes the healing power of crystals, as they're part of nature and of our stone kingdom. Can't you see that we're the same energy as yourself? We're light and we're love, in a denser format that makes our movement less detectable than your own. We're positioned to capture maximum sunlight and moonlight, which when charged into any being, can unleash its healing properties. We who are charged with sun and moonlight can unleash these energies upon one who has been indoors for too long.*

"Those who are sick should seek to commune with nature in silence, much as we do. Do not discount the power of sunlight, moonlight, starlight, and fresh air! Water is an essential property to wash away fungus accumulated in the body from breathing too much still air. Crystals can certainly amplify the natural healing energies of the sun, moon, stars, air, and water, but they're not necessary. In fact, when too much emphasis is put upon a healing apparatus, it impedes the flow of hope and faith that comes from simply being outdoors.

"The ancient healing temples and places of worship were always outdoors. It was your ancient Catholic church that invented dark temples with roofs in the name of protecting you from the elements."

"Didn't the ancient Buddhists worship indoors?"

"They spent much more time in gardens of worship, and are more in tune with the sanctity of nature than those practicing traditional and modern Western religious practices. One throwback to your past is the erection of stain-glassed windows in places of modern worship, which filters the sunlight through healing colors of glass. Much better, still, is to get the full spectrum of colors that natural sunlight—including sunrises and sunset—affords."

So there was the same message I'd heard during my journey through Greece about the healing power of natural light. Once again I vowed to research scientific studies about sunlight's effect on health. After all, most people equated sunlight with health dangers, not health benefits.

I then asked the stones, "What message would you like to give to me, and to anyone who reads your words?"

Their instant reply was: *"Reclaim your manifestation and healing powers immediately! Religious practices have discouraged individuals from seeking power by inflicting labels of heresy and treason upon them. The guilt and fear still permeates deep in the subconscious mind. This includes the fear of standing out, of being unique and distinctive. You've associated this attention with being vulnerable, so you sabotage yourselves again and again by not publicly addressing the truths and problems that you see. You rein yourselves in, and only allow so much attention to be cast in your direction before you hide in your protective cloaks.*

"Pass along this information: Healing energy is freely available to <u>everyone.</u> No one is specially gifted. There are only those who are free to choose to capitalize upon their inner strengths <u>or</u> to shrink from them.

"The world is colder and darker each time an individual shudders from the thought of speaking up. Even if your message isn't well received, the properties involved with the message are spread energetically throughout the land for time eternal.

"To each and every one of you: Your words, your thoughts, and your feelings are pure poetry. Do not rush to hide or discount them, but instead capitalize on them to make each other stronger. You will energetically evolve at much faster rates through this sharing and swapping of thoughts and ideas, so speak of them openly and comfortably. Do not shy away from public appearances where you tell your stories and give teachings.

"Bless everyone you see, no matter how they treat you. Your spiritual daily vitamin comes from this practice: Visualize blessings coursing through your bloodstream, cleansing and vitalizing your body. Fill up your mind, your lungs, and your entire being with sunlight on a regular basis."

Their words made me pause. Still, I had so many more questions to ask. "What about the advances of science, including using soap to eradicate bacteria, and the fact that humankind's life expectancy is much longer today?"

"That is your assumption," they replied. *"Actually, many ancient peoples of the sunlit world lived well into 3- to 400 years of age and beyond. They were happy and vital their entire lives. Surely, you know that your scientists say that the human body is built to last this long.*

"The Industrial Age, which rightly should be called 'The Indoor Age,' is what spawned your modern diseases and ailments. And deaths by accident come from industrial inventions such as cars and guns."

"Even the plague?" I asked.

"Check your history books—that was during the Indoor Age.

"In Babylon, you spent your lifetime outdoors, in a roofless temple without walls. In this lifetime, you must create the space and freedom in your schedule to spend time outdoors. Or at least bring the outdoors into you, with lots of open doors and open windows at all times!"

The stone's words reminded me of the new Crystal Children, who crave spending time outdoors. In fact, the only time that these children exhibit crankiness is if they're indoors too long. Once in nature, the children are captivated for hours as they stare at trees, plants, insects, and animals.

HEALING IN SCOTLAND AND IRELAND

Our tour of the United Kingdom took us to Edinburgh (pronounced *Edin-bur-oh*), Scotland, where I conducted an all-day course called "Healing with the Angels." The sold-out workshop audience included many healers interested in new ways of treating illness and helping their clients.

The seminar was based on my book *Healing with the Angels,* a collection of case studies about angels, as well as my experiences with spiritual healing. I'd received thousands of letters from readers who had experienced healings as a result of reading it (many of their stories are in Part II of *this* book), so I knew that the methods were teachable. I also planned to teach techniques that hadn't yet been published in any of my previous works.

I first led the audience through angel healings so that they could experience the methods themselves. Next, I explained the techniques so that they could write the steps in their notebooks. One of the methods that the angels had taught me was a way to heal from the pain of psychic attack, which occurs when someone becomes enraged with us, curses us, or wishes pain or ill will upon us. As I guided the audience through this method called "Curse and Dagger Lifting" (which I discuss in Part III), I heard several people cry, and watched their expressions change.

After the Curse and Dagger Lifting experience, many members of the audience reported that they had been instantly alleviated of chronic back pain and headaches—something I'd heard sporadically from other audiences to whom I'd taught the method. Yet, in this group, virtually everyone told me that engaging in this practice made them feel lighter and more positive. Since my work as a spiritual healer and former psychotherapist was geared toward helping people feel happier and healthier, this method appeared to be a most effective tool.

The next morning, Steven and I ventured through Edinburgh to see the castle there, as well as a knoll called Arthur's Seat. As we walked through town, Steven and I thought that *everything* looked like a castle! "Is that the castle?" Steven would ask.

"Maybe, although that building over there looks like it could be the castle," I replied. Finally, we walked around the corner and saw a gothic structure built into the side of a wildly overgrown hill. This time there was no question—we'd found Edinburgh Castle.

We spent some time marveling over the structure, but my true desire was to climb Arthur's Seat. (Legend has it that when King Arthur was worried about his kingdom, he'd climb the high hill above Edinburgh so that he could think clearly.) On this particular day, the hill was covered with enchanting yellow wildflowers. Steven and I sat down at the top of it, feeling very peaceful. Instead of receiving profound ideas or insights, I realized that the hill was a place of retreat. It was a location where the mind and body could be relaxed and quiet.

Afterward, we traveled to Ireland, where I taught the Angel Therapy Practitioner course in a Dublin suburb called Newtownmountkennedy. Instead of being called New Town Mount Kennedy, the name was all run together, reportedly the longest name for any Irish city. We held the event in a charming area of town called Druid's Glen.

Steven and I stayed in a beautiful two-story house on the beach of County Wexford, about an hour's drive south. The use of the house was a gift to us from a wonderful Irish couple—a woman who was a healer married to a successful businessman. We commuted to the seminar each day in a rental car that Steven drove.

As many of you know, automobiles are driven on the left side of the road in the United Kingdom, in contrast to the United States, where cars are driven on the right-hand side. So, Steven would start out each drive by repeating, "Left side, left side," to remind himself to stay on that side of the road. Only once did he forget and veer into oncoming traffic. Each day we'd invoke Archangel Michael and the other angels to oversee our drive. As a result, our daily commute was a lovely experience where we could truly enjoy the Irish countryside on our way to Druid's Glen.

Since we were staying at a house instead of a hotel, I was able to cook healthful vegan meals for Steven and myself. Although not a vegan, my husband does enjoy flavorful vegetarian cooking. To make my meals, I needed the right ingredients, so we headed off to Tesco, the neighborhood grocery store.

We found some beautiful organic produce, soy milk, and other foods. The only additional item I needed was tofu, but when we asked the employees at the store where they kept their tofu, they said they'd never heard of this word. Finally, Steven asked Tesco's manager if she knew where we could purchase it, and she directed us to a new health-food store in a nearby town.

ALL A-TWITTER

As we walked into Mrs. Bee's health-food store in the town of Gorey, I knew that we were in the right place. The energy of the small, clean, efficiently run shop seemed magical. Steven and I had noticed in our travels that the term *health-food store* usually meant a vitamin shop that carried little, if any, food. But Mrs. Bee's was well stocked with nuts, beans, juices, and dried mixes. And she had tofu in her refrigerator! She also sold ecologically safe cleaning supplies, which I joyfully put into our basket. The thought of polluting Ireland's beautiful waterways with chemically based detergents had bothered me a lot. I also selected an olive-oil-based skin lotion, since I'd learned about the oil's magical healing and cleansing properties while in Greece.

As Steven and I filled our shopping basket, we walked by a shelf filled with angel products: statues, wall hangings, and—I gasped with surprise—my own oracle cards and books! I quickly thought about introducing myself to Mrs. Bee. I usually keep a low profile during my off-hours when not speaking or teaching, as I don't like people making a fuss over me, especially when I'm engaged in everyday activities like shopping, dining, or exercising. But for some reason I decided to be more open with Mrs. Bee that day. Perhaps it was because she was the spitting image of my mother, or maybe it was her loving aura—there was just something about Mrs. Bee that I could trust.

So when I placed my groceries on the checkout counter, I said, "Thank you so much for carrying my angel cards and books."

She looked at me and her face flushed. "Are you Doreen Virtue?" she asked.

I hesitated momentarily and then answered, "Yes, I am."

Mrs. Bee shrieked so loudly and hugged me so hard that I briefly regretted introducing myself. Yet her reactions came from a pure and childlike place of love.

"Oh, I'm all a-twitter!" she exclaimed. Then she told me a story that helped me understand her excitement. "This morning we had no customers in the store. None at all. So I looked at my wall-hanging of Archangel Uriel, and I said, 'Uriel, please send customers to the store.' That was just 30 minutes ago, and here you are!" She hugged me again. "Your books taught me to ask the angels for help, and look what happened!"

As Mrs. Bee, Steven, and I conversed, the store began filling with other customers. Mrs. Bee asked me to sign my books and card decks, which I was happy to do for such a lovely person. By the time we left, Mrs. Bee's store was packed with shoppers.

ANGEL EARTH

I was anxious to bring in my newfound knowledge of Atlantis and the healing temples to help my students in the workshop heal and learn. Mark Watson and Shaun Wise of the Detroit-based band Angel Earth had traveled to Ireland to play music at our Angel Therapy Practitioner course. All the students lay down on blankets on the floor, and while Mark played keyboards, I took everyone through a guided meditation based upon my memories of the crystal healing beds of Atlantis.

I watched as psychic debris lifted from everyone's bodies and floated just below the ceiling, but the dark gunk wasn't leaving the room! Then I realized that the staff had psychically sealed the room to keep out energy intrusions from the outside. However, the seal was also keeping psychic debris from *leaving* the room. The staff was in a circle around the students, and I motioned for them to lift the energy up through the ceiling. When they did, the seal opened up and the room cleared.

The Atlantean healing temple meditation was so powerful that everyone began asking me for copies of it on a tape or CD. The meditation, along with Mark Watson's music, is now available, and it's called *Angel Medicine: A Healing Meditation CD* (also published by Hay House).

The band Angel Earth had worked with me periodically for three years. We'd traveled throughout North America together and had become close friends. Originally, Angel Earth had a third member, Michael Wise, whom I first met in Pittsburgh around 1998.

Michael had worked in a Detroit factory, but he really wanted to devote himself to music and spiritual studies, so he asked the angels for a sign. That day, he saw his birth date and initials on a license plate and knew that the angels were giving him the go-ahead. Michael quit his job the next day and became a full-time musician.

Michael, his son Shaun, and childhood best friend Mark traveled with Steven and me to our workshops in Canada and throughout the United States. They drove a rented motor home and took side trips to the Grand Canyon and other magical locations. Michael was a devotee of Paramahansa Yogananda, and he also worked closely with Jesus and Archangel Michael. He wrote most of the words to the band's songs, which were all uplifting and spiritual.

A sweet, even-tempered man, Michael was always in good spirits. He'd drive endless miles, set up his band's equipment, and interact with audience members without ever saying a negative word. Michael always talked about his dream of moving from Detroit to a sunny beach area, yet his family and friends were in Detroit, and it would have been tough to leave them. The band's song "Oceans" reflected Michael's passion for the sea.

Then in August of 2002, while Steven and I were conducting the Hawaiian Healing Retreat in Kona, I received an e-mail from Mark with the phrase "With Deepest Regrets" in the subject line. I hurriedly opened the e-mail and was shocked to read that Michael had died that morning. He had been in his yard reading a book about aliens, and was up to the chapter called "Crossing Over." Then, Michael simply fell over and passed away, leaving his wife and high school sweetheart, Sandy, to find him. He was only 48 years old, with no history of health problems; and he didn't smoke, drink, or do drugs. Two autopsy reports were unable to find any cause of death.

Michael came to me in several lucid dreams that let me know that he was very happy in the spirit world. He was with his beloved Yogananda and Jesus, and he told me, "It was my time."

Whenever the remaining members of Angel Earth played, I saw Michael so clearly standing there, playing his guitar and singing his heart out. He was the embodiment of joy that came from living his passion. Michael lived the last years of his life ideally, instead of compromising himself by working at a job that he couldn't stand. (You can see Michael's photos and read about him by looking up the band's Website: **www.AngelEarth.org**).

At night after class, I'd soak in a bath of water created from sea salt purchased at Mrs. Bee's. (Soaking in sea-saltwater is a fast way to ground and clear yourself at the end of the day.) The sea salt absorbed psychic debris and other toxins, and led to a feeling of tranquility that I'd often experienced while swimming in the ocean.

My readings were always the clearest when I was close to saltwater. For instance, at one Hawaiian workshop, I gave individual readings to all the participants while sitting outside in the sun next to the sea. My readings were so detailed and clear that even I was shocked. I chalked the clarity up to my proximity to the sea and my daily ocean swims. After all, salt was a crystal, so soaking in salty water was actually like bathing in crystalline water!

At Mrs. Bee's, I'd purchased three small polished rose quartz crystals and one amethyst stone. Actually, Mrs. Bee insisted on giving them to me as gifts, making their energy even more special. The angels had asked me to place the crystals in my drinking-water bottle during my trip, as insurance against stressful energy. I placed the stones in my water bottle, and I transferred the stones as I changed water bottles during my trip. Although my schedule was intense while in Ireland, my health and energy levels remained high—and I attribute partial credit for that to those crystal stones. Once we left Ireland, I put the crystals in a special pouch and haven't yet been guided to use them in drinking water since that time.

I visited Mrs. Bee's a few more times during our time in Ireland and was pleased to find out that some of the graduates of our Angel Therapy Practitioner course would be giving angel readings at her store.

CHAPTER 8

The Sunshine Report

When Steven and I returned to Southern California, I delved into researching scientific studies on sunshine. I resolved to stay unbiased, no matter what the angels had told me. After all, I wanted to write responsibly about the topic, and not impart opinions unsubstantiated by hard data.

But then, while researching the topic, a personal situation occurred that made me take the topic all that more seriously: My mother was diagnosed with a mild form of skin cancer on her face.

A week before she and my father had visited my home to celebrate their 50th wedding anniversary, my mother had gone in for the first of her tests. She was scheduled for more tests on her return home. Mom had always been a sun worshiper, like many California girls. She'd spent her teenage years baking in the rays, getting a deep tan—now she regretted having done so and had vowed to completely steer clear of the sun.

The weather was mild and sunny while Mom was visiting Steven and me, and the entire time she wore sunglasses, sunscreen, long-sleeved shirts, long pants, and wide-brimmed hats. My father fussed over her, making sure that his beloved wife wouldn't come in contact with sunshine and possibly have a recurrence of the skin cancer. Since they were scheduled for a Hawaiian vacation the following month to celebrate their wedding anniversary, I worried that they'd miss out on the joys of the good weather.

As we sat out on the balcony—my parents in the shade of an umbrella, and me sitting in the sun—my father asked what I used to shield myself from the ultraviolet rays. When I told him nothing, he seemed concerned. Then I told him about the research I'd found:

"Sunlight has been demonized because of its correlation to skin cancer and cataracts," I said. "Some in the scientific community believe that ozone depletion is a major factor in these conditions. People are warned to stay out of the sun, to slather on sunscreen, and to wear sunglasses. Yet I've always found that sunshine warms my soul and elevates my mood."

Mom smiled and said, "Yes, me, too!"

"And everyone knows that reduced sunlight is associated with debilitating depression and seasonal affective disorder," I added.

I told my parents about the scientific and historical studies pointing to the sun's healing properties, as well as its unhealthful side. After reviewing the research, I felt as if we'd collectively thrown the baby out with the bathwater by shunning sunshine. After all, articles published in respected journals such as *The New England Journal of Medicine* and the *Journal of the American Medical Association* report that people who work outdoors are significantly less likely to get skin cancer than those who are indoors all the time (and who *occasionally* go out in the sun and then get sunburned). One such study came from the University of Western Australia, an institution in a country that reportedly suffers from one of the atmosphere's biggest ozone holes.

I told my parents about research showing that women who live in northern latitudes are more likely to develop ovarian and breast cancer than those who live in sunnier southern locales. In a similar study, women who worked outdoors were significantly less likely to develop breast or colon cancer. Scientists know that lack of sunshine creates vitamin D deficiencies, which is correlated with ovarian, breast, and colon cancer. Vitamin D protects against these types of cancers. Vitamin D deficiency is also associated with bone loss and fracture.

My parents listened intently as I said, "Scientists have also discovered that the recommended daily allowance for vitamin D is insufficient for people who don't get daily sunshine exposure. In fact, two studies of Middle-Eastern women living in sunny climates found that they suffered from vitamin D deficiencies because their outer clothing prevented sunlight from converting into vitamin D in their systems."

I was on a roll (and a little bit on a soapbox), but my passion held my parents' interest. "Most studies on skin cancer and sunlight have been conducted on fair-skinned individuals, and darker-skinned races that have higher incidences of cancers may need additional sunlight exposure. Studies on the link between sunlight and melanoma also have no consistent design or standardized measures, which could explain why they show conflicting results. Many studies show that sunscreen only protects against the nondeadly types of skin cancer, but that it doesn't produce significant protection against melanoma, which is the deadly skin cancer. In other words, the jury's still not in on whether, or how much, sunlight affects melanoma.

"So, are you saying that everyone should spend more time in the sun?" my mother asked.

"I'm saying that the research shows that sunlight is a double-edged sword that's both necessary for good health in moderation, and unhealthy in excess—especially for fair-skinned individuals. People should definitely avoid getting sunburned, but they also should spend at least one hour daily getting fresh air and direct exposure to sunlight.

"After reviewing all the research, I really believe that it's healthiest to go out in the sun in the morning or late-afternoon hours without wearing any eye shields or sunscreen. After all, the healthful sunlight rays enter the body through the eyes. Fair-skinned people should limit their exposure to no more than one hour daily while they build up melanin-based tans.

"I also think that we need to be outdoors for the sunrises and sunsets, and step outside at night to absorb the moon and starlight."

I gave my parents a copy of the book *The Healing Sun* by Richard Hobday. Since the book was written by a British doctor of engineering who cited the latest scientific studies about sunshine's connection to both health and illness, I thought that my father would respect the work.

One week before my parents were scheduled to leave for their Hawaiian vacation, I asked my mother if she'd relaxed a bit about exposing herself to sunlight.

She replied, "We're still reading the book, but we're already feeling much better about the sun. I still think I should take precautions when it comes to my face and not get the side of my face where the stitches were sunburned. But we will enjoy the sun and follow the 'moderation in all things' advice. The book makes a lot of sense. Relating it to *A Course in Miracles,* I'm really thinking that all the negative publicity about the sun is causing guilt and that could be the real (rather illusory) culprit behind what happened to me!"

I also thought about the fact that, if we don't spend much time in sunlight, we must take vitamin B-12 supplements. If our bodies are low on B-12, our ears begin to ring—which is the sound that our angels make when they're giving us messages or uplifting us through toning.

FINDING LIGHT IN THE BLACKOUT

We were on our way to Toronto, where I was to give an evening workshop and where Steven would present one the following day. The flight attendant had requested that everyone close their window screens to allow for better viewing of the in-flight movie, yet I couldn't bear to fully shut out the daylight and beautiful views of the clouds. After all, it took all day to fly from California to Toronto. With the time-zone change, we'd be landing at night. So I kept my shade at half-mast to enjoy at least part of the day's light.

"Our captain has informed us that there will be severe turbulence ahead, so he's turning on the seat-belt sign. Please remain in your seats, with your seat belt tightly fastened."

I sighed and called upon the angels to buoy up our airplane and keep it steady in the air. I saw dozens of angels next to the belly of the airplane, bolstering it on their upper backs. I'd invoked angels to help with turbulence for many years, and it had always worked. (Many of my audience members have told me similar stories.) This time was no exception, and soon the flight attendant announced that we were "free to move about the cabin."

My Toronto workshop went well, and I was enjoying my time in Canada. The Learning Annex had put Steven and me up in a wonderful hotel that served vegan food and had a great gym— two things that made traveling infinitely more bearable. The next evening, August 14, 2003, Steven was set to give a workshop on his fifth book, *Sacred Ceremony*. During the event, participants would conduct a group ceremony, involving building an altar, drumming, dancing, and delving into active ways to pray and meditate.

At 4:11 P.M., Steven was relaxing before his workshop when the lights and music went out in our hotel room. We assumed that the hotel's electricity had gone out. Then we heard a loud screeching sound and a woman's voice came over the loud-speaker in our room, announcing that power was out all over the city. A few minutes later, there was the screech again, calling our attention to the following announcement: "This blackout is wide-spread, affecting much of Northern Canada; as well as New York, New Jersey, Connecticut, Ohio, and Michigan."

She explained that the power station in nearby Buffalo, New York, had malfunctioned. There was no telling when the lights would be restored. The elevators were out of service, as was the running water, which was electrically pumped up to the hotel rooms.

The sun was still high in the northern sky, so Steven and I walked downstairs to go outside and investigate. We went inside a nearby Starbucks coffee establishment, where no hot drinks were available, but where they did have bottled juice and water. Everyone inside the coffee shop nervously chatted with one another, speculating about the future of the blackout situation.

Steven and I noted how tragedy unified strangers, then took our purchase of water outside.

The city was eerily quiet. Downtown shoppers sat on sidewalks, pondering how to get home. Taxis, buses, and limos were unable to operate without computers in their main offices, so all public transportation was suspended. And cars were no longer allowed in the city, to prevent looters from driving in and taking advantage of the situation.

Our hotel was restricting food service to registered hotel guests only in order to conserve its provisions, since no new deliveries could come in. Dining fare was limited to sandwiches, salads, and other meals not requiring cooking. As the sun set, Steven and I ate salads and prayed for angelic intervention in the candlelit restaurant.

As we climbed the ten flights to our room, I silently gave thanks that we were both in good physical shape. Many of the hotel guests huffed and puffed on the stair climb, unaccustomed to exertion. The angels had told both Steven and me how important it was for everyone to get into excellent condition for upcoming situations where we'd all need stamina and strength. As we climbed the final flight of stairs, we were both thankful that we'd listened.

Steven had brought candles for his *Sacred Ceremony* class, which had now been cancelled because of the blackout. We gratefully lit the candles as darkness descended upon our room.

"This is how life was for many years before the invention of lightbulbs," I remarked to Steven.

"Yes, before lightbulbs artificially extended daylight until the wee hours of the night," he agreed. We discussed how the human's natural circadian rhythms were built to wake up at dawn's light, and then sleep soon after sunset. I later discovered that the onset of modern diseases such as diabetes, cancer, and heart disease occurred precisely at the time that the lightbulb became widely used in homes and offices in the 1920s.

My previous studies had taught me that important brain chemicals, especially serotonin, were created during our sleep time. If we were collectively sleep deprived because of artificial lighting, it stood that we were also collectively serotonin deprived. Since serotonin regulated mood, energy levels, and appetite stimulation (especially for carbohydrates such as sweets and breads), artificial lighting could be the culprit behind epidemics of obesity, depression, and life-impairing disease.

Sitting there in the dimly lit Toronto hotel room, looking over a darkened landscape, it was easy to imagine the old days when people went to bed much earlier, a time when there was no electronic stimulation such as television or e-mail to keep people awake. After dinner and perhaps conversation by the fire, it would be natural to fall asleep around 8 or 9 o'clock.

I thought about all the modern prescription drugs that artificially created or mimicked serotonin production, such as Ritalin, which is used for attention deficit hyperactivity disorder (ADHD); and Prozac, used to treat depression. Low serotonin was also associated with premenstrual syndrome, bedwetting, and obesity. *Sounds like we all need to sleep more at night!* I thought. Then I had an idea.

"Honey, let's go outside and gaze at the moon and the stars," I said to Steven. "Let's take advantage of the city lights being out and look at the nighttime sky."

I didn't need to ask Steven, a nature fanatic, twice. We raced down the stairs and on to the vacant street. The blackened sky back-dropped the sparkling diamond stars like a velvety canvas. As we walked around the corner, the nearly full moon greeted us brightly. We stared in awe at the way the moon and stars popped out of the sky, seeming much closer than they normally did when they competed with streetlights. Soon, other people noticed us staring at the moon. They gathered around, and we all admired Mother Nature's light show together.

When we returned to the room, Steven and I prayed and asked the angels to help us get to our travel destination. I was scheduled to speak in Atlanta before 2,000 people on Saturday morning, and I had to leave Toronto the next day, Friday, to ensure making my speech. Yet the Toronto airport and all surrounding airports were closed. Not only that, but, no taxi, bus, or limo company was able to drive us anywhere. We needed a miracle if I was to make my speech.

I thought about our dependency on electricity. Everything, it seemed, was contingent upon the juice. I was experiencing what our world would be like if there were no electricity. It made me realize that the blackout was a test run and a sign. We needed to shore up our use of solar power and also lunar power, or completely reduce our dependency on electronics.

At 10:45 that night, a small strip of Toronto regained power. That strip included our hotel. The lights were back on! Miraculously, we found a car company to drive us to the Buffalo, New York, airport, which had resumed takeoffs and landings. Inside the airport in the waiting area, I found a white feather on the seat next to mine. *"The angels are here helping us!"* I told Steven, and showed him the sign. And when we checked into our Atlanta hotel and I found a second feather right inside our room, there was no doubt that our prayers had been heard and answered.

Within a few days, the rest of the Eastern Seaboard resumed power, and the biggest blackout in history—affecting 50 million people—was over. But the signs warning us to seek alternative power options continued, as London and Italy experienced major blackouts over the next two months.

CHAPTER 9

The Wizard of Atlantis

It was September, time for our annual visit to the magical land of Australia. For the first part of our journey, I toured with three psychics: Gordon Smith (aka "the Psychic Barber" of Scotland), John Holland, and Sonia Choquette. I called our event "Psychics on Parade," but Hay House, our publisher and sponsor, officially called it "Intuitive Messengers." The four of us would share the stage for all-day workshops where we'd give random audience readings and brief lectures.

After the other three speakers returned to their respective countries, Steven and I stayed in Brisbane to prepare for the three-day certification course I was teaching. A highly condensed version of the Angel Therapy Practitioner training, the "Angel Intuitive" course was being offered in Brisbane, Melbourne, and Sydney.

At the same time, I was finishing this book. I would feel anxious at times, which occasionally made me procrastinate when I thought about sitting down and typing. Finally, after prayerful discussions with my angels, I concluded that these anxieties were related to past lives, where I'd been killed for revealing the type of information I present in this book.

Steven did past-life work with me, and we found that I'd had my throat slit in one life and had been hung in another for being a teacher of this kind of work. Immediately after he revealed this, a deep, craggy red line with dry skin formed around my neck. It took a full week for it to disappear. When it did, the anxiety healed along with it.

* * *

During my stay in Brisbane, I researched some of the messages from the angels of Atlantis and from my Atlantean past-life regression. I was intrigued that during my regression, I'd recalled that Hermes had infused the healing temple's pyramid with light. *Who was Hermes?* I wondered. He appeared to be a powerful mortal man who lived in and benevolently ruled over Atlantis. Yes, he was also known as a Greek god and thought to be the Egyptian deity, Thoth. He was credited with creating "hermetic science," the art of manifestation through visualization and alchemy, and his work is said to be the basis for the secret knowledge of groups such as the Freemasons and the Rosicrucian societies. The pyramid containing an eye, on the back of American currency, was said to spring from the Freemason founders of the country. *How interesting that this eye and pyramid are identical to what I saw in the Atlantean healing temple,* I realized with a gasp!

I'd e-mailed Nicholas, the psychic historian I'd met in Greece, asking him for any information on the connection between Hermes and Atlantis. But Nicholas never returned any of my e-mails. My angels told me that he was afraid to commit himself in writing. After all, in his past life, he'd suffered greatly for disseminating esoteric secrets.

So, in meditation, I asked Hermes to fill in the blanks. I immediately heard a deep male voice say that Atlantis has ascended. *"That's the place of crystalline castles where you visit during your soul travel dreams."* Hermes reminded me that he'd coined the famous phrase "As above, so below," which refers to the fact that Atlantis was an attempt to bring Heaven to Earth. However, it couldn't stay in this dense energy and had to ascend.

The next day, I taught a course in Brisbane for graduates of the previous year's Angel Intuitive Course. I decided to take the class through the Atlantean crystal-bed healing meditation. While I did so, I saw the seven high-priestesses who were each in charge of radiating colored light through the crystal points positioned above the chakras. Then I psychically saw a male high-priest come in. At first, I worried that he might upset the meditating students, since my past experiences with Atlantean priests hadn't been that positive. But when I took a good look at the high-priest's face, I gasped. It was definitely Merlin! I'd worked with him for many years and knew him well. He had the "wizard" look, and in this vision—which I was continually describing to my meditating students—Merlin outstretched his hands over the individual in the crystal healing bed. Merlin released old psychic wounds and toxic debris from the person.

And then he transformed before my eyes into Hermes! I gasped again as I described what I was seeing to the class. *Merlin and Hermes were the same man!*

As soon as I walked in the door of my hotel room after the class, I went straight into a channeling session and asked Merlin/Hermes to explain.

"How is Hermes related to Merlin?" I asked.

"You caught us when you reverted back to Atlantis this morning! My shape-shifting couldn't take place fast enough to fool you! Just kidding, darling. It really was a revelation for your audience's enjoyment. Remember that we told you that Avalon and Atlantis were simultaneous? Well, I was overseeing both traditions, both sides of the alleyway, if you will.

"The Egyptian pharaoh Ramses was also calling upon me, and I was visiting him in my dreamtime. That's when I was invoked by the name that he called me: Thoth or Radah, and I became a legendary figure because I wasn't showing up in the physical form, but in the mystical dreamtime form. Many of the 'gods' and 'goddesses' were apparitional figures because they were highly evolved living persons, coming to mystics in dreams and meditations."

"What about the golden light that I see in the pyramid in the Atlantean healing temple?" I asked.

"Yes, that is the eternal flame of the God-truth, which I tipped upside down and invoked and imbued into the earth's core and crust to ensure its continuation into eons in the future. It was sent to the various centers of worship and prayer, what you now know

as power spots, and this is why its trail—what you call ley lines— leads to each location. It is simply a way for all of us to collective- ly hold hands in unified spirit. The flame can be called upon by anyone and at any time, and I welcome your interest in fanning the flames by intending to send down the golden light that is within everyone, into the earth's inner atmosphere.

"Remember, too, that the hole in the roof of the temple fun- neled the golden sunlight downward into the crystal pyramid. As above, so below! The healing golden light of the sunshine is a mir- ror of the God-love that you seek. Bask, warm yourselves, and heal in it, and teach others not to shun the sunshine, nor to shun the love that they seek."

"Was Atlantis where Santorini now stands?" I asked.

"Atlantis was widespread in various locales throughout the earth. It is closer to what you call Shambala now, off the Indonesian coast, and into central Bali. It had an Australian con- nection as well. The peninsula you sense connecting Greece to Egypt is correct, and that was for many eons the predecessor and also the successor to Atlantis. It was in an in-between period of human function, and the Greeks were idealists who propelled humankind forward in many directions.

"Pythagoras was a student of mine, both etherically and physi- cally. You knew him well in ancient Egypt, where you once studied with him. You were a student of his in many ways and in many life- times. Pythagoras listened well, and he was fearless in putting this wisdom into practice.

"My life in Egypt was well after the time that Atlantis sank. By that time, I was able to step into my physical role there as Thoth, which amazed many people who had only previously witnessed me in dreamtime. I brought all of the healing and intellectual wisdom we'd amassed in Atlantis with me to Egypt."

THE ANGEL AND THE SERPENT

Our Brisbane hotel was near a botanical garden that sported a duck pond, ancient ficus trees, and lots of birds and possums.

Every day, Steven and I jogged through the park, enjoying the sunshine and fresh air.

Since Hermes, the angels of Atlantis, and the Stonehenge stones had lectured me about the importance of the sun, stars, and moonlight, I'd been going outdoors a lot more. Both Steven and I made sure to spend at least an hour outside without sunglasses each day. When indoors, we'd open the windows and balcony doors to allow in fresh air and unfiltered sun and moonlight. We'd begun limiting our hotel stays to locations with windows that opened, and preferably, with balconies where we could open a door and really connect with the outdoors.

I'd always found that when I jogged, the increased oxygen flow created a stronger connection between the angelic realm and me. The angels had told me that on the Earth plane, their messages were carried on the molecules of oxygen. The more air we breathed, the stronger the connection. So I wasn't surprised one day while jogging through the Brisbane park to begin receiving a download of angel messages.

"The human body is comprised of both the serpent and the angel," they told me. This was a consistent message that I'd been receiving for nearly a year. *"The serpent's head is your medulla oblongata, known as your 'reptilian brain.' The serpent's body is your spine, and also your alignment of the chakra system. The serpent is your instinctual nature, which serves you well and is aligned with the intention of survival. The serpent needs sunshine and warmth to survive, so care for it well. It represents your light body. It is composed of pure light.*

"The angelic side of humanity is that part of everyone that is pure love. No matter how a person acts or behaves, remember that they have an angel within them. This part is the soul and the spirit. It thrives on love, both giving and receiving. Ideal health is achieved when you pay attention to both the serpent and the angel within. Ignore neither side, but feed them both with abundant light and love.

"The ancients of Atlantis knew this wisdom about the coupling of the serpent and the angel, and they symbolized it in their healing medallion called 'the caduceus,' which is a melding of the angel and the serpent."

I couldn't quite recall what a caduceus looked like, except that I knew that it was a snake wrapped around a pole. I couldn't wait to finish my run so that I could log on to the Internet and look at the symbol. Dripping with perspiration, I went onto the **Google.com** "Images" section and typed the word *caduceus.*

As hundreds of images popped up, I gasped: The caduceus, which you can see below, had angel wings at the head of a pole, with two snakes wrapped around it! Just as the angels had told me during my run, it was the perfect symbol for the melding of the serpent and the angelic!

And how perfect that the medical community had adopted this symbol as a sign of health. It showed the ancient wisdom of taking care of both the lower and the higher self, the earthly self and the celestial self, and of balancing physical and spiritual needs. It also showed the acceptance of the human shadow. Instead of trying to deny our shadow side, or feel ashamed of it, true health meant accepting the dark side of our psyche. These shadows were instinctual in nature, after all.

The two snakes also represented our double-helix DNA. I thought of my friend Gregg Braden's book, *The God Code* [Hay House, 2004], in which he'd correlated the code of DNA to ancient Hebrew language. Gregg discovered that although everyone's DNA is unique and individual, each pair is numerically encoded with the value equated to the Hebrew word for *God.* In other words, God has been encoded in everyone's genes.

Then I explored the history of the caduceus and discovered that it was *the* healing wand that Hermes carried in Atlantis and ancient Egypt! Everything had come full circle. The ancient secrets of the Atlantean healing temples had resurfaced, and they were embodied in the simple, commonsense words that Dr. Chronis had spoken to me on Santorini Island:

Light plus love equals healing.

PART II

Angel Medicine Steps and Stories

CHAPTER 10

Introduction to the Principles of Angel Medicine

In this part of the book, I'll discuss the practical application of "light plus love equals healing." Angel medicine means paying attention to both the physical (light) and spiritual/emotional (love) of ourselves, or whomever we're intending to heal. Both components are very real, and both are equally important to bringing balance, harmony, and health to a person's physical, emotional, intellectual, and spiritual health. These methods also bring healing to one's material life, and can heal finances and even so-called inanimate objects, as you'll read about in these pages.

There are many ways to work with both light and love, and you can select among the examples when choosing a healing modality. In many of the healing stories in Part II, you'll notice that the most dramatic and fastest healings usually occur when several components related to light are mixed with several components that address love. Simply put, the more you use these components, the better.

COMPONENTS OF LIGHT HEALING

Light is that part of us that's connected to Earth life. It comprises our instincts, our physicality and health, and our chakra systems. Light comprises vibrations, so it involves energy healing such as Reiki or Therapeutic Touch. Light is also composed of colors, so visualizing and intending colors for protection and healing also falls under this category. Light refers to our physical energy bodies.

Here are some ways to introduce more light into a situation when conducting a healing for yourself or others:

- Hold crystal-clear intentions of the desired outcome.

- Work with crystals.

- Absorb unfiltered daylight; or light generated by sunrises, sunsets, stars, or moonlight.

- Send healing energy, such as Reiki, pranic, Qigong, Therapeutic Touch, and so on.

- Practice chakra clearing, including etheric cord cutting, spirit releasement, and vacuuming.

- Visualize and surround yourself or another person with light and colors.

COMPONENTS OF LOVE HEALING

Love comprises our soul and spirit, as well as our emotional body (which is the bridge between our physical and spiritual self). Some examples of working with love include:

- having faith and trust;

- releasing fear;

- feeling compassion;

- feeling gratitude;

- prayer and meditation; and

- acting kindly toward yourself and others

ANGELS: BOTH LOVE AND LIGHT

Perhaps one reason why calling upon angels is so effective as an instrument in healing is because angels bring both light and love to any situation or person. When you ask angels to be at the side of someone in need (you or someone else), they come in with the warm glow of a bright inner light coupled with unconditional love and a calm, faith-filled nature.

When dire circumstances put us in a state of alarm, faith may be the first thing to go out the window. We can lean on angels to bolster our confidence and assure us that everything will be all right. We can tap in to their faith in Divine order. The angels can help release us from fear so that we're filled with trust. And as the master healer and teacher, Jesus, taught throughout his life: "As is your faith, it is done unto you."

In the next several chapters, you'll find out how to work with light and love to effect healing. You'll also read real about people whose health and lives were healed through the process of calling upon light and love.

CHAPTER II

Seeing the Light—
Crystal-Clear
Decisions

With any manifestation, it's essential to be certain about what you desire. Angel medicine can work instantly, and you can be immediately healed. The key is that you're completely clear that you require an instant healing. You need to release any doubts or fears that this is the right thing. Some may worry that commanding Heaven is blasphemous, and this fear can short-circuit an immediate healing. It's clarity about your desires that brings about results.

Our inner light stems from that part of us that is instinctual. Animals and birds use instinct for survival. When a snake sets his sights upon his prey, he has the crystal-clear intention of eating. He doesn't hesitate, thinking, *What if I don't deserve to eat?* or *What if this isn't God's will for me?* Without clear intentions, the snake would starve and die. While we don't need to stalk live prey for survival, we do need the same clear intentions to manifest our earthly needs. We still have instincts within us that need honoring and attention.

This isn't the same thing as straining or forcing an outcome to occur. Anytime we *try* to make something happen, we become blocked as far as achieving our desired goals. That's because the negativity associated with force and strain attract the very thing we fear. These fears might include anxieties about whether you'll be able to achieve an outcome, whether you "deserve" it, whether you'll be able to keep and maintain the desired outcome in the future, and what other people may think about your success.

Having crystal-clear intentions means having a relaxed, confident attitude. It may help to keep in mind that as you're healed, you're in a better position to help your loved ones and community. As a strong, healed, secure person, you've got more resources that allow you to give more freely—with joy and passion.

OVERCOMING THE FEAR OF HEALING

If a part of you wants to be healthy but another part of you is afraid of it, this will block your manifestation. To heal, you need a crystal-clear intention of health. With clear intentions, miracles such as instantaneous healings are possible.

A Course in Miracles says that instant healings are normal; however, many people think it's too weird to immediately be healed from a malady. That's because Western medicine believes that healing occurs over time . . . slowly . . . after regular visits to the doctor and taking medication for weeks or months. As much as we want an instant healing, this would scare us as much as seeing a ghost. So, we have one foot on the gas pedal and one on the brake as we pray for healing—while simultaneously (unconsciously) praying that it doesn't occur, since it would scare us.

I've also had clients express deep-seated fears that they didn't *deserve* instant healings, so they wouldn't accept it when it occurred. I remember one woman who asked me to heal a boil on her ear. I placed my hands on her earlobes and sent energy through the ear while simultaneously affirming that it was healed. The boil instantly started draining and disintegrating. The woman held her ear and kept exclaiming that she couldn't believe the healing occurred so quickly! I reminded her of a famous Louise Hay story along the same lines:

Louise recounts that she once helped a client instantly heal from the need for corrective lenses—that is, the woman now had perfect vision. The woman was naturally pleased; however, she was so amazed at the immediacy of the healing that she kept exclaiming, "Oh my! I can't believe I don't need glasses anymore! I can't believe it!" The woman affirmed so many times that she couldn't believe that her eyesight was improved that she soon manifested the need to wear glasses again.

Why would anyone be afraid of health? In my healing work, I've seen the following reasons:

— **Fear of "God's will."** Some people fear that God is *willing* their ill health, and they're afraid of violating a greater will than their own.

Yet, if we truly believe that God is loving, and if we trust that God is good, then why would the Creator will anything but love and goodness for us? One who is all-love would never "test" us, or use pain as a way to make us grow. Wouldn't we be more useful to God's plan if our energy and health were vibrant and radiant?

When you pray for health, be very clear that this *is* God's will for you. You are one of the much-needed troops of Earth angels on this planet. All hands are needed for the smooth operation of God's plan of peace. When one lightworker opts out of his or her appointed task, it leaves another lightworker to do the work for two.

— **Ambivalence about suffering.** Some individuals believe that all life is about suffering and that suffering is inevitable. Freedom from suffering isn't achievable, in their opinions, so why bother working on its attainment?

Many people have told me that they believe suffering is the only route to personal and spiritual growth. Their souls will be shortchanged if they try to bypass the important life lessons inherent in pain. The angels have told me, though, that while we can definitely become stronger through suffering, we can also grow much faster through peace.

When we become peaceful, we make an important contribution toward *world* peace. We also inspire others through our peacefulness. Being ill or injured never inspired anyone. But transcending or healing physical limitations is always uplifting to witness.

— **Fear of change.** Chronic illness or injury can become a lifestyle—and a long-term project. Being healthy would leave an empty gap, which some people instinctively fear. *A Course in Miracles: Manual for Teachers* says that "all forms of sickness, even unto death, are physical expressions of the fear of awakening." In other words, ill health can keep our minds and schedules so busy that we avoid looking inward at ourselves and our life's purpose.

— **Secondary gain.** Let's admit it: We're rewarded for illness and injury with lots of sympathy, cards, and bouquets. We might also receive time off from work or school, as well as payment for long-term disabilities. We may unconsciously desire the continuation of these rewards, and resist mending our bodies as a result.

— **Self-esteem.** Many of the people whom I've counseled have admitted that, deep down, they don't believe that they deserve happiness and health. They also wonder whether they warrant Heaven's attention, having lived less-than-perfect lives.

I help them see that, while none of us live perfectly, we're all still God's perfect children. We're all equally loved, unconditionally.

— **Fixed ideas about health.** Some folks have firm beliefs that they'll inherit a genetic family trait, that illness is inevitable, or that a certain condition is untreatable. In a way, doctors put curses on patients when they give firm diagnoses, and if we buy into these diagnoses, we may manifest the symptoms. We can also be influenced by advertisements about illness and medications, and media hype about epidemics.

CLEAR EXPECTATIONS, CLEAR RESULTS

Clarity about your desire for an instant healing, and your *acceptance* of an instant healing are both equally important. A busy spa owner from San Francisco told me that she'd been diagnosed with cancer. As she was being wheeled into the operating room, she exclaimed loudly, "I don't have time for this!" She meant it, too—her business demands kept her occupied every day, and she had no time for an operation or recovery time. The doctors opened her up and were amazed to see that there was no evidence of cancer.

Put your foot down to the Universe and tell it your conditions.

But what about God's will? some will ask. This is an individual concern. I truly believe that each of us has a "time" when we're to go home to Heaven. We preplanned this time, in conjunction with God and our angels before incarnating.

I also believe that God is omnipresent, within each of us. This means that God's will is everywhere, overlapping your own. And a loving God would never want you to suffer in any way, just as you'd never will your own children to suffer.

It's true that you can grow through pain, but it's also true that you can grow through peace. Demand, command, and expect peace in all ways, and it shall be yours.

Some people are afraid of health because they have an investment in illness. One woman I worked with had her whole life wrapped around her illness: It was her project, her love, her child. If she healed, what would fill this vacancy? The very thought of a healthy body left my client anxious. She worried, "How will I spend my new free time?" and "What meaning will my life have?" With free time, she'd have to search for a meaningful project, and this might mean failure or success . . . two of her biggest fears.

Other clients have confessed that they equate health and peace with a life of boredom. Problems are exciting and create a nice adrenaline rush, yet peace and health yield opportunities to experience different types of excitement—such as devoting yourself to helping a pet cause, traveling, or assisting your family.

A woman named V. J. Williams put her foot down to the Universe and received an instant healing. Her neighbor's young horse had jumped its fence and was loose near a busy roadway, so V. J. helped herd the horse back into its pasture.

The animal became spooked and kicked back with both hooves. V. J. remembers, "One of his hooves hit my rib cage and sent me to my knees, fighting for breath." An emergency room x-ray found a fractured rib.

Doctors wrapped V. J.'s ribs and sent her home to rest for two days. She was in pain and tried to remain motionless. On the third day, V. J. went to a job that she'd only recently begun. She was in pain, but still able to function—but she soon developed symptoms that indicated her injury was worse than imagined.

"I noticed that every time I bent over and sat back up when retrieving papers from my desk, I would feel a gurgling run up and down my back in my lung area. When I bent down, the bubbling would run down my back and then would gurgle back up as I came upright. This continued Wednesday through Friday, and I knew without being told that one of my lungs was punctured. This meant another emergency-room visit, and a lot of expense since I didn't yet have health insurance at my new job."

Since the first hospital visit had cost her $2,500 and V. J. already wondered how she'd cover *that* bill, she was very anxious about incurring any additional medical expenses.

That night, V. J. packed her overnight bag to take to the hospital. She began crying hard and prayed for help. She needed a miracle healing, and she needed it now! Her clarity while praying allowed her to fully receive her wish.

V. J. describes what happened next. "I bent over, and there was no gurgling sound! I bent over several more times, and still no gurgling! It had stopped, and it never returned. I started crying harder than before in gratitude to my angels and God for healing me. What a truly blessed miracle!"

She never experienced any further problems with her lungs, and her ribs healed quickly and completely. V. J. says, "I learned a valuable lesson that day: We are *never alone* in our times of turmoil and trouble. All we have to do is ask."

Expect a Miracle

The angels *want* to help us, but they can't intervene unless we specifically *ask* for help with everything we need assistance with. Don't tell them *how* to help; just ask for what you want. Be very clear about what you desire. Remember: Crystal-clear intentions create light, which illuminates your desired manifestation.

For instance, if you're bleeding, call upon Archangel Raphael and tell him, "Raphael, stop this bleeding immediately!" Don't worry that you're being bossy, pushy, or disrespectful. The angels respond well to a clear request. I find that if I call on Raphael in this way while simultaneously putting pressure on the cut, the bleeding stops rapidly. Just wash away the excess blood and any grime around the former incision, and be sure to tell Raphael, "Thank you."

Sixteen-year-old Alex Woburn used to suffer from nose-bleeds. One day he called upon his guardian angels to stop the bleeding. Alex reports, "My angels stopped it as soon as I asked."

The angels will also help you to lessen, or eliminate, physical pain. Completely surrender the situation, and say to God and the angels, "I give all of this to you. You take the pain. I can't take it anymore." This often yields fast results.

Again, Alex Woburn tells of how his angels eliminated pain when he asked them to.

"One day at school, a huge trampoline fell on my foot! My toes were black-and-blue, and the nail was coming off my big toe, with skin ripped across my feet. I had to stay home for two days and could barely walk. Finally, I asked my guardian angels to intervene and heal my toes.

"Within ten minutes of asking for help, the bruising faded from my large toe, and the nail became cleaner and hurt less. I was able to walk properly again without limping. This was no coincidence—I'd received some major help on healing my big toe.

"Still, the toenail hung partially off of the nail base and had to be removed by a doctor. The doctor told me that the procedure of removing the nail would hurt, so I prayed to the angels to alleviate any pain. Before I knew it, the nail was removed, without any pain whatsoever! The doctor's expression was one of shock, since I hadn't even cringed, and she asked whether I had a high pain threshold. But I knew that my guardian angels had surrounded and helped me, and I thanked them greatly."

PUT YOUR FOOT DOWN

Crystal-clear intentions mean that you won't accept anything but your desired outcome. As I've been saying, it's important not to tell Heaven *how* to create your desired outcome . . . but you must be really clear on what you will and won't accept.

If you need to, imagine that you're protecting a loved one. Sometimes we're more apt to be the protective mother bear on behalf of a pet or child than we are on behalf of our own selves. If you can't do it to heal yourself, then remember how many more people you can help when you're healed.

The point is to be very clear and put your foot down about your desires, as Wendy Eidman did.

Wendy was making waffles one morning and accidentally pressed her finger directly on the hot surface of the waffle iron. The pain was terrible, and a large blister quickly formed on her finger. As she ran cold water over her hand, Wendy prayed that Archangel Michael would heal her burn. The pain temporarily ceased but soon returned. So she prayed again, with the same results.

After about an hour of this ping-ponging between pain and peace, Wendy finally sat down and *demanded* that the pain be taken away, and that it not be allowed to return, no matter what!

Wendy says, "Lo and behold, it worked! I was instantly healed and the blister went down. I could do dishes and give my kids a bath, and you know how hot water feels on a burn—it's unbearable. I didn't feel anything at all! I was completely and utterly healed—and completely convinced that it was through Michael's healing grace."

Holding crystal-clear intentions means that your whole system is geared toward the manifestation of your desire. All of your energy is placed in that direction, and positive results are inevitable.

If You're Unsure about What You Desire . . .

What if you don't know what you want, or you're afraid of asking for the "wrong" thing? If that's the case, then think of the best possible scenario that you can imagine. If you can't imagine yourself manifesting so much goodness, imagine a loved one manifesting it. Then transfer yourself into the scene.

If you're afraid of making a "wrong choice," keep in mind that you *can't not* make a decision. In other words, if you make no choice . . . that's a decision to keep things as they presently are. The best way to handle this fear is to think of the best possible scenario and then say, "This, or something better, God."

That way, if you've limited your choices to one that is less than great, you leave room for improvement. You've also opened the door for the angels to help you choose the best possible options. And you'll be able to release any fears of making an unwise choice, and your fearlessness will help you manifest faster and more efficiently.

Once you've made your clear choice to have health in all areas of your life—physically, emotionally, spiritually, intellectually, romantically, financially, and so on—the more methods to bring light and love into your life, the better. In the next chapter, we'll look at the use of crystals to amplify light for healing.

CHAPTER 12

Crystal Healing

Since the time of Atlantis, and perhaps before then, crystals have been used to conduct healings. Crystals amplify natural energy in a process called "piezoelectricity." Today, hospitals use quartz crystals, microbalancers, and piezoelectric crystal sensors in diagnostic and healing work. Crystals are routinely used in radios, watches, and other electronic devices.

I place large, clear quartz crystals near my telephone to boost my connection when I give psychic readings over the phone. There's no doubt, in other words, about crystals' power to boost energy.

For instance, I once purchased a sugilite pendant at an expo a few minutes before a speech I was giving was to begin. I put the pendant on as I walked into the auditorium, and immediately began trance-channeling Archangel Michael for the first time publicly. Since then, whenever I'm called upon to channel Michael before an audience, I always wear sugilite, as I've found that the stone is aligned with his energy.

I've also discovered that if I wear a large amethyst or aqua aura stone next to my throat, then I have an easier time giving lengthy lectures (such as my three- or six-day certification cours-es, where I lecture daily). The large crystals near the throat chakra boosts its energy, and help me avoid throat fatigue or hoarseness. Whenever I've worn *small* crystals during a speech, my speaking energy lags.

Crystals can boost the light and energy of our chakra system and also of our energy body, and they can heal imbalances as well.

An Australian nurse named Elisabeth Jensen experienced a profound healing with the help of a crystal and the angels. Eleven years ago, she was severely depressed and suffered from a nonmalignant pituitary tumor that affected her entire hormonal system; she also had chronic back pain. If that weren't enough, Elisabeth's boyfriend was very violent and abusive toward her, and he also suffered from a chronically draining wound that hadn't responded to any treatment.

Elisabeth had a clairvoyant ability to see energy and auras, and one day she purchased a clear quartz crystal. As she was showing the crystal to her boyfriend, something magical happened: The crystal seemed to trigger an outpouring of white light from Elisabeth's crown chakra and hands toward her boyfriend.

Elisabeth says, "I felt very calm and blissful and put my hands on him as directed by an angelic voice. After about half an hour, the energy disappeared, and we both felt wonderful and peaceful. He and I were changed forever that day. His wound was completely healed over the next day, with only a tiny scar, and he stopped all physical abuse from that time onward."

Elisabeth's pituitary tumor also disappeared as a result of the one session with the crystal-directed white light, along with her depression and pain, and she became more psychically aware of angels. She now teaches workshops on the topic.

CRYSTAL CHILDREN

The newest generation of kids, the Crystal Children, are naturally interested in, and gifted in, crystal healing. This is one of the reasons why the generation earned its name. These young people are innately wise about which crystals to use for healing, and the ways in which they can implement this knowledge.

Stephen and Karen Williams noticed that their five-year-old daughter, Sabrina, showed a strong interest in crystals. She quickly learned the names of different crystals and often selected them for the family to bring home from stores.

One evening, Sabrina told her parents that she needed a crystal healing. After she'd chosen some crystals, Karen began teaching her daughter how to place them upon the major chakras. Sabrina interrupted her mother and said, "Mummy, I know where they go; I've done all this before," and proceeded to place the crystals on her chakras for self-healing.

Karen says, "Her connection with the crystals is a natural and comfortable one that I'm sure extends beyond this lifetime."

Did children like Sabrina live during the time of Atlantis, where they learned how to use crystals to boost the energy of chakras along the spinal column? So many of the present generation of toddlers exhibit an uncanny knowledge of crystal healing that one begins to wonder . . .

Carri Lineberry reports that her three-year-old daughter, Maia, keeps an amethyst crystal under her bed. "I found it there one day," says Carri, "so I put it away. Maia promptly discovered that the amethyst was gone, put it back, and informed me that it was to stay there."

The super-sensitivity of the new generation of children makes them extra aware of the therapeutic value of having crystals nearby. At age three, Maia is displaying the knowledge of working with crystals that's normally reserved for seasoned veterans of the healing art.

Maia's five-year-old sister, Shailyn, is also innately knowledgeable about crystal healing. One morning, Shailyn found her mother's newly purchased rose quartz crystal. Without any prompting or teachings, Shailyn picked up the crystal and placed the point at the center of her mother's forehead. Then Shailyn said, "Mommy, I can fix people with this. You can do surgery with this, you know."

Where did children like Maia and Shailyn access this healing knowledge, which they display with complete confidence? They either learned it in a past life or received the information in a dream or as channeled information. Perhaps healing with crystals is innate knowledge that all souls intuitively know but that we sometimes forget. Regardless, the information about crystal healing "from the mouths of babes" is worth paying attention to.

RECAPTURING ANCIENT WISDOM

Crystal healing is an ancient practice that has recently reemerged, and healers are beginning to incorporate the use of crystals in their healing practices with more frequency. Recollections of Atlantean healing wisdom is inspiring more and more massage therapists to put crystals beneath their clients as they lie on massage tables; Feng Shui practitioners suggest placing specific crystals in the home to effect positive change; and spiritual healers are using particular crystals on their clients' bodies to balance, clear, and heal disharmony and disease.

K. G. of New Brunswick, Canada, visited a crystal healer for help with neck pain. The healer, who used Therapeutic Touch and Reiki treatments along with crystal work, identified K. G.'s neck pain as stemming from blocked energy in that region.

During their first session, the healer placed a smoky quartz crystal under K. G.'s neck, explaining that this would help ground (release and balance) the problem. At first, K. G.'s pain was relieved, but within a few minutes, it returned. The healer said, "The crystal is full." Like a vacuum-cleaner bag filled with too much soot, the smoky quartz needed clearing, so the healer cleansed the crystal and once again began extracting pain energy from K. G.

In addition to the smoky quartz, the healer gave K. G. a calcite stone to hold in one hand and an amethyst in the other. The healer explained that these crystals helped keep the energy moving down and out of K. G.'s body.

K. G. says, "Once I started using my healing gifts more, things improved. From time to time my neck will still bother me, so I will use my crystals, which now also include hematite, clear quartz, and smoky quartz to clear up the pain." K. G. says that when pain arises, it reminds her that she's not using her healing gifts enough in the world. The pain motivates her to take action, which— together with the healing properties of the crystals— helps her neck to heal.

Like K. G., I've discovered that smoky quartz is excellent for removing toxins, psychic debris, entities, and unhealed situations from the past. Just by placing a smoky quartz crystal point at my bedside, with the point directed away from me, I've had some of the most clearing and therapeutic dreams of my life. This crystal's ability to draw darkness out of the body is unparalleled.

Sixteen-year-old Fiona from Scotland used crystals to heal a migraine headache. She lay upon her bed and held a green agate crystal in her left hand and a bloodstone in her right. She also placed a heart-shaped clear quartz crystal upon her forehead, a great stone for clearing the third-eye area.

Fiona visualized a circle around herself and asked this circle to provide perfect protection against any lower energies. Inside the circle, only high energies of love were allowed. Then, Fiona visualized her green agate sending green healing light energy into her body, clearing away anything that was causing her migraine. Fiona asked that all pain and negative energy be sent into the bloodstone in her right hand. She breathed deeply and calmly, and very soon her migraine disappeared.

As Fiona got up, she noticed that the bloodstone had turned black! All the negative energy and pain had been transferred into the stone, just as she'd requested.

Green stones, such as the agate that Fiona used, or malachite, are wonderful amplifiers of the healing green light that comes from the heart chakra . . . and also the Archangel Raphael.

THE 15 ARCHANGELS AND THEIR CORRESPONDING CRYSTALS

Archangels are the overseers or managers of guardian angels. They're extremely large, powerful, and loving. Although archangels are genderless, their specific specialties and purposes lend either a male or a female energy to them.

Like all the angels, archangels are nondenominational and help anyone who calls upon them. Since archangels have no time or space restrictions, each one can simultaneously be with many people. Anyone who calls on an archangel is granted the request, without exception.

Each of the archangels radiates a particular aura color, related to the specific purpose of that angel. You can use certain crystals to invoke, and develop a closer relationship with, each archangel. The crystals can be worn, held, or placed nearby to elicit this effect.

Following are the 15 major archangels, their purpose related to healing, their corresponding auric colors, and associated crystals. (For more detailed information on each of these archangels, please consult my book *Archangels & Ascended Masters*. In addition, the chart in Part III of this book gives detailed information about which crystals to use for different maladies, health conditions, and types of emotional distress. It also discusses how to care for and clear your crystals.)

Everyone is qualified and able to call upon archangels by simply holding the intention in mind. You can't make a mistake in invocation. You can invoke an archangel by: visualizing that archangel with you or a loved one, saying or thinking the archangel's name silently or aloud, reading a prayer concerning the archangel, asking God to send the archangel to you or a loved one, praying for the archangel's help, writing a letter to the archangel, looking at a painting or a statue of the archangel, or even singing to the archangel. The point isn't *how* you ask, but that you *do* ask in some way. And remember that the archangels have no time or space restrictions, so they can be with you and everyone who invokes them simultaneously. They have unlimited time and energy, so don't worry that you're bothering them with your request.

The Healing Purpose, Aura Color, and Associated Crystal of Archangels

Archangel	Meaning of the Name	Specialty	Aura Color	Related Crystal
Ariel	Lioness of God	Heals and helps wild animals and the environment	Pale pink	Rose quartz
Azrael	Whom God helps	Heals grief	Off-white	Creamy yellow calcite
Chamuel	He who sees God	Heals anxiety and brings peace	Pale green	Green fluorite
Gabriel	Messenger of God	Heals during pregnancy and childbirth, and heals anxiety regarding creative projects	Copper	Citrine
Haniel	Glory of God	Heals female cycles	Bluish white	Moonstone
Jeremiel	Mercy of God	Heals emotions	Violet	Amethyst
Jophiel	Beauty of God	Heals negativity and chaos	Dark pink	Pink rubellite or pink tourmaline
Metatron	The prophet Enoch	Heals learning disorders and childhood issues	Green and pink stripes	Watermelon tourmaline

THE HEALING PURPOSE, AURA COLOR, AND ASSOCIATED CRYSTAL OF ARCHANGELS CONT.

ARCHANGEL	MEANING OF THE NAME	SPECIALTY	AURA COLOR	RELATED CRYSTAL
Michael	He who is like God	Heals fear and nervousness, and clears energy	Royal purple	Sugilite
Raguel	Friend of God	Heals personal and professional relationships	Pale blue	Aqua aura or aquamarine
Raphael	He who heals	Heals physical illnesses and guides healers	Emerald green	Malachite
Raziel	Secrets of God	Heals spiritual and psychic blocks	Rainbow stripes	Clear quartz
Sandalphon	The prophet Elijah	Heals aggressive tendencies	Turquoise	Turquoise
Uriel	God is Light	Heals away resentment and unforgiveness	Pale yellow	Amber
Zadkiel	Righteousness of God	Heals memory and mental functioning	Dark blue	Lapis lazuli

One additional way to invoke the archangels is by visualizing their aura color surrounding a situation or a person in need of healing. For instance, if someone needed help for menstrual issues, you could visualize bluish-white light around that person, or around the ovary area. This would invoke Archangel Haniel's healing power, which is specifically geared toward women's health concerns.

In the next chapter, we'll examine the healing colors of the angels' auras in further detail.

CHAPTER 13

Healing with Light and Colors

Our body is composed of moving electron particles, and electrical vibrations that are measurable on CAT and PET scans and other diagnostic equipment. These devices show our brain's and body's varying electrical surges as differing colors, so it's not surprising that we're recovering the memory of the healing properties of colors, too. Hospitals are beginning to use colored lights for healing. For instance, blue fluorescent lamps are commonly shined upon infants to speed their healing from jaundice. And a new study from Italy has found that turquoise fluorescent lamps work even better than plain blue when it comes to alleviating jaundice symptoms.

In addition to using actual colored lights, visualizing or intending (thinking or feeling instead of seeing) certain colors around a physical ailment can also significantly speed its healing.

RAINBOW LIGHT

As discussed in the previous chapter, each archangel has a different color associated with its aura, so calling upon these colors can invoke the particular archangel associated with that hue.

For example, visualizing rainbow-colored light around your-self or someone else helps heal blockages from past lives, as well as karmic imbalances that are causing negative patterns. By invoking all the colors in the rainbow, deep healing occurs on many levels simultaneously.

Rainbow coloring is associated with the Archangel Raziel, who's known as the "wizard archangel." Raziel is very wise and magical—think of Gandalf from *The Lord of the Rings*, with large angel wings. He helps those with high-level spiritual purposes (such as spiritual teachers and healers) lose their anxieties about their gifts—especially those who've been punished in this life or a past one because of their psychic and healing abilities.

Meredith of Australia never really believed in angels until a psychic told her that she had two guardian angels. The psychic gave Meredith detailed descriptions of both a male and a female angel surrounding her. Still, Meredith didn't believe it until two days later when a friend said that during meditation he saw a male and a female angel next to her. The angels perfectly fit the psychic's previous descriptions of Meredith's guardian angels. Since Meredith hadn't told her friend about the psychic reading, she was amazed and thought, *Maybe there's something to this angel business!*

Shortly after, Meredith bought and started using my angel oracle cards. As she became more familiar with them, Meredith developed the ability to feel, sense, and even see angels around others.

Meredith's daughter suffered from epilepsy and learning disabilities. Soon, the five-year-old would begin school, and Meredith worried about how her daughter would cope. She recalls the morning of her daughter's first day of school: "I had her sitting on my lap, telling her that her angel would look after her. Suddenly, I felt an energy standing close by. When I tuned in, I saw the most beautiful angel and felt her calming energy. She told me that her name was Mary and that she'd look after my daughter. It was a great comfort for me to send my daughter to school, knowing that she was being looked after. To this day, nearly three years later, she's never had a seizure at school!"

Yet, Meredith's daughter continued to have three to four seizures a month at home. Naturally, Meredith was extremely concerned, so one night when her daughter was asleep, Meredith went into a deep meditation. She called upon her own angels, her daughter's, and any others that were available. Meredith visualized her daughter lying on a table, encircled by angels all sending out healing energy.

Meredith asked the angels what color healing energy to send to her daughter, and she received an intuitive reply of "rainbow colors." Meredith then had a vision of rainbow healing energy pouring out through the hands of all the angels and herself, into her daughter.

Meredith then received another intuitive message from the angels. She recalls, "I was so worried about my daughter, and I felt so helpless. But the angels told me that my daughter had chosen this lifetime to complete certain things to do with her evolvement. The angels said that all I had to do was love her. They stressed that her health was *her* stuff to deal with." This wasn't easy for a caring mother to hear, yet the angels' words helped her fully surrender the situation to God.

The next morning, Meredith told her daughter about the angel healing circle. She then asked her daughter, "What healing color do you suppose we sent you?" Meredith expected her daughter to reply, "Pink," her favorite color. Instead, the little girl said, "Rainbow!"

Meredith says, "My heart leapt! I realized that my daughter, at some level, knew exactly what was going on."

After the rainbow energy healing, Meredith followed the angels' guidance to stop worrying and just love her daughter, and the little girl has gone more than a year without having any seizures.

Rainbow light is also associated with Reiki healing energy, which is a special vibration that healers begin emitting after they're attuned. Attunement occurs when an already-attuned Reiki teacher shows cryptic symbols to a student. The teacher "draws" these symbols on the student's crown and other chakras with her finger. The student then learns certain hand positions to send the Reiki energy to herself, or to clients whom she'll treat with the energy. Reiki is taught in four levels, with new symbols given for each level. The final level is called "Reiki master."

Reiki energy feels soft and velvety, like a shower of soft water. When I meet Reiki masters, I see rainbow stripes in their auras. I've also seen a group of angels completely covered in bright rainbow coloring next to Reiki masters. I call them the "Reiki angels."

In Chapter 14, I'll discuss Reiki, Qigong, Therapeutic Touch, and other energy healing modalities in greater detail. You'll read about scientific studies on the effectiveness of energy healing in treating illness and injury.

EMERALD-GREEN LIGHT

Emerald-green light is associated with the Archangel Raphael, who's the chief healer among the archangels. When you call upon Raphael, he spreads his emerald-green light over the affected person. The green light is absorbed like a healing balm or fast-acting medication. Conversely, you can visualize emerald-green light around yourself or someone else, with the same healing effect. Invoking light is the same as invoking an archangel, since light is the true essence of all angels.

Immediately before her appointment with an energy healer, Shannon asked that the Archangel Raphael be present during the session. Shannon asked Raphael to oversee it and to guide the healer so that she could be healed emotionally, physically, and mentally.

Throughout the two-hour session, Shannon kept seeing the color emerald green in her mind's eye. Without

Shannon mentioning this color, her healer said, "I keep seeing the color emerald green around you."

About a week later, Shannon bought *Archangels & Ascended Masters,* which explains that Raphael's aura color is emerald green. She was amazed!

Raphael's presence at the session was profound for Shannon, who says, "It was one of the most powerful and beautiful healings I've ever had."

When Raphael is nearby, you may see emerald-green light in your mind's eye, or sparkles of green light with your physical eyes. The emerald-green light stays covered over the injured or diseased body part until the situation is healed. Many times during my psychic readings, I've noticed that my client has, for example, green light covering her kneecap. When I ask her about it, she'll tell me that this area was injured and that she's been praying for a healing. The green light next to a body part indicates that one's prayers for health have been heard and answered.

Sending colored light to an injury or illness is a highly effective method. It works especially well in healing children and animals, since their perfect faith speeds up healing. The next two examples can teach us all about becoming more like the trusting and faith-filled children and animals.

Louise Ring O'Hanley's 11-month-old daughter, Caitlin, developed a strange growth in her mouth. Four different doctors were unable to identify the growth, so they referred Louise and Caitlin to an oral surgeon, who recommended surgery (with anesthesia) for the following week.

Louise was terrified of bringing her baby girl in for this procedure. Fortunately, she'd just read a book about angels the previous day, so she prayed all weekend prior to the scheduled surgery. Louise asked Raphael to send his emerald-green healing light to Caitlin's mouth, and to heal her completely.

By Monday morning, the growth had completely disappeared (and has never returned), so the surgery appointment was cancelled. As Louise now says, "I believe in the power of prayer!"

Caitlin, like most children, was open and receptive to the loving light from her mother and Raphael. When *you* desire a healing for yourself, ask the angels to help you be open and receptive. Remember: The angels can help you with *everything*, including having more faith and greater receptivity to healing.

✳   ✳   ✳

Donna Mead of New Zealand was helping her best friend, who'd just moved to England, by taking care of her fox terrier, Daisy. Daisy was in a new program that allowed pets to be quarantined at someone's home before being flown to the United Kingdom, so Donna was taking care of Daisy at her home during the six-month quarantine program.

Daisy had some health concerns from a recent stroke that had affected her lower body and created skin problems and blood clots. Donna worked with Daisy rigorously, using special shampoos for her skin, taking her to the veterinarian's office for checkups, and walking her regularly. Daisy was doing fine until the fourth month, when she became completely lethargic. Donna couldn't even lure her out of bed with her favorite doggy treat.

Donna took Daisy to the vet for testing to see why she'd lost all her energy and vitality. The test results were grave: She had blood cancer, and the vet said that they'd probably have to put Daisy to sleep, especially if her condition worsened. However, Donna wasn't ready to give up, so she took Daisy home that night.

Donna decided to work with the angels. She says, "I asked Archangel Raphael to heal Daisy with his green and white light, using me as the conductor. What I saw was amazing: This illuminating green and white light seemed to run throughout Daisy's body in circular movements. At first there were large circles engulfing her entire body. Then the light turned into smaller circles. I intuitively knew that as the light was removing the disease, the circles got smaller until I could no longer see any color. I opened my eyes and looked at Daisy, who just stared back at me. I thanked Archangel Raphael and then carried on with my evening."

The next morning, Donna dropped Daisy off at the veterinarian's office for another checkup. When Donna returned to the office later that day, she was greeted by Daisy bounding up to her, jumping up and licking her. The vet explained that although he couldn't understand or explain it, all the tests now showed that Daisy's blood was completely normal.

But Donna understood it, and she thanked the angels aloud right there in the vet's office! Fully recovered and healthy, Daisy was able to fly to England to be with her owner, who reports that Daisy now has the energy and disposition of a puppy. When Daisy's new vet in England reviewed her chart, he said that the healing was nothing short of a miracle.

Donna invoked both the emerald-green light of Raphael, as well as white light, for a beautiful and effective healing of the dog. Emerald-green light is a physical healing color, good for any bodily ailment. White light is a protector color and can help in any situation where there seems to be harsh energy affecting a person. In Daisy's case, the white light may have protected her from the doctor's unwitting "curse" of the diagnosis of a terminal illness—that is, the doctor's thought-forms of seeing Daisy as untreatable were blocked by the white lights.

WHITE LIGHT

When you visualize or invoke white light, you're calling on an intelligent, living being. White light is the color of guardian angels, while colored lights are the colors of archangels and some of the ascended masters (such as Quan Yin, the Eastern goddess of compassion, whose color is cherry red). White light is the halo glow of angels.

Anything that you surround with white light is perfectly protected, for white light is invincible. It's also a very powerful color for healing away deep-seated fears and illnesses, much like a steam-cleaning with a powerful water hose.

As you'll read below, Kaiisha was healed when she visualized white light cleansing her chakras.

Five years ago, Kaiisha Taylor of Australia was seriously ill. Emaciated and drained of energy, Kaiisha was undergoing extensive medical testing to pinpoint her condition so that it could be treated.

Her test results would be ready on Monday during her doctor's visit. As she waited for the verdict, Kaiisha became very frightened as she considered the prospect of an early death. After all, she was only 23 and still had a lot of living to do.

Instead of succumbing to fear and pessimism, however, Kaiisha decided to take action. She began meditating twice a day, for an hour at a time. During meditations, Kaiisha visualized filling her chakras with healing white light. She imagined love energy radiating from her body so intensely that it filled the room. Kaiisha made sure that her meditation room was a sacred and peaceful location; and she kept fresh flowers, candles, and crystals near her while meditating.

On the Saturday before her doctor's appointment to find out her test results, Kaiisha prayed with all her heart that she would be okay. She recalled, "As I was praying, I became aware of a bright light in the room, and I felt the room warming up. I could hear beautiful, soft music, and in front of me was a huge golden-white light that was pure love in the shape of an angel!

"The angel came over to me and put her wings around my back in an embrace. I felt the message telepathically that everything was going to be okay. I could see two more angels behind me, and the love I felt was so amazing and powerful that tears ran down my cheeks. I had absolutely no doubt that everything was going to be fine as the angels left. I felt so happy that I didn't have cancer, as I'd previously feared."

Kaiisha immediately phoned her mother to report that her health was fine. Her mother cried with relief, as she'd also been worried. When Kaiisha arrived at the doctor's office on Monday morning, she felt completely confident that the test results would show that she was in perfect health. So when the doctor told her that she didn't have cancer after all, Kaiisha replied, "I know."

Notice how Kaiisha worked with both the energy of light and love in her healing. She also had crystal-clear intentions, which manifested in her praying with all of her heart for health, coupled with acting in faith by meditating twice a day. When love is invoked, along with light and crystal-clear intentions, the power of both the light and the love are amplified by each other. Love plus light is the most effective medicine of all.

As you work with white light regularly, you'll learn to trust its consistent power to heal and protect.

Lhasa Compton often uses white light, and has had many experiences to support her faith in its power. One day, for example, Lhasa noticed the symptoms of a sore throat, so she cupped her hand to her throat and pictured a ball of white-gold light in the area. Within a minute, the discomfort was gone and didn't return.

The most dramatic healings occur when we have crystal-clear intentions about healing a condition. This often happens when someone we care about is ailing. Sometimes, though, the people we're so clearly trying to heal resist our healing efforts because of their own fears or agendas. As stated earlier, animals and children don't resist healing work—they welcome it and, as such, are privy to miraculous healings.

Brenda King found a lump on the throat of her newly acquired dog, Minnie. The veterinarian said that tests would have to be performed, followed by surgery, with a cost exceeding $400. To spare Minnie the trauma, and herself the expense, Brenda decided to try a spiritual treatment first.

Tuning in to Minnie's energy, Brenda realized that the dog was extremely hungry for love. So, Brenda encircled Minnie in white light and Reiki energy, and sent the dog lots of love. Brenda's mother and boyfriend also joined in, sending Minnie love and light. Two hours after they surrounded Minnie with this energy, the lump noticeably shrank in size. By the next morning, it was one-third smaller. From Thursday through Sunday, Minnie received intensive white-light treatments from Brenda, her mother, and boyfriend; and by Sunday, the lump was almost gone. It eventually shrank to nothing the next week, and Brenda noticed that Minnie seemed very light and happy.

Brenda says, "I've used white healing light for some time; however, this experience was such a testament of what can manifest with openness, and the willingness to give and receive. Minnie was also very receptive to the light and love. It was obvious that she wanted to let go, and we were simply aids to her own healing. This experience has taken my breath away."

Here's another sweet story of white light healing an animal. While you might not consider a rat as a cute, cuddly pet, I think you'll feel the love within this story about a mother caring for her daughter's feelings—as well as their pet's comfort.

Elizabeth Seer's daughter, Aspen, has pet rats named Zelda and Princess Gimpers. One morning, Aspen was distraught because Princess Gimpers was ill. Elizabeth saw that the rat was actually close to death, with rapid, shallow breathing; half-lidded eyes; and a lethargic demeanor. She was also cold to the touch and refused to eat or drink.

Wanting to spare Princess Gimpers any further suffering, and also to help her daughter avoid the grief of losing her pet, Elizabeth went to work. She carried Princess Gimpers into her meditation room and held her. Elizabeth says, "I prayed that if she were meant to live, she should be cured swiftly. I prayed for the warm, healing angelic white light to surround her, and help her through her obvious trauma."

Princess Gimpers responded almost immediately to the prayers and white-light treatment. She recovered completely, and returned to normal eating, as if she'd never been ill or close to death. Elizabeth said, "I know that the angels came to us that day. The loving, all-encompassing light of the angels helped Princess Gimpers recover, and spared my daughter from the torment of losing a beloved pet."

White light has dual purposes: cleansing to evoke a healing, and also protection. The intention that you hold as you invoke the light determines which purpose will be manifested. The next two examples show the protective power of surrounding a person or an object with white light.

Kate was expecting two friends for dinner at her home in Saskatchewan, Canada. The first friend arrived on time, but the second friend was late. Kate and her friend worried that their late companion might be struggling to drive on the snowy, slippery roads, so they both visualized white light around their friend and his car.

When he finally arrived, the friend explained that while driving around a dangerous curve, his car had begun swerving toward a deep ditch. Then the car suddenly straightened itself out and carried on as if had never lost control. Kate and her first guest looked at each other, both calculating that the time he'd been driving around that curve was the exact moment they'd white-lighted him. Kate says, "It was a small but powerful reinforcement on a physical level that white light has a tangible effect on life as we know it."

*   *   *

Shelly Bassett, an Angel Therapy Practitioner in Canada, realized that she'd forgotten to lock her car one evening. It was late and she was tired, so instead of going outside to lock the car, she asked Archangel Michael to watch over her car and the wallet she remembered leaving on the seat. Shelly also surrounded the car and wallet with white light. She envisioned her car and wallet in a beautiful white bubble, and sent this light across her neighborhood. Shelly went to bed, peacefully knowing that her belongings were safe and secure.

The next morning, Shelly's doorbell rang. It was her neighbor, holding Shelly's wallet. He explained that he'd found it on the roof of his house. Shelly was amazed that even though the $20 bill she'd had in the wallet was gone, her driver's license and credit cards were still there along with a few gift certificates.

Her neighbor explained that there had been several break-ins the previous night in their neighborhood. Even though other cars were also broken into that night and other items were stolen, all of the stolen items were mysteriously returned, intact, to the owners a few days later.

Since Shelly had prayed for the entire neighborhood's safety and had surrounded it with white light, she realized that white light was an energy field that you could trust, love, and honor. She also realized that she'd gotten exactly what she'd asked for: the safety of her wallet. Shelly says that she'd forgotten to ask that the money in her wallet be protected as well. Shelly now surrounds her neighborhood with white light every night, since she's received proof that it really does work.

White light can also be invoked in times of impending danger to provide instant protection.

On the morning of July 22, 2003, the city of Memphis, Tennessee, was devastated by fierce winds. Laura Montanaro woke up to the sound of the storm, looked out her window, and saw debris flying through her yard. Laura immediately asked the angels to protect herself and her family, and she surrounded the house with bright white light. The sight of huge old oak trees towering above her house, swaying violently in the wind, was quite an ominous sight! Yet Laura felt so protected by the light that she lay back in her bed and just listened as the storm passed. Her home lost electricity, just like hundreds of thousands of other Memphis residents, but she still felt a sense of calm.

After the storm passed, Laura drove around and saw unbelievable devastation everywhere. Trees were in the streets, on power lines, and had crushed many people's homes, even killing a few. But nothing happened to Laura's property.

Laura says, "I felt so blessed and watched over. We even got our power back 18 hours later, whereas many others didn't have theirs for nearly two weeks in the sweltering heat of a Memphis summer! I have no doubt whatsoever that when you call upon your angels and surround yourself with white light, you're protected. I pray every night, and surround our planet with white light, and I encourage others to do the same."

White light is an old, tried-but-true method that empowers all of us to heal and protect ourselves, our loved ones, and our property. I recently received a message from the angels requesting that we all visualize the planet covered in white light as we fall asleep each night. With all the different time zones, the earth is continuously protected. Since white light (and all the other colors) fade with time, this nightly ritual ensures that the earth is always covered and sealed.

GOLDEN LIGHT

Golden light is the energy color of the Christ—not necessarily the man or the religion, but the spirit of forgiveness and powerful, unconditional love. It's the sign that everything's going to be okay. It means, "Have faith, because all is well." People who experience "Jesus sightings" report seeing a golden glow around him. I normally see golden light around those who either work closely with Jesus or who live by the principles he taught.

Many people see golden light right before a car accident. They report that the glow comes from nowhere, and that it brings them comfort immediately before the collision.

Donna Flavell and her friend Ann commuted monthly to a training course that was a four-hour drive from their homes in Auckland, New Zealand. Normally they surrounded their automobile with white light for protection during the drive. One day, though, they forgot to do so—and they also had ignored a friend's cautionary warnings about making the drive. On that day, a speeding car crossed the center divider and came straight toward Donna and Ann's car. Both women saw a bright glow of golden light between the two cars, even though all sunshine was obliterated by a heavy cloud covering.

After the head-on collision, Donna awoke to hear Ann calling her name. Ann was certain that Donna was dead and was praying for her to come back to life. Both women were then helicoptered to a hospital and put into braces and hospital beds. Scans and tests showed that Donna had spinal injuries and a ruptured spleen.

In the following hours, Donna did a lot of praying. She also visualized her cells, nerves, veins, and entire body repairing and restoring itself. When Donna was wheeled in for a CAT scan, the specialists were baffled by the scan results, so they repeated it. Her spleen had completely healed!

Donna was kept in the hospital overnight for observation. During this time, she continued to pray, and to affirm her health. She wished that she had her homeopathic medicine with her, until she received a psychic message that she could self-administer the medication telepathically, which she did.

The next day, Donna's doctors said that she'd need to stay at the hospital another day. Donna prayed for help to be released from the hospital so that she could be near nature. Ten minutes after this prayer, she was released to go home—just as she'd asked.

Donna's osteopath later told her that she was less than two millimeters from having her spinal column severed during the accident. And her tow-truck driver said that he couldn't believe anyone had survived the accident. Donna credits her health and life to the angels.

Faith is an aspect of love, because it's the absence of doubt and fear. Those who have read the gospels will recall that Christ continually gave credit to faith for all of his healing work. Modern substantiation of his words has been provided by numerous studies showing that patients' faith in their doctors' competency was a crucial variable in determining whether or not the patients healed.

So, you can invoke golden light to help you or whomever you're healing have increased faith. Golden light can also be invoked along with other colors. Invoke golden light along with white light if you're afraid and you need protection. The golden light will buoy your faith, and the white light will ensure your safety.

> Lhasa Compton (whom you met earlier) was driving during flash-flood warnings in Arizona. Since the sky was darkening with rain clouds that threatened a downfall, Lhasa asked that an angel fly ahead of her and spread white-gold light to keep her path safe and clear. As rainwater began to flood the road, Lhasa's car moved smoothly through the water. After she safely reached her home, Lhasa heard a news report that the roads were impassable and several motorists were stranded in the flooded conditions. She thanked the light for allowing her a safe passage.

When invoking colors, you can't make a mistake and choose the wrong one. You may wonder, *Why don't I invoke all the colors just to make sure?* This method will work well, too. However, the best method is to pray for guidance about which colors to invoke and/or to follow your intuition's directives about color selection. Again, you can't make a mistake. Your crystal-clear intention to heal while sending colored light—coupled with love—is the true power that heals.

ANGEL LIGHTS

One way to know that your healing prayers are being answered is by the presence of "angel lights." These are sparkling lights (similar to trails of fireworks) or flashes of light (like a camera's flashbulb). White lights are the auric sparkles of guardian angels, and the sparks act like friction as the angels move across time and space. Colored lights are the auras of archangels and ascended masters. Those who have never heard of angel lights may suspect that their eyesight is malfunctioning when they see sparkling lights, as Melanie did.

When Melanie was expecting her child, she began seeing white and red lights through the day. She'd never heard of angel lights, so she had her eyes examined by two different doctors. Both physicians said that Melanie's eyes were perfect and that the lights must be a complication of her pregnancy. Yet, after the birth of her daughter, Melanie continued seeing the sparkling lights.

One evening as she sat outside looking at the nearby trees, she saw huge blue and red lights flying near her. The lights glowed brighter than anything she'd ever seen, and she didn't know what to make of it. She now realizes that she was seeing archangels, and that the blue lights were from the Archangel Michael.

Melanie believes that her daughter brought more angels into her home and her life. Melanie credits her daughter for opening her own spiritual gifts.

The white lights that Melanie saw were the extra angels that accompanied her daughter's birth. The red lights were most likely from the Eastern goddess of compassion, Quan Yin (also known as Kuan Yin). Quan Yin is a Buddhist divinity whose name means "she who answers all prayers." She's especially nurturing toward mothers and children, so her presence in Melanie's life makes sense.

White lights also appear whenever angels gather to protect us from harm, as Nicole Herrera discovered.

When Nicole was boogie-boarding in the San Diego surf, a huge wave picked her up and smashed her face-first underwater. Nicole struggled to find her way to the surface, disoriented as to which direction was up or down.

Suddenly, her head broke through the water, and she saw sparkling white lights all around her. One week later, she read that these kinds of lights are associated with angels.

Angel lights also appear when we need comfort and reassurance.

> Annie of Queensland, Australia, remembers that as a child she was often frightened of bedtime, worried about the danger in the darkness. She says, "Then these lights would come into my room and hover around my bed. There were colored lights and also white lights. They were only little lights, not so big as to fill the room. Along with these lights, I would also hear a noise in my ear." The light and humming sound would comfort Annie, and she'd sleep peacefully.
>
> Annie would tell her mother about the angel lights, but her mother didn't understand them, so Annie now takes great care to support her own young son, who reports seeing the lights himself.

As Annie's story indicates, children are especially adept at seeing angel lights. The angels want us to be at peace, and they come to us whenever we feel upset or afraid. They show us that—while the darkness seems to be genuinely frightening—the lights of the angels are always nearby. In the next story, a mother's prayers for her daughter are answered by the presence of angel lights.

> Tina Markarian's five-year-old daughter, Lindsey, became quite ill with a high fever, so Tina had her daughter sleep with her so she could monitor the temperature. Neither one of them slept as Lindsey tossed, turned, and moaned all night.
>
> Tina lay in bed, very worried, and said a silent prayer that God would send some angels to help her little girl. She didn't mention the prayer to Lindsey, since she didn't want her daughter to think that she was more ill than she was. Her dad had recently died of a heart attack, and Lindsey was afraid of dying suddenly herself.

A couple of moments after Tina's prayer, Lindsey began crying. She said, "Mommy, I'm so afraid." Tina asked what Lindsey feared, assuming that it was her usual fear of dying.

The little girl said, "I'm afraid because I see all these lights floating around my head. They look like stars or fairies."

Tina wept tears of joy, explaining that the lights were angels helping her daughter get well. Tina says, "I knew my prayers were being answered, so I then told Lindsey about the prayers. My little daughter said that she knew it was true."

Then mother and daughter both fell asleep and had a peaceful night's rest. The next day, Lindsey felt much better, and she never again feared dying like her daddy again.

While Tina didn't see the angel lights herself, her daughter's innocent testimony that the angels were there was enough reassurance for the healing to occur. The angels heal us by alleviating our fears, and also by sending healing light into our bodies to wash away negativity and imbalances.

Belinda Warren of Canada received this type of healing from the archangels, who showed their characteristic and colorful angel lights. In Belinda's case, Raphael, the Archangel of Healing, appeared as a green light. And Archangel Uriel, the "wise uncle" who helps us come up with creative solutions, worked in tandem with Raphael to effect a deeply powerful healing.

The year 1999 was a difficult one for Belinda. She was exhausted from the demands of raising two young children, felt financially strapped, and didn't seem to have any emotional support from those around her. All of her relationships, including her marriage, felt emotionally abusive and restrictive to her. Just when she was about to give up hope, Belinda began to see evidence of angels surrounding her.

She first saw them as a glowing light without form. They'd enter Belinda's bedroom and spread their love across the room as if they were soft, powdery blankets. Belinda says, "I'd always feel completely safe in their presence, and I began to look forward to their visits, which always occurred at the same time of night."

The angels emitted a green light, and Belinda also saw some that glowed in a yellow tone. One time, she was awakened by the green lights and intuitively received a message from them to stop worrying about her children and finances, and that everything would be okay. She was told that the angels were healing her of pain from this life and past lives.

Belinda watched a light-being travel up her body, beginning at her feet, as if it were clearing her chakra energy centers. The angel slowed down near the solar plexus chakra near her navel, and it felt as if a knot in her stomach melted away. The light continued upward through her chest, throat, and face. She fell deeply asleep after this healing session

Afterward, Belinda felt a greater sense of personal strength and self-esteem. She began asserting herself in her relationships, and felt safe to be herself around others. Belinda says, "Little by little, I began to stand up for myself on a regular basis. It was very frightening at first, but I just kept up with it. Now I only have wonderful and incredibly loving relationships in my life, and the angels are completely responsible for making it happen."

CANDLE HEALINGS

You can invoke additional light with candles. Staring at a lighted white candle is a wonderfully effective way to focus the mind upon your desires, and away from fearful thoughts. Look into the flame, imagine all of your greatest desires, and then say, "This or something better, God." Call upon additional angels to give you guidance and protection for your healing and manifestation work.

Jackie Stevens of Australia was sitting in church, praying for a healing. Her whole body ached from illness, and she silently prayed, "God and angels, how do I get my energy back, move onto my path, and feel strong and healthy?" Within a couple of minutes, a distinct whisper in her ear said, "Look into the candlelight, send love and light, receive love and light, and bless and release."

Jackie followed the guidance and focused on the candlelight. She says, "It felt as if the light was growing within me. As I sent love to the candle, I felt love build within me. As I blessed and released, I felt the aches and pains go away, along with the tension I normally carry in my shoulders."

Angel Orbs

Angel lights are showing up more frequently in photographs. Many of my audience members regularly show me photos with white orbs and wispy shapes that clearly mimic the outline of angels and fairies. The increased frequency of this phenomenon is probably due to the advances in cameras and digital photography. I also believe that the phenomenon can be credited to the "thinning of the veil." This means that as we're collectively ascending and becoming more spiritually aware, we more easily notice the spirit world's presence around us.

Ten-year-old Ryan Reynolds of Cincinnati, Ohio, often spoke of seeing angels. Ryan, who had been diagnosed with an inoperable brain tumor, told his family that he saw angels during a hayride. Three different people took photos of Ryan at the hayride, using three different cameras. One photographer was a reporter for the local *Community Press* newspaper, using a company camera for a news story she was covering.

When the film from all the cameras was developed, the photos each showed orbs of light surrounding the little boy. Each camera used different types of film. The family didn't know what to make of the white spots on the photographs. One photo showed small white spots around Ryan, another photo was of him with a fish-shaped white image, and the third photo showed a large white orb next to him.

But Ryan instantly recognized the angels in the photographs. His mother recalled that he pointed to the large white orb on the third photo and said, "Mom, this is why it felt so good to go on the hayride. Because right there is my guardian angel . . . I knew she'd be there. That's my angel, Mommy. She talks to me all the time." His mother said that Ryan spoke of angels frequently.

Ryan died peacefully two months after the hayride, knowing that he was surrounded by his guardian angels. With all those angels around him, you may wonder why Ryan didn't recover and live. Well, I believe that his life purpose was to call attention to the presence of angels through his touching death. His story made international news, and Ryan's life caused quite a stir in newsrooms that normally don't report on incidents involving angels. If he'd healed, the newsrooms probably wouldn't have even noticed his story, as they tend to only concentrate on dramatic accounts. The brave soul of ten-year-old Ryan Reynolds went to Heaven so that adults worldwide would contemplate the reality of guardian angels.

Angels appear on film because cameras are able to capture light and energy with increasing degrees of accuracy and sensitivity. In the next chapter, we'll talk about energy and its relationship to physical and emotional health and healing.

CHAPTER 14

Energy Healing Work

Since our body is electric, it makes sense that we could call upon this natural electricity and send it to others. Healing results when we couple the action of sending energy with love and crystal-clear intentions. Energy healing is a form of light.

Today, hospitals and doctors' offices worldwide offer in-house or referral treatments with "complementary" and "adjunct therapies" that include energy healing work. As the studies below show, their faith in this work is well founded.

SCIENTIFIC STUDIES ON QIGONG

The ancient Chinese energy healing practice known as Qigong (pronounced *kee-gong*), has received a lot of attention from medical science. The practice is based on bodily movements, which push qi (or chi, the life-force energy of the universe) through the body, removing energy blocks that can create illness. Studies that have been conducted primarily in Chinese university hospitals show significant results when Qigong is used to treat illness, pain, and addictions.

For instance, researchers at the Tongji Medical University in China found that Qigong treatments significantly inhibited tumor growth, and stimulated anti-tumor immunologic functions in rats. This effect was amplified even more when Qigong was used in conjunction with chemotherapy.

Qigong showed remarkable healing effects in a study of male heroin addicts at the Guangzhou University in China. Eighty-six such men were divided into three groups. Those in the first group learned how to practice Qigong (the movements are similar to Tai Chi or yoga), and also received Qigong energy treatments from an experienced practitioner. The second group of addicts received detoxification medication, and the third group received no treatment. The results were exciting and statistically significant: The Qigong group went through withdrawal much quicker and easier, with lower anxiety levels. Most significant is that the Qigong group had no traces of heroin in their urine within five days of the onset of Qigong treatment, whereas the medication group took nine days to be heroin free, and the no-treatment group took 11 days.

Equally impressive results were found in research conducted at New Jersey Medical School. The study compared two groups of chronic pain sufferers: One group received Qigong instructions and treatment from a Qigong master, while the other group received instructions and treatments from an unqualified person. After three weeks, a whopping 91 percent of those who'd received genuine Qigong reported less pain, compared to only 36 percent of those in the "sham" Qigong group.

"Qigong walking" is a form of moving meditation. In an interesting study in Kyoto, Japan, diabetic patients were randomly assigned to either a group that engaged in Qigong walking, or those who went for a conventional walk. After both groups walked for 30 minutes following lunch, those in the Qigong group showed a significantly greater decrease in plasma glucose.

Other scientific studies on Qigong have shown the following:

- A 20 percent improvement in ventilatory efficiency for oxygen uptake and carbon dioxide production after engaging in 20 minutes of Qigong breathing exercises for ten consecutive days, in a Marietta, Georgia, Life University study.

- A significant reduction of harmful cholesterol in the blood of hypertensive patients, accompanied by an increase in helpful HDL-C serum levels among those who practiced Qigong for one year. A similar study done in Shanghai found that Qigong had a regulatory effect on hemodynamic alteration as well as on improvement of the left ventricular function in hypertensive patients.

STUDIES ON REIKI, THERAPEUTIC TOUCH, AND OTHER ENERGY TREATMENTS

As mentioned earlier, Reiki and Therapeutic Touch are energy healing practices similar to Qigong, except that instead of working with breath and movement, healing energy is sent solely through the hands. Both have received attention from researchers at hospitals and nursing colleges. While the results for Reiki and Therapeutic Touch aren't quite as impressive as those for Qigong, they still warrant notice.

Twenty people who suffered from chronic pain were given Reiki treatments in a study conducted at the Cross Cancer Institute in Edmonton, Canada. The study found a highly significant reduction of pain reported by the subjects who received Reiki.

At a center in Quebec, 20 people diagnosed with terminal cancer received three Therapeutic Touch treatments. Those who received the treatments reported reductions in pain, nausea, depression, anxiety, shortness of breath; and increased activity, appetite, relaxation, and inner peace.

Could the Reiki and Therapeutic Touch treatments' benefits come from a placebo effect, or from the patients receiving extra attention from loving energy workers? Another study from the University of Southern Maine lends clinical support to the efficacy of energy healing work. In this study, chronic pain sufferers were given cognitive behavioral therapy to learn how to manage their pain; then half the group were also given Therapeutic

Touch treatments. Those who received the additional treatments reported a higher degree of "self-efficacy," meaning that they felt more optimistic about their power to overcome pain. Those who received the treatments also were more likely to stick with their cognitive behavioral therapy program—again, probably due to the increased hope, faith, and optimism that Therapeutic Touch offered them.

Of course, one could argue that these three studies were based on subjective reports from the patients. In other words, the people who received energy treatments told the researchers that they felt better. But could they have been exaggerating the benefits they received? Researchers at the University of Texas Health Science Center in Houston decided to conduct biological tests on people who received Reiki treatments. They discovered that subjects who received 30 minutes of Reiki showed significant drops in systolic blood pressure, their skin temperature increased, and electromyographic activity (a measurement of muscular tension) decreased during their sessions. In addition, the subjects reported a significant decrease in anxiety.

Perhaps human touch is enough to trigger these healing effects. To test this theory, researchers at the University of Alabama at Birmingham (UAB) Burn Center divided a group of 99 burn patients into two groups: One group received Therapeutic Touch treatment daily for five days. The other group received a similar treatment for the same amount of time, from untrained persons posing as Therapeutic Touch practitioners.

Statistically significant results appeared for those who received Therapeutic Touch treatments from trained practitioners: Patients reported greater reductions in pain and anxiety, compared to the sham-treatment group. In addition, those who received Therapeutic Touch showed a significant drop in blood lymphocytes, revealing the physiological benefits of the energy treatment.

One striking note in most of the studies on Qigong, Reiki, and Therapeutic Touch is the way that they all significantly reduce anxiety. Since anxiety is both a cause and an effect of mental and physical illness, the healing effect of energy treatment is valuable in its ability to reduce anxiety.

I've studied Reiki (and am attuned at the master level); as well as polarity therapy, based on working with the positive and negative poles of the body (similar to jump-starting a car battery); and pranic healing, involving deep cleansing of the chakras. Countless other new forms of Reiki, healing touch, and energy healing work have also been developed. These energy-healing systems give natural healers additional confidence about their innate spiritual gifts. In addition, these systems provide organized frameworks for conducting energy healing work.

Of course, like any other profession, some energy healers give the practice a bad name due to their lack of integrity. Your best bet when seeking out an energy healer or teacher is to get referrals from people whom you trust, and also follow your own intuition when you meet and work with the person. If you feel physical or emotional discomfort when you're with the energy worker, if you feel that their focus is primarily money oriented, or if they pressure you to undergo sessions or take classes that don't feel right to you, then find a different practitioner.

THE SPIRITUALITY OF ENERGY HEALING WORK

Many people turn to the spiritual path when they're under stress of some sort. They decide to turn inward to find relief and answers. Jennifer Hull is an example of someone who found spirituality as a result of the pain stemming from an illness.

The 63-year-old Hawaii resident had suffered from fibromyalgia for many years and had tried different forms of treatment. One day she visited a new medical doctor who suggested that Jennifer try receiving healing-touch therapy—a form of energy healing. This was a new idea for Jennifer and her husband.

On the day of the healing, Jennifer and her husband were escorted into a small room, and she immediately felt a profound sense of relaxation. The healing-touch

practitioners were a married couple who worked together, and Jennifer was struck by their soothing voices and
facial expressions. While her husband sat in a corner of
the room, Jennifer was helped to lie down on a massage
table made up with comfortable cushions, blankets, and
a soft pillow.

The therapists explained that they were going to say a
short silent prayer and then run their hands over
Jennifer's body without actually touching her. After this
warm-up period, they'd begin laying hands on her.
Jennifer felt little electrical sensations as the couple sent
her energy.

As they laid their hands on her, Jennifer began having
intense visions. She saw herself in a night scene in Maui,
with palm trees everywhere. Behind one tree was a
woman, and as Jennifer stared into her eyes, the background scenery changed to a clear blue sky. Then the
woman disappeared.

Jennifer waited patiently to see what would happen
next. In a few minutes, another face appeared. Jennifer
said, "It was a young girl, about 12 or 13 years of age, very
pretty, with short dark hair, a heart-shaped face, and del-
icate features. It felt as though a healing light shined
from her eyes that matched the color of the blue background. She was smiling at me and looking at me with
such love that it gave me a wonderful feeling of happiness. The euphoria I felt enveloped me and gave me an
overwhelming sense that she understood and recognized
my pain—and all the physical and mental anguish that
I've endured over these last few years.

"Then my sweet little angel disappeared, but not
without leaving me something else to think about. In the
distance, I could see a small object appearing and moving
toward me as if it was an animated computer object. I
waited to see what it would be, and when it arrived, I had
another unbelievable surprise. It was a head-and-shoulders
image of Jesus.

"The angels had both appeared in very lifelike colors, but Jesus was similar to a photo negative or an etching, all in different shades of black, white, and gray. The vision of Jesus disappeared the same way it had arrived, slowly rolling into the distance. As it vanished from sight, the male therapist asked me to turn onto my stomach, and I remained silent until the session was over."

At the end of the session, Jennifer's husband was in tears. As they left the room, he cradled her in his arms and told Jennifer how much he loved her, and apologized for being difficult to live with lately. Jennifer says the session changed her life.

Soon after, Jennifer purchased the last remaining copy of my *Healing with the Angels* book at a wholesale store. The following month, she bought the last copy of my *Healing with the Angels Oracle Cards* at a bookstore. She placed both items into a drawer and forgot about them. Then she went to the hair salon, where an Angel Therapy Practitioner was giving readings with my angel oracle cards. The practitioner encouraged Jennifer to use the cards to keep in touch with her guardian angels.

Today, Jennifer talks to her angels regularly, with the help of the cards and through prayer and meditation, and she's constantly aware of their presence. She now has peace of mind, as the angels gave her the reassurance that there's more to life than this earthly experience. She was given a sign that she'd always hoped for, and now she now longer feels alone.

ENERGY HEALING ON PETS

Animals are very sensitive to the energies around them, and they often become ill when there's stress in their household. If a family member is upset, the animal may absorb the energy and manifest an illness.

Conversely, animals respond very quickly to healing energy that's sent to them. They heal rapidly in response to anyone who holds the crystal-clear intention to be a conduit of healing energy. This energy is sent through the hands and is coupled with profound love.

Rachel Ann Pernak-Brennon of Great Britain was heartbroken when her beloved pet collie, Ben, was diagnosed with cancer. Overwhelmed with grief, Rachel sat down and began verbalizing her feelings. She wasn't praying or talking to anyone in particular; it was more like she was venting her emotions.

Within minutes, Rachel sensed a benevolent spiritual presence next to her, so Rachel asked the angel, "If there's anything I can do to help heal my dog, please tell me what to do and I'll do it."

Rachel recalled what happened next: "My hands began to tingle and pulsate, as though they were almost stretching out of the skin. I felt boiling hot, and I also felt someone there, so I opened my eyes. I couldn't believe it, but I saw loads of sparkling, glittery little lights.

"My hands were still tingling, and by this time, Ben had come into the room and had sat down by my side. So I held both my hands over his body. He seemed a little unsure at first, but then he settled down and fell asleep."

Although Rachel had no prior experience with hands-on healing, she trusted her inner guidance. Rachel held her hands over Ben for ten minutes, until the tingling sensation left her hands. Later that night, she found a white feather and knew it was a sign of angelic intervention. She found two other white feathers in the upcoming days.

This experience motivated Rachel to begin talking to her angels frequently. She felt guided to continue sending healing energy to Ben. Shortly afterward, Ben's tests showed that the cancer was completely gone.

Rachel has gone on to become a holistic therapist so that she can conduct angel healings with other animals and people, too.

The following story shows how well animals respond to energy healing coupled with crystal-clear intentions, spoken in the form of positive affirmations.

Jerry Hirshfield, a California psychotherapist, noticed a large wart on the neck of Joy, his cat. During a veterinarian visit later that day, the doctor shaved the growth off. He told Jerry that the wart would probably regrow, which it did a couple of months later. Again, the vet shaved away the wart from Joy's neck.

When the wart regrew a few weeks later, Jerry decided to try sending love energy with his hand. Jerry stroked Joy's neck while simultaneously feeling waves of love going into the wart and dissolving it into nothingness. He mentally repeated, "God's love is all-powerful and is healing this growth right now. Your neck is whole, perfect, and complete. It is healed by the Infinite Power of Love, which heals everything, and in which everything is perfect. This wart, which is only an appearance, is *dis*appearing into the nothingness which it is."

Jerry repeated this treatment twice daily, and within three days, the wart had shrunk. Within a week of continued treatments, the wart completely disappeared. It reappeared once more, so Jerry applied the same prayer-and-love energy treatment, and once again, the wart went away.

However, when the wart reemerged later, Jerry turned to the angels for help. He'd recently read a book about angelic healings, so this time, Jerry added to his previous prayers: "Dear Angels, please help me in applying God's love to Joy's neck." The wart disappeared faster than previous times, and to date, has not returned.

Since then, Jerry has administered the same treatments, with his angels' help, to his own aches, pains, and ailments. With these treatments, a bout of flu disappeared within three days, whereas for other people, the symptoms seemed to last a week or two. Almost any pain he applies these treatments to either goes away completely or is greatly reduced.

Jerry says, "I now know that God's energy is always available to us and heals instantly if we place ourselves consciously in the flow of the energy field. Calling on the angels helps us do this better because they're already in the field at all times."

He has applied treatments to other people, and finds that healings occur in direct proportion to the recipient's faith. "Those who are open to the possibility that they can be helped in this way are indeed helped the most," says Jerry.

ENERGY HEALING ON SO-CALLED INANIMATE OBJECTS

Energy healing isn't limited to healing the physical bodies of people and animals, it also heals seemingly inanimate objects. Since everything is composed of atoms and energy, then everything can be affected by energy healing.

Kristen, who's an Angel Intuitive and Reiki healer in Australia, discovered that a virus had infected her computer. She tried using a virus scan to delete the infected files, but the damage had been done. After trying other methods to resolve the problem, Kristen went to bed annoyed and disappointed.

The next morning, she decided to scan her computer for viruses again, while sending her computer some Reiki energy. She also asked Archangel Michael and Uriel to help clear her computer of all viruses. She explained to the archangels that an infected computer would negatively impact her spiritual work.

Meanwhile, Kristen's husband, Tim, suggested that she call a computer expert for assistance, but she announced with conviction that she didn't need to, since the angels had the situation under control. Within a few minutes, the scan summary appeared announcing, "No infected files." Kristen and Tim thanked the angels with great joy and gratitude. When Kristen pulled an angel oracle card later that day, she wasn't surprised to draw the "Archangel Michael" card.

The reason that energy healing work is so effective is because everything in the Universe is composed of energy. By sending healing energy, we reconfigure energy systems back to their natural state of health and order.

An important part of energy healing work involves cleansing and balancing the chakras—the body's inner energy centers. Chakra work can help us heal physically and emotionally, as I'll discuss in the next chapter. Those already familiar with chakra healing work may particularly want to read the sections on some new forms of chakra work involving addictions, past lives, and psychic-attack clearing.

CHAPTER 15

Taking Care of the Energy Body and Chakras

These days, many people are familiar with chakras (*chakra* means "wheel" in the ancient Eastern language of Sanskrit). As mentioned earlier, chakras are energy wheels within the body that push along life-force energy, in much the same way that paddles push the balls along in a game of pinball.

Most systems discuss the seven major chakras, which are illustrated on the next page. They include the root chakra at the base of the spine; the sacral chakra midway between the navel and the spine's base; the solar plexus, located behind the navel; the heart chakra in the chest; the throat chakra in the Adam's-apple area; the third eye, located between the two physical eyes; and the crown chakra at the top of the head. I also include the "ear chakras," located above the two eyebrows.

✳ ✳ ✳

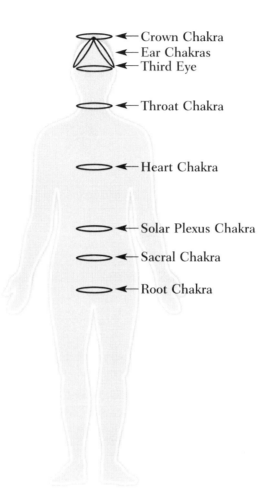

Each chakra has a different color vibration, depending upon whether the chakra wheel spins slow or fast. The cooler colors (such as purple, blue, and green) come from faster-moving light vibrations and faster-moving chakras. The warmer colors (yellow, orange, and red) stem from slower-moving light and chakras.

Each chakra has a specialty that it regulates. Many are located next to a hormonal gland, and those chakras are involved with regulating and balancing the glands. Four of the chakras influence the psychic abilities known as "claircognizance" (knowing facts without knowing how you received the information);

"clairaudience" (hearing the voice of the Divine); "clairvoyance" (seeing psychic visions); and "clairsentience" (intuitive feelings).

THE CHAKRAS			
CHAKRA NAME	BODY LOCATION	ASSOCIATED COLOR	SPECIALTY
Crown	Top of the head	Purple	Claircognizance
Ear	Above each eyebrow	Violet	Clairaudience
Third eye	Between the two eyes	Indigo blue	Clairvoyance
Throat	Adam's apple	Light blue	Speaking truth to self and others Creative projects
Heart chakra	Chest	Green	Clairsentience Relationships Spiritual love
Solar plexus	Navel	Yellow	Power and control
Sacral	Between solar plexus and root	Orange	Bodily health and appetites
Root	Base of spine	Red	Career, finances, home, and material security

CLEARING THE CHAKRAS

Chakras are very sensitive, and they can absorb negative energy, causing them to become dark and unbalanced in size. In healthy individuals, the chakras are equally large in size (balanced) and are free of dark energy (clear). Dark energy comes from being around negative people or situations, or from holding negative thoughts yourself. Shrunken chakras come from having fears about the issue related to that chakra; while obsessions related to a chakra's issue will cause that chakra to swell disproportionately when compared to the other chakras.

Keeping your chakras clear and balanced is one of the easiest ways to develop your psychic abilities. Yoga and meditation are two powerful methods to clear and balance the chakras. I also have an audiotape (or CD) called *Chakra Clearing*, which is quite effective if you'd prefer a guided meditation. And in Part III of this book, you'll find several methods that help clear and balance the chakras.

ETHERIC CORDS

Whenever we have relationships involving fear of any kind, we form an unhealthy attachment to one another. This attachment is like a leash that says, "Don't change!" "Don't leave me!" or "Don't hurt me!"

These attachments are both palpable and visible when you notice them. I call them "etheric cords," because they look like surgical tubing attached from one person to another. (In some cases, the cords go from a person to a material object that they're afraid of losing.) Etheric cords are hardened forms of dysfunction, which you can notice with your psychic senses.

Etheric cords create a conduit for energy to run between two people. The person at the other end of the etheric cord can drain energy from you without your conscious awareness. Or, the person can send negative energy through the cord to you, causing physical pain that seems to have no medical cause.

Helpful people often have lots of cords attached to the people they assist. It doesn't matter whether they're paid to help people; the cords are formed when the "helpee" becomes dependent upon the helper for assistance. So if you have a best friend who continually calls you for advice, you probably have an etheric cord attached to that person.

Many people with chronic shoulder, neck, and back pain have large cords in these areas that are the true culprits. The longer your relationship has existed, the larger the cord. Therefore, the larger cords run the most energy back and forth. That's why I often find that people with chronic pain have large cords to primary family members.

A woman named Samantha attending my Melbourne Angel Intuitive Course came up onstage and allowed me to cut large cords that I saw protruding from her back. When I asked Samantha if she had back pain, she answered that her pain was chronic and resulted in frequent insomnia. I intuited that the cords extended to her ex-husband, with whom she had a contentious relationship involving shared custody of their children. Samantha instantly agreed that her ex-husband had "been a pain."

I called on Archangel Michael to cut Samantha's cords, but found that they resisted being sliced. This always indicates that a person is hanging on to anger, unforgiveness, or a desire for revenge. So I asked Samantha to take a deep breath. I then said, "Would you like to finally be rid of the pain associated with your ex-husband and with your back? Would you like to trade pain for peace?"

As she exhaled and said yes, Michael and I were easily able to cut through the cords. The next day, Samantha told me and the students in the class that she'd had the best night's sleep ever, without any pain. And, for the first time since their divorce, she was also able to think of her husband without anger.

In addition to causing physical pain, etheric cords are the cause of chronic fatigue syndrome and healer's burnout syndrome. In these cases, the person has too many cords attached to needy individuals, who are draining that person. If you're in this position, you may fear that these needy people really do depend upon you completely. However, if their neediness is making you ineffective, then they've brought you down to their level. They've sapped your strength, which does no one any good.

To heal this situation, mentally affirm to those people: "All of your needs are met by God, just as they are for me. You are strong, vital, and healed—just as I am." Then ask the angels to give you the strength to say no, and the self-esteem to take breaks when you need them. Keep your throat chakra clear, to give you the courage to be honest with these draining individuals.

(In Part III, you'll read about the specific methods to cut your etheric cords and vacuum your chakras of psychic debris.)

Jeannine Proulx was going through a difficult time and used the etheric cord-cutting method in desperation. Her fiancé had relapsed from an addiction and was admitted to an inpatient treatment center. This left them financially strapped, so Jeannine had to move in with her fiancé's parents.

When her fiancé returned home, his mother confronted Jeannine and accused her of being the cause of her son's addiction and relapse. The mother's fury was so intense that Jeannine left to stay with her brother for a few days.

Jeannine was reading my book *The Lightworker's Way* at the time. While driving to her brother's home, she thought of the etheric cord-cutting technique described in the book. Jeannine was curious to see what her tie to her mother-in-law looked like. She instantly had a vision of a huge, slimy cord from her belly, extending outward toward the sky and her mother-in-law. The vision was so vivid that it scared Jeannine, who normally doesn't consider herself to be clairvoyant.

She visualized herself cutting the cords and saw that the layers of slime came off easily with an etheric handsaw. However, inside the outer layers were rows of steel cables, so Jeannine visualized using a chainsaw to cut through the steel. The cables broke away in the same way that steel does—with a twang, twang, twang sound! Jeannine found the process eerie yet freeing. She kept it up until the last cable—which put up the greatest resistance to being cut—broke under the power of her chainsaw. Jeannine then pulled the remainder of the cord from her belly, and she felt a painful tug that left a hole inside her. So she filled it with white light and love, which alleviated the pain.

Jeannine says, "The freedom I got that day as I released the cords that attached me to my fiancé's mother and her fear has given me more power in my self-healing abilities than I ever thought possible. It has allowed me to let go of other people's fears and claim my own power."

Jeannine and her mother-in-law now have a mutually respectful relationship, devoid of the chains of steel.

Cutting etheric cords and vacuuming the chakras can have profoundly deep healing effects, which sometimes extend back to past lives. While reincarnation is still a controversial topic, what's not so controversial is how many healings occur from past-life-regression work. Phobias, anxieties, and addictions heal rapidly when a person discovers a past-life basis for the problem. Whether you believe that person actually lived in the past life, whether you think it's a metaphor for a current-life situation, or even if you decide that the past life belongs to one's spirit guide, the healing results of past-life regressions are impressive.

Cordelia Brabbs had attended my all-day "Healing with the Angels" workshop in Edinburgh, Scotland, where I guided attendees through a very deep and intense session of cord-cutting and vacuuming with Archangels Raphael and Michael. Cordelia says, "During the process, I felt as though large lumps of gunk were being sucked out of my chakras, and I was overwhelmed by intense emotions that left me sobbing."

Five days later, Cordelia was struck by a sudden and violent illness that felt like food poisoning. Since Cordelia is a teetotaling vegan with perfect health, she knew that the cause was not physical. She realized that she was going through an energy detoxification process resulting from the workshop clearing. Eventually the symptoms subsided, and Cordelia was able to go to bed.

The next morning, she felt as though an enormous weight had been lifted from her. She felt light and joyful, without knowing how or what had actually occurred. Cordelia was so intrigued that she asked a mediumistic friend to channel an explanation. The friend said that Cordelia had cleared out leftover energy from a past life as a working-class boy in 1812 New York, when she'd died of cholera at age 13.

Cordelia immediately researched cholera on the Internet and found that her previous day's symptoms exactly matched those of cholera! Cordelia says, "Since my experience, I've found myself reclaiming my power as a light-worker, and I'm in the process of manifesting my Divine life purpose—something that had terrified me before. I truly believe that I have Michael, Raphael, and Doreen's clearing exercises to thank for my new fear-free life."

HEALING ADDICTIONS THROUGH ETHERIC CORD CUTTING

In addition to pain relief and increased energy, those who cut their etheric cords report being healed of addictions, including alcoholism, smoking, drug dependency, and compulsive overeating.

Archangel Raphael taught me the addiction-healing method (on page 233 in Part III) in late 2001, and I immediately began using it during my workshops. I guided audiences through the methods, both for their own addictions and also to use with their own clients who struggle with them. Although I haven't had time to conduct scientific studies on its efficacy, the empirical case studies I've received have been very impressive.

OVERCOMING OVEREATING

The addiction to food can be as serious as any other form of addiction. Since food is necessary to life, and it's legally and socially sanctioned, people who struggle with overeating often struggle more than someone battling other addictions. Archangel Raphael's method of cutting etheric cords to the addictive substance works well with any form of addiction.

Carolyn B. of Los Angeles is a healer and a therapist who decided that her excess body weight was interfering with her life's purpose. Besides the fact that she'd been getting Divine guidance to lose weight, Carolyn wanted to live a healthier lifestyle. She decided to lose 17 pounds without knowing why she'd selected this number.

Carolyn tried a number of different weight-loss methods with only minimal success. Then she attended my workshop at the Agape Church in Santa Monica, California, where I took the audience through the addiction cord-cutting method.

Carolyn put food, procrastination, and other addictions on her lap to release. She says, "I literally felt a shift in my awareness. I also called the 'Angel of Weight Loss' (my own idea) to help me. I lost the urge to overeat as much and was drawn to more healthful foods." Carolyn no longer craved meat or alcohol, and she began eating a more vegetarian diet.

She rapidly lost 17 pounds and two dress sizes and has kept the weight off for several months. Having struggled with her weight for six years, Carolyn says, "It's nothing less than a miracle that my weight came and stayed off with the angels' help. At first I couldn't believe it, and I was constantly checking my scale to be sure it was real. With the weight loss, I feel healthier and happier. The angels are truly magical."

Weight isn't the only issue with food cravings. With any addiction, part of the suffering comes from feeling like you have no choice but to indulge. Cravings can haunt and control the addicted person, so healing from an addiction gives the person the freedom to choose, and usually results in increased self-respect.

Carol Manetta is an Angel Therapy Practitioner who struggled with daily chocolate cravings. Not wanting any substance to have control over her, Carol asked the angels to help her. Immediately, she felt a strong reduction in her cravings and no longer felt that she had to eat chocolate daily.

Carol still ate chocolate occasionally, but since she'd invited the angels to help her with this issue, she felt them around her whenever she'd indulge. Her chocolate binges diminished more and more, and after two weeks of not eating any, Carol binged on chocolate candy one night. About an hour later, Carol's heart began to pound like a hammer in her chest. The strong heart palpitations kept her awake all night, and Carol was very anxious due to her history of arrhythmia and mitral valve prolapse. When she had a similar reaction to non-chocolate candy, Carol decided to stay away from chocolate and sugar altogether.

Carol says it's a miracle that she no longer craves sweets. She reports, "Now, God's love and fresh fruit provide sweetness in my life. I no longer crave sugar. In fact, when I go to grocery stores and health-food stores, all those candies and other sweets have no appeal. I feel a strong pull away from all the sugary items on the store shelves. My health has never been better, and I have God and the angels to thank for this."

HEALING FROM DRUG AND ALCOHOL ADDICTIONS

Usually when we think of addictions, drugs and alcohol come to mind. Just as with Carolyn and Carol's healings from food addictions, cutting the etheric cords to mind-altering substances also has profound and often miraculous results.

Holly Andrews-Rising had been using large amounts of cocaine to cover up all of her emotional pain. She knew that her habit was killing her and that she needed to quit, so she began seeing a psychotherapist who suggested that she read my book *Healing with the Fairies,* which Holly did in three days. She felt guided to search the archives of my newsletter and found the September 2002 issue, which detailed Archangel Raphael's addiction-healing method (as outlined in Part III of this book).

Holly says, "I knew deep down that if I was ever going to help anyone as a lightworker, I had to get rid of the constant craving for cocaine. So I did everything in just the way Archangel Raphael outlined. I will never be able to explain the way it felt!"

Eight months later, she's still clean, sober, and free of cravings. Holly is now completing GED courses to earn her high school diploma and plans to attend college afterward. Holly also tells her stories at various churches to inspire others. She thanks God and her angels daily for healing her.

Having previously worked in drug-and-alcohol inpatient and outpatient facilities, I can attest to how miraculous Holly's healing is. Cocaine addiction has one of the highest relapse rates, and it's a life-destroyer—its exorbitant expense causes the addict to engage in destructive activities to obtain money. And its impact on the body is corrosive and dangerous.

This method also works with addictions to other drugs, including alcohol, caffeine, and cigarettes.

Eva of Norway also followed Archangel Raphael's prescription for healing from addictions after reading the September 2002 *Angel Therapy* newsletter. A smoker for 30 years, she followed the steps of this method, and has been smoke free for 15 months.

I've also talked to people who've used the method to successfully heal addictions to workaholism, gambling, chronically unhappy relationships, debt, procrastination, and any other behavior that interferes with health and happiness.

CURSE AND DAGGER LIFTING

When someone is angry with us, they may unwittingly or consciously send negative energy our way. A very powerful person who's upset about something can send psychic fireballs. We can also curse *ourselves* when we become angry or disappointed with how things are going in our lives.

Intense anger energy can manifest etherically into a "psychic attack." When this happens, there are etheric daggers, knives, arrows, and other sharp objects lodged in the attacked person's body, usually in the back. Even though these weapons are non-physical, they can create real physical pain.

I learned about this phenomenon after a former student of mine became angry when we wouldn't let her volunteer at one of our seminars. She attended the seminar anyway, sitting outside the entire time. After the seminar, I received a healing massage treatment. Midway through the session, I saw about a dozen daggers being lifted out of my back. I tuned in to discover what they were, and immediately knew that the former student had psychically attacked me. The next day, I found that my assistant had also been attacked by her.

I did additional research and conducted sessions with audiences. I found that most people are unknowingly carrying these weapons of psychic attack in their etheric bodies. Using the method in Part III of this book, my audience members were able to see and feel the weapons being lifted from their bodies. The

Archangel Raphael would then heal the former psychic wounds and incisions, and Archangel Michael would send loving energy to heal the attacker and prevent subsequent attacks.

While the topic seemed a bit heavy and dark to me, I nonetheless found my audience members healing whenever I employed this method. Many people told me about their instant relief from back pain and headaches after I helped them lift the weapons from their etheric bodies.

And a woman who hadn't even heard me discuss this method sent me the following story.

When Rochelle was at church one day, she began praying that her life would improve. She then saw a very large angel in front of her with its wings folded behind its back. Rochelle heard a disembodied voice that told the angel what to do. The angel reached over to Rochelle and began pulling daggers from her throat, ears, and heart. When the angel completed the job that the voice commanded it to do, it left as suddenly as it had come. The light of the angel was so bright that Rochelle couldn't open her eyes.

One evening about a week later, Rochelle awoke to find a dark presence in her bedroom. She then saw an angel appear, who chased away the darkness. Rochelle fell peacefully asleep with a vision of angels sitting all around the roof of her home.

Rochelle hadn't mentioned either incident to her husband, so she was thrilled the next day when he said that he'd also seen an angel in their bedroom the night before. He said that he was certain it hadn't been a dream. The angel had protected Rochelle and her husband from further psychic attack.

Bringing in More Light

When we cut etheric cords and clear our chakras, we allow more Divine light to shine within ourselves. It's the equivalent of dusting off a dirty lightbulb so that its full wattage can be projected. Our inner light also responds to the warmth and brightness of outer light from the sun, moon, and stars, as I'll talk about next.

CHAPTER 16

Angels and Sunshine

Since light plus love equals healing, it makes sense to bring in as much light and love as possible into any situation that calls for a healing. The more light from any of the methods (clearing chakras, energy healing work, crystals, and so on), the better.

In the Atlantean healing temples, we worked with crystals by directing sunlight and spiritual light from ley lines toward patients' chakras. As patients lay down in a bed made of crystal, large crystal points were situated above each chakra. Priestesses took turns directing the light through each crystal into successive chakras. During these healing sessions, we also prayed and called upon the angels. The results were that people from all over would traveled to the healing temples to experience profound healings.

Sunshine has been a healing treatment dating back to ancient Greece, Rome, and Egypt, in addition to other countries and cultures. For instance, in Greece and Rome, physicians would send their patients to a "solaria" for exposure to healing sun rays. Hippocrates, the Grecian "Father of Medicine," prescribed "heliotherapy" (healing with sunshine) in his writings, and for his patients. And in the late 1800s, doctors treated tuberculosis with sun exposure, because of the sun's ability to kill bacteria associated with this disease and its related infections.

Many ancient civilizations literally worshiped the sun. Those in Aztec, Mayan, Egyptian, Celtic, Persian, Greek, Roman, and other cultures prayed to sun gods for help and healings. Solar ceremonies praised the sun for its life-giving force. The early Christian and Catholic churches called this pagan worship a sin, and began strongly discouraging its practice. Yet the references to sun worship are still evident, especially on every *Sun*day of each week.

＊　＊　＊

The love part of the healing equation comes from prayer and calling upon Heaven's help. Angels, as pure, egoless beings, bring both light and love into any situation. When angelic invocation and intervention is combined with additional sources of light, it opens the door to profound healings.

Jackie Stevens was feeling lost, confused, and lonely. Her energy level was low, and she couldn't sleep—classic signs of depression. She stayed home from work one day and sat outside in the sunshine under a tree. She prayed for help from God, the angels, the archangels, her higher self, and the fairies. As Jackie closed her eyes and took deep breaths, she felt the sun warm her body, penetrating through her winter clothing. She sat for quite a long time, enjoying nature. Then Jackie felt the loneliness and feelings of vulnerability lift. She experienced increased energy, which brought a smile to her face and lightness within her heart. She realized that she wasn't alone then, and wouldn't be in the future.

Jackie continued her natural light treatment by sitting under the moon and stars that evening. She felt the light from the moon and stars cleansing her deeply. She says, "I felt a cleansing of my mind, body, and soul like never before. I also felt fully connected with the universe. Now I make it a point to enjoy at least a short walk outdoors every day. And each night I sit outside to look at the moon and stars, particularly if I can't sleep. I've discovered that as the sun replenishes our energy, so does the moon cleanse our heart, mind, and soul."

Today, Jackie helps others get in touch with their angels and heal with the angels' help. Like Jackie, the woman in the next story also conducts private angel healings and readings, as a result of her personal healing involving the sunshine.

Angie Hartfield was at a low point in her life. She was going through a difficult divorce, and her father was ill. On top of that, Angie had begun having seizures accompanied by painful swelling and shortness of breath.

Angie's symptoms got so bad that she finally checked herself into an emergency room. Her test results showed a diagnosis of an autoimmune disease called systemic lupus erythematosus. She began steroid therapy and was told to stay indoors, with the drapes closed and away from all sunlight. She became very depressed, couldn't eat, and slept most of the day.

Her young daughters were understandably upset by their mother's illness, especially since their grandfather was also ill. So Angie began praying. She says, "I wasn't sure what to pray for at first. I just wanted relief, and I desperately needed support. I knew that I had angels, and I finally asked them to help me. They motivated me to go to my local bookstore, and the angels strongly told me to purchase *The Messengers* by Julia Ingram and G. W. Hardin and Doreen's book *Angel Therapy*. I read *Angel Therapy* first, and I sat and cried as I realized that I wasn't alone and that with the help of my angels, I would survive this disease."

Next, the angels guided Angie to switch to a doctor who used a homeopathic approach. Much to Angie's relief, her new doctor took her off the steroids. The doctor also helped Angie work toward a healthy remission and showed her ways to manage her symptoms.

This progress encouraged Angie to talk to her angels more frequently. They guided her to eliminate unhealthy behaviors from her lifestyle. This resulted in even higher self-esteem and confidence, which further motivated Angie to get completely well.

The angels instructed Angie to use positive affirmations and to visualize herself being happy and healthy. She was soon able to stop taking medication altogether, except for an anti-inflammatory pill, which she only used in extreme circumstances.

She says, "My angels assured me that I would soon be completely free of all medication. I felt like I was in 'angel training,' as they taught me about life and how to become a healthy individual."

Angie has been symptom free for more than three years. She knows that the disorder is completely gone, and she no longer acknowledges it as a part of her. She also moved with her daughters and new husband, Duke, to Hawaii. "I'm out in the sun constantly now," she says. "The angels tell me that I will wilt like a flower if I don't get sunshine."

LET THE SUN SHINE

An Italian adage says: *Dove il sole non entra il dottore,* which means, "Where the sun doesn't enter, the doctor does." As mentioned earlier, scientific studies show that while exposure to the sun may have some harmful effects, one can experience even greater health risks by *not* going out in the sun. Statistically, more people die of diseases associated with sunlight deprivation than do people with skin cancer. As with everything, moderation is important when it comes to sun exposure—it certainly isn't wise to get sunburned, yet it's also unwise to avoid the sun completely.

While skin cancer scares have caused many people to shy away from the sun—after all, *cancer* is an ominous word—it's important to consider all the scientific evidence regarding the pros and cons of sun exposure. After reviewing the latest medical research reported in prestigious journals such as *The Journal of the American Medical Association* and *The New England Journal of Medicine,* the general consensus about sunlight's relationship to health can be summarized as follows:

— **Sunshine is associated with nonfatal types of skin cancer.** Excessive ultraviolet (UV) light exposure is correlated with the development of basal cell carcinoma and squamous cell carcinoma, two types of skin cancer that are easily treatable and rarely fatal. These cancers primarily develop in fair-skinned individuals who have intermittent sun exposure. In other words, they spend most of their time working and living indoors, so when they *do* go outside, they become sunburned instead of allowing their body to adapt to gradual sun exposure.

— **Potentially fatal skin cancer may be dietary, not UV, related.** The relationship of UV exposure to malignant melanoma, the potentially fatal type of skin cancer, is still not understood. There's some evidence that says that becoming sunburned several times is related to melanoma. However, another study has shown that the biggest factor was dietary fat imbalances, especially among people who don't ingest enough omega-3 fatty acids.

— **The ozone's role is unclear.** The negative buzz about the ozone's connection to skin cancer may be more of an urban myth than a scientific fact. A study on ozone depletion's role in skin cancer found that, although the ozone layer hasn't changed in Norway's skies, their rate of malignant melanoma has increased anyway. Reports about Chilean sheep developing eye cataracts because of their proximity to the Antarctic ozone hole are scientifically unfounded. Interestingly, further studies in Chile found no significant change in the animal or human population's health.

— **Vitamin D depletion is dangerous.** People with vitamin D depletion are more likely to develop breast, colon, ovarian, and prostate cancer; and heart disease, high blood pressure, multiple sclerosis, jaundice, and osteoporosis are also associated with vitamin D deficiencies. Many studies show vitamin D depletions among those who live in sunshine-deprived locations, those who are homebound or hospitalized, dark-skinned individuals, and women who customarily dress in clothing and veils that hide their skin's exposure to sunshine. This is true even in people who take vitamin D supplements. Another study found that elderly women suffer from vitamin D deficiencies during the winter months when sunshine levels are low.

— **Low sun exposure is linked to cancer.** Many well-documented scientific studies show that women who live in northern latitudes are up to 150 percent more likely to develop ovarian and breast cancer than those who live in sunnier southern locales. One study also found that women who worked outdoors were significantly less likely to develop breast or colon cancer, compared to indoor workers. Scientists know that a lack of sunshine creates vitamin D deficiencies, which is correlated with ovarian, breast, and colon cancer. Vitamin D protects against these types of cancers.

— **Seasonal Affective Disorder (SAD) affects millions.** During winter months, people with SAD experience depression, become lethargic, sleep excessively, crave carbohydrates, gain weight, lose interest in doing things with other people, often feel guilty, and feel a lack of excitement about life in general. Symptoms improve when SAD sufferers are exposed to full-spectrum lighting.

— **Sunlight increases mental and physical performance.** A study of 22,000 American students found that when they were in classrooms exposed to natural sunlight, their test scores rose by 26 percent. Sunlight has been shown to lower blood pressure, increase the blood supply to organs and muscles, increase oxygen supply in body tissue, and increase glycogen (stored energy) in the muscles and liver.

— **Sunlight has health benefits.** In addition to increasing our vitamin D supply, sunlight has an insulinlike effect that is beneficial for diabetics. Exercising outside in the sun lowers the lactic-acid count, which can reduce muscular pain from a workout. Sunshine exposure also lowers serum cholesterol and seems to increase our tolerance of stress because it lowers our resting heart, blood pressure, and respiratory rates. According to Zane Kime, M.D., author of *Sunlight,* when we're under stress, we produce too much cyclic adenosine monophosphate (cAMP), which impairs our immune system and lowers our resistance to cancer. This is especially true in individuals whose diets are high in polyunsaturated fats. It seems that cAMP is very sensitive to sunlight exposure, and sunshine reduces and destroys cAMP. This has a sedative effect, which is one reason why we often feel sleepy when we're out in the sun.

— **Sunlight provides benefits for children.** Studies show that sunlight may heal neonatal jaundice and increase bone mass in prepubescent children. Also, mothers who are exposed to the sun during pregnancy are more likely to give birth to infants who are taller than mothers who rarely go out in the sun during this time.

THE PINEAL GLAND CONNECTION

Sunlight enters into the body primarily through the eyes, which direct the light to the brain's pineal gland. The pineal gland then uses the sunshine to produce the helpful hormone melatonin, which triggers the production of serotonin.

Serotonin is important in keeping us calm, helping us to get a good night's sleep, decreasing symptoms of premenstrual syndrome and bed-wetting, and reducing carbohydrate cravings. Since many psychoactive medications work by increasing serotonin, sunlight exposure could lead to a reduction in the use of these prescription drugs.

Studies show that sunglasses, contact lenses, and eyeglasses reset our eyes' ability to detect sun rays. When we wear sunglasses, the brain doesn't realize the extent of sun exposure we're getting, so it doesn't secrete as much melatonin as it would in full sunlight. Melatonin, which makes us tan, provides natural sun protection. Our body doesn't realize that it's getting maximum exposure to sunlight when we wear sunglasses, so the body doesn't produce its natural defenses that enable it to prevent sunburn. This is because the eyes help the body adjust melatonin production according to the sunlight exposure. The melatonin provides natural sun protection. Glass of any kind—whether it's glass in windows, car windshields, eyeglasses, contact lenses, or sunglasses—filter out the healthful rays of the sunshine.

Biologically, we're meant to be exposed to sunlight for health and happiness. Our hemoglobin pigments (red blood cells) are virtually identical to the chlorophyll in plants. Chlorophyll absorbs sunlight and converts it into energy and food for the plant's growth and health. In a similar way, our body benefits from sunlight exposure.

So, enjoying a moderate amount of sunshine in the morning or late afternoon (when UV levels aren't strong), without sunscreen or sunglasses appears to be important for health. Office workers and housebound and hospitalized patients would be wise to open their windows and allow full sunshine to stream in, if possible. If this isn't practical, a walk outdoors during a break is a good idea.

Sunscreens aren't a panacea, as studies show that people stay out longer in the sunshine than is advisable, because they assume that the sunscreen is protecting them. Commercial sunscreens are also laden with chemicals that the pores absorb into the body. These lotions also block out UV rays, which are important in the production and absorption of vitamin D, as well as lowering blood pressure and serum cholesterol.

SUNRISE, SUNSET

The angels of Atlantis were very clear in their conversations with me that we also benefit from exposure to the colors and light of sunrises and sunsets. They told me that being outside during a sunrise awakens the upper chakras, and energizes and prepares us for the upcoming day.

The angels of Atlantis also said that bathing in the colors of a sunset (by being outside and watching the sun go down) prepares us for a wonderful night's sleep. The sunset stimulates the lower chakras.

This makes sense, since the colors of sunrise turn from the warmer colors of the lower chakras to the cooler, upper chakra colors of the dawning blue sky. And the sunset does the opposite—going from the day's upper chakra colors to the warm colors of the sunset. So, the sunrise stimulates the chakras upward, from lower to upper (perfect for energizing you for the upcoming day); and the sunset stimulates the chakras downward, from upper to lower (to help our bodies settle down from the day's activities and prepare for the evening's rest).

Exposing ourselves to sunrises and sunsets connects us to natural earth rhythms, which helps us have better timing and puts us in the synchronistic flow of life. Ideally, we should witness the sunrises and sunsets outdoors without sunglasses so that our bodies can absorb the light fully. However, even watching the sun rise and set through a window is better than not seeing it at all.

STARLIGHT AND MOONLIGHT

In addition to the sun's light, the angels of Atlantis also say that exposure to light from the stars and the moon are also health- and life-enhancing.

The cycles of the moon have long served as benchmarks for us to know when to plant and reap farm crops. These lunar cycles are associated with fertility and harvest celebrations, which also correlate to spiritual and religious holy days.

On the three evenings of the full moon (the evening prior to the full moon, the evening of the full moon, and the evening following), taking a moon bath is refreshing and inspiring. Sitting outside while bathing in the moonlight feels mystical. It revives ancient memories of the "old ways" of connecting to spirituality through nature before organized religion demonized these practices.

— **The evening prior to a full moon: recharging night.** Like a breast freely giving milk, the near-full moon gives moonlight to recharge our crystals, oils, and bodies. Place your crystals and other items outdoors if possible, or next to a window where they'll receive maximum exposure to the moonlight during the night.

— **The full moon: releasing night.** When the moon is completely full, give it anything that you want to release. You can do this mentally, or through an action such as writing what you'd like to let go of and then burning or burying the paper beneath the full moon.

— **The new moon: manifesting night.** On "dark-moon" nights, the energy is ripe for manifesting your dreams and desires. Meditate about your desires, and either tell the dark moon of your intentions, or write them in an affirmative way (meaning that you write positive statements describing how you've already achieved your desires). Ask the new moon and Archangel Haniel to guide your actions in manifesting these intentions, and affirm that they work out for the highest good.

— **The half-moon: courage and power night.** The half-moon is symbolized by a bull's horns and is a sign of power. On this evening, make a commitment to move forward fearlessly. Ask Archangel Michael to boost your courage to take steps to manifest your life's purpose.

— **Starlight.** Starlight awakens the imagination and opens the mind prior to sleep. This allows our dreamtime travels to reach even higher and farther into the astral plane, gives us greater access to ascended masters and departed-loved-one dream visitations, and helps the unconscious solve problems and create new ideas during our dreams.

We're spirits incarnated upon a beautiful planet that has physically based light sources—the sun, moon, and stars—that are designed to support and heal us. Light is a tool available to everyone, free of charge. When this is coupled with love, the possibilities are unlimited. In the next chapter, we'll look at one aspect of that love: prayer and faith.

CHAPTER 17

Prayer, Faith, and Angels

In the Atlantean healing temples, we prayed for our patients. We also prayed for ourselves and each other. We knew that the more love we expressed outwardly from the heart, the more power was built and contained within the temple. What was good for one was good for all—we made no distinction between praying for the health and happiness of a patient versus praying for the same for ourselves. We knew that our own strength, health, and happiness would ultimately benefit our patients.

SCIENTIFIC STUDIES ON PRAYER

Hundreds of scientific studies have documented the healing benefits of prayer. Studies have found that a person who prays for his or her own health—or who is prayed for by others—is more likely to survive a serious health condition, need fewer pain medications, heal faster, and live longer than people who don't incorporate prayer. Studies show that prayers of *any* denomination have a significant and measurably positive effect upon health. Scientists have ruled out mere positive thinking as the cause, as prayer studies have been conducted upon plants, bacteria, animals, and infants—who theoretically don't know that they're being prayed for.

For example, a Columbia University Study conducted in 2001 at the Department of Obstetrics and Gynecology at New York's Presbyterian Hospital found that women being treated with in vitro fertilization embryo transfers were significantly more likely to become pregnant if people were praying for them. The study was double-blind, meaning that the doctors, researchers, and women didn't know who was being prayed for.

And a famous study conducted at San Francisco General Hospital in 1988 found that 192 coronary-care patients who were prayed for suffered from significantly fewer incidents of congestive heart failure, cardiopulmonary arrest, and pneumonia after ten months, compared to a matched population of 201 patients who weren't prayed for. They also required fewer medications and less ventilator support. A similar study of 999 coronary-care patients conducted in 1999 at the Mid America Heart Institute at Saint Luke's Hospital in Kansas City, Missouri, found similar results.

Another study revealed a significant reduction in symptoms of rheumatoid arthritis among patients who were prayed for, compared to those who weren't. And an Israeli study concluded that patients with bloodstream infections had shorter hospital stays and durations of fever when they were prayed for.

Most prayer studies are based upon *intercessory* prayer, in which the patient is prayed for by someone else. This is because it's more difficult to measure a person's own prayers for him- or herself. At Bloomsburg University in Pennsylvania, researchers found in 2002 that students who were prayed for showed significant reductions in anxiety symptoms, compared to those who received no intercessory prayer.

Unexpected Healings

When we pray for anything, it's best that we don't outline *how* we want our prayers answered. When we effectively hand

God a script and say, "This is how I want You to handle this situation," we create limitations. The Divine infinite wisdom of the Universe often has wonderful surprises in store for us when we pray with crystal-clear intentions and then release the situation in full faith.

Julie Maggi of California had injured her back so seriously that her doctors only allowed her to sit upright for one hour daily. Her three slipped disks kept her bedridden and in constant pain, yet Julie instinctively knew that she needed to heal her mind and emotions, as well as her body, so she prayed daily for her angels to assist her with this healing. As an act of faith that her prayers would be answered, she also refrained from all drugs, including painkillers, and refused to have surgery. Julie did her best to listen to her body's needs and take care of them.

Two years after her injury, as Julie slept in her bed, she heard someone enter her bedroom. Since Julie lived alone, she struggled to wake up and see who was there. Julie saw a woman with dark brown curly hair and brown eyes. She was wearing a dress that glowed with golden-white light, and she also had a wreath of light around her head.

The woman knelt beside Julie and gently pulled back her blankets. She then placed the palms of both hands on Julie's back, right at the point of her injury. After a few moments, the woman replaced Julie's blankets and disappeared.

Julie says, "I realized that an angel had visited me—it most certainly wasn't a dream. I believe the encounter was a sign that my prayers were heard and answered. Today, although my back still has some limitations, I'm much stronger, and for that, I give thanks to all my angels."

Julie could have never anticipated that a physical angel would visit her, so she was wise to simply pray and allow the Universe to decide how her healing would occur. She was also wise to follow Divine guidance to listen to her own body. Like

Julie, the man in the following story trusted his own inner guidance, which came to him following his prayers for health.

Prayer and light instantly cured liver cancer for
Salvador van Drimmelen of Holland in 1970. Salvador
and his wife were living in South Africa when he fell seriously ill and was admitted to Johannesburg Hospital.
After extensive testing, Salvador was diagnosed with liver
cancer, and the consulting physician recommended
immediate surgery.

Much to the doctors' disapproval, Salvador decided to
delay surgery while he consulted God, Jesus, and Mary
for guidance on how to proceed. Salvador traveled to the
mountainous woods, where it was quiet enough for him
to clearly hear Divine guidance.

Salvador engaged in strong prayer in the woods. His
heart opened and his tears flowed during his days of
prayer and meditation. One day, while kneeling on a bed
of pine needles saying the Lord's Prayer and clasping his
Mother Mary pendant, Salvador watched the sunlight
change into a ball of intense white light.

He says, "It was like a thousand suns, it was so bright.
In this blinding Heavenly light appeared the Divine Mother
in all her glory. In this sacred moment, my heart was filled
with the everlasting joy of my soul." Salvador heard Mary's
reassurance that he would experience salvation.

Then, Mary's image slowly vanished. While Salvador
was still kneeling, a holy silence fell upon his surroundings. In order to stay in the Heavenly moment as long as
possible, he didn't move at all.

Salvador said, "Suddenly I realized that my constant
pain had left me. I felt energy streaming through my body
again. Filled with gladness and completely healed, I
returned back home, praising God."

Salvador has expressed his vision of Mary, and his
gratitude to her, in intricate embroidery art, which I've
been privileged to see. His beautifully colored designs are

breathtaking, and a true testament to the miracle he experienced.

The light that Salvador experienced was a direct result of his prayers and his willingness to follow guidance to sit quietly and meditate. This isn't always easy, as health challenges can create so much fear that we're temporarily unable to hear the voice of the Divine. The next story shows how the *fear* of hearing can actually create the physical result of not being able to.

Four-year-old Mikaela Bachas seemed to have hearing difficulties, so her mother, Stephanie, took her for an examination. The doctor found that Mikaela was suffering from "otitis media," otherwise known as "glue ear." The condition required the surgical insertion of a small grommet tube into each ear to help drain the trapped liquid.

Mikaela had the surgery, but three months later, her hearing was low again. A new test revealed that the grommets had been pushed out, so the doctor said he'd again have to perform surgery to insert new tubes.

Stephanie was concerned about putting her daughter through another surgery. She'd recently read my book *Healing with the Angels,* and her mother had just finished reading *You Can Heal Your Life* by Louise L. Hay. Stephanie and her mother decided to pool what they'd learned from these two books and come up with a spiritual alternative to surgery. Together, they concluded that Mikaela was hearing things that she didn't want to listen to. When Stephanie asked her daughter about this, Mikaela replied that she was hearing frightening voices. Many sensitive children report hearing voices, according to my research.

So, Stephanie and her mother created a list of healing affirmations and prayers. Stephanie explained to Mikaela that—if she wanted to—she was capable of healing her ears with the help of the angels. The three of them then recited prayers and affirmations related to hearing with love, and about being safe and secure.

Mikaela prayed that Archangel Raphael would heal her ears, and she also asked Archangel Michael to keep voices away from her while she slept. Mikaela excitedly announced the next morning that the prayers had worked! Archangel Michael had kept the voices away all night.

She faithfully recited her prayers and affirmations each day and night. About a week later, Stephanie noticed a reduction in the volume of the television, and other indicators that Mikaela's hearing had improved. A subsequent doctor's test showed a 20 percent improvements in Mikaela's hearing! Without Stephanie's prompting, the doctor suggested delaying Mikaela's second grommet surgery for six weeks.

Stephanie recalls, "Mikaela was just as excited as I was about the news. I congratulated Mikaela on her achievement, and we thanked the angels for their work and for guiding the doctor to willingly postpone the surgery. We continued to pray to God and the angels, and after the six weeks, Mikaela's hearing was 100 percent. This experience confirmed my belief in the work of the angels. I hope that people will feel inspired to believe in God and the angels, and to teach their children about them—as well as to look at their own health issues from a deeper level."

FOLLOWING DIVINE GUIDANCE

The above stories all illustrate an important point: It's often not enough to simply pray and then wait for results. We're given inner instructions, in the form of repetitive thoughts, feelings, inner words, or visions, as a result of prayer. When we follow this Divine guidance, we literally co-create the answer to our prayers, along with Heaven. Many people whom I've counseled have mistakenly believed that their prayers were ignored, when *they* were actually the ones who were ignoring the Divine guidance instructions that Heaven gave them in answer to prayers.

The next story illustrates how one woman's willingness to listen to her inner guidance proved to be a lifesaver for her sister.

In early 1993, Jen Wesolowski kept having visions that something horrible was going to happen, and she got so frightened that she just blocked out the full communication. On February 12, her sister, Sandie, was hit by a speeding car while walking across the street. Sandie flew into the air and hit the car windshield headfirst. The doctors said that Sandie had severed her brain stem, and they gave her no hope of recovery or survival. The hospital chaplain recommended making funeral arrangements.

By February 14, Valentine's Day, Sandie's blood pressure was so low that the hospital staff asked if the family wanted to donate her organs, or conduct resuscitation procedures. Since Sandie was the mother of three young boys, the decision required a lot of consideration.

A few moments later in prayer, Jen had a vision of an illuminated hospital bed in a darkened room. She heard a soft voice say, *"Everything will be all right."* Jen also heard the month of May stated by this voice. The angels' message let Jen know that her sister would recover.

That same day, Jen asked the hospital's priest to lead the family in a healing prayer at Sandie's bedside. Jen says, "The minute we all gathered and held hands and he spoke to her, Sandie's face started to come alive. The priest touched her forehead and said, 'Sandie, my name is Father Frank, and your family and friends are here, and I know you can hear me.'"

Sandie furrowed her brows, and the healing began! Even though she had no broken bones, she *did* have a severe injury. Nevertheless, Sandie eventually learned to walk again. Although she's unable to smell or taste, she's made a full recovery, with her other abilities and memory intact.

Jen gives thanks that she listened to the angels and had faith in Sandie's recovery. Jen says, "Since that day, I listen to my angels, and although I may not hear as clearly as possible, I don't push their messages aside anymore."

Like Jen's example, the next story about Leisa Machado shows the miraculous results that can occur when someone prays, and then follows the guidance she receives.

I met Leisa at a workshop I gave in the seaside town of Santa Cruz in Northern California. When I clairvoyantly looked inside of her, I was awestruck (not an exaggeration) by how clean this woman's insides were. All of Leisa's organs looked as sterile as an operating room. Her chakras were pristine, and she absolutely glowed from the inside. Never before or since have I seen such a clean internal body!

Leisa told me that she ate organic foods exclusively, avoided all chemicals, and drank only distilled water because she felt that all other water had potentially harmful organisms. Leisa explained that she and her husband wanted to conceive a baby, and she thought the best way was to prepare her body as well as possible. Still, she was having difficulty conceiving.

She'd had three tubal pregnancies, a miscarriage, and one failed attempt at in vitro fertilization. After six years of trying to conceive, Leisa worried that she was getting older and was still without a child. That's when she decided to use a holistic approach to child conception. Leisa embarked on a path of spirituality, which involved praying, eating organic meals, and holding positive thoughts.

She attended my angel workshop shortly after beginning this process. I psychically saw that Leisa would successfully conceive and birth a child; however, it would be at least two years in the future. Leisa didn't like this news—she wanted a child sooner. So I asked the angels for a message, and they said Leisa could perhaps conceive sooner with the help of Archangels Michael and

Gabriel. Michael helps to clear the energetic body of any effects of fear, which could potentially delay any goal—including the conception of a baby. And Gabriel has been helping expectant mothers since before the biblical annunciations to Elizabeth and Mary.

Leisa recalls what she did after the workshop: "I began to meditate and pray on the situation and felt guided to call on not only Archangel Michael, but Gabriel and Raphael as well. Doreen had mentioned that Gabriel was known for helping during pregnancy. Michael had always been there for me in the past, and I called on Raphael—the healing angel—for help to be physically ready for conception and pregnancy.

"I started meditating twice a day, visualizing each angel doing his unique work on my body and spirit to prepare me to conceive. During one of these meditations, my angels told me that my child could come sooner than Divinely planned as long as I continued to train as a child counselor. My guardian angel urged me to surrender my fears to God, and I would take my fisted hands and unclench them up to my angels, saying, 'I can't do this anymore; you need to take this for me.'

"Finally, I got my miracle. Although second in vitro attempts are successful only about 20 percent of the time, it worked for me. I was finally pregnant with a healthy embryo! I can only thank my angels for this—both my guardian angels and the archangels—and acknowledge that it wouldn't have happened had I not remembered to *continually ask* for support.

"Thank God I learned this lesson, too, because I would need angelic help throughout most of my pregnancy. During the first few weeks, I started to bleed. My doctor put me on bed rest, and I put my three special archangels to task, calling on them continually. I could (and still can) feel each one near a certain side of my body, keeping me at peace.

"After a few weeks, I was permitted to get up. My second trimester was fine, but at week 31, I began to go into labor. In the hospital, I felt an incredible outpouring of love and healing. The angels told me that this baby was a pure spirit and that he needed me to stay as pure as possible in order to honor his arrival into the world. I was again reminded to surrender and 'let him go.' The wording was unusual and quite frightening, however. I was terrified that it meant I would lose him. I *re*-learned that I needed to let go of trying to hold on to him myself. At week 34, I had Jaren—a strong and healthy baby boy, named for the Hebrew word for 'outcry of joy.' He was premature, but breathing on his own and very cognitive."

But Jaren wasn't out of the woods yet. About eight hours after he was born, he took a turn for the worse: He stopped breathing and went into a coma. The doctors couldn't figure out what was wrong with him. In her grief and panic, Leisa turned to her angels. She thought, *This can't be happening! They've guided me through every step. I can't lose him now!*

As she sobbed in her hospital bed, Leisa felt a gentle presence that calmed her with warmth and love. Leisa and her husband sent out a call for prayers. They called friends, who in turn called and e-mailed other friends. They soon felt numerous prayers, and an abundance of Reiki energy and angelic assistance, coming in to help them.

Leisa says, "I could actually see Jaren surrounded by layers and layers of angels. At times I could see his spirit float up with them, but his feet always stayed grounded in his body. Two days later, doctors were amazed by his miraculous recovery. And just a week and a half later, my husband, Jeff, and I took our little miracle home with us, where he belongs."

Leisa's story reminds us of the importance of talking to our angels continually, and then adhering to the Divine guidance that they give us. An important part of Leisa's journey was her willing-ness to surrender and let go. This wasn't always easy for her. Often, Leisa had to ask the angels to help her surrender, since the goal of pregnancy was so dear to her heart.

Her story also illustrates the principle of surrender. Even though Leisa had a crystal-clear desire to have a baby, she was also willing to have the faith necessary to surrender this desire and trust in Divine order completely.

The next story is remarkable because the woman's angels gave her guidance that was contrary to the messages she was receiving from medical doctors. It truly took courage for her to follow her angels' advice, and yet the results were lifesaving.

Lucretia, my original psychic development teacher at the Learning Light Foundation in Anaheim (I wrote about her in my book *The Lightworker's Way*), received lifesaving information from her angels.

Lucretia meditates regularly and uses angel oracle cards to keep in close contact with her angels. In May of 2002, Lucretia clearly heard her angels repeatedly tell her to have two moles removed, one on her left arm and one on the right side of her chest.

As her doctor shaved off both moles, he commented that he was concerned about the one on her left arm. Lucretia heard her angels softly say something about a mix-up, but Lucretia didn't understand the message at that time.

A week later, Lucretia's primary-care physician called to tell her that she had a melanoma on her chest that called for excise surgery immediately. Lucretia's angels reassured her that everything would be okay.

Lucretia noticed that her surgeon looked like a cherubic angel. The surgery went well, and a week later, the doctor told Lucretia that no melanoma had been found on her chest. As she drove home, elated by this good news, Lucretia heard her angels tell her three times: *"The melanoma is on the left arm; they mixed it up."*

The next time she was at her surgeon's office, Lucretia asked him to check the mole on her left arm for melanoma. When the results took longer to be returned than expected, Lucretia's angels told her that this was because of the mix-up. The pathologists couldn't match the original tissue sample that they'd taken with the second sample. That's when Lucretia mustered the courage to tell her surgeon that her angels had told her about the tissue mix-up. The surgeon was surprisingly open to hearing Lucretia's angelic message, and he acknowledged that some people have the ability to receive information from the beyond.

When the pathologists were told about the mix-up, they were able to complete their report, which *did* show a melanoma in Lucretia's left arm. The angels had been right! She then had a third surgery, and everything was successfully removed. Lucretia hasn't had any trouble since.

ANSWERED PRAYERS

Why are some prayers answered, while others are seemingly not? The reasons are beyond human comprehension, but they might have to do with the following situations:

- Praying for someone to live when it's their soul's choice to cross over.

- Not noticing, trusting, or following the Divine guidance instructions that come in response to prayer.

- Sabotaging answered prayers as the responses come to you because you fear the paranormal or feel undeserving of Heaven's attention.

- Not noticing when a prayer is answered, since the answer comes in a different way than you expected.

- Believing that only "special," "pure," or "chosen" people have their prayers answered.

Even though not every prayer seems to be answered, the number of scientific studies and empirical case studies show that prayer is an effective and reliable healing method. Most likely, more people have experienced answered prayers than we'll ever know.

I've met some people who are afraid of asking for Heaven's help too often, or bothering Heaven with trivial requests. This is projecting our belief in human limitations onto Heaven, which has no limitations. The angels want to help us create peace on Earth by helping us in whatever way they can. We can't ask for help too often, and we certainly aren't bothering the angels when we request their assistance. In contrast, it's their sacred honor and sincere pleasure to bring smiles to our faces and peace within our hearts.

Some people are angry with the Creator because of previous prayers that seemed to go unanswered. Afraid of being disappointed again, they stop praying. Yet under dire circumstances, they may return to praying . . . with different results, as the next story shows.

Rina Waaka's 18-month-old son was in the intensive-care unit with respiratory problems. Twice, her son almost died, and Rina was frantic. She thought about praying, but she was angry at God. Her dad had died two years earlier, despite her fervent prayers, so Rina had vowed never to pray again.

All that changed when Rina felt utterly helpless to heal her son. She went into a little room in the hospital, closed the door, and fell to her knees to plead that God save her boy.

Two days later, a middle-aged woman whom Rina had never seen before approached her at the hospital and inquired about her son's condition. Rina ignored her and went outside to smoke a cigarette.

When Rina returned to the hospital ward, the same woman stopped her. She told Rina that she had nothing to worry about, as she'd just visited Rina's son and the Holy Spirit was looking after him. Rina became irate and stopped at the nurses' station to see why a stranger had been given permission to see her son. The nurses said that no one had been on the floor or in her son's room, except for the nurses and Rina.

When Rina went in to see her son, his room felt different, and she felt a presence around him. Two days after the angel's visit, her son was discharged from the hospital. The doctors couldn't understand how he'd healed so rapidly! They'd expected his recovery to last considerably longer.

Rina's willingness to give prayer a try proved miraculous, and renewed her faith. The following stories are also inspiring, and are helpful reminders of the miracles that often result from prayer.

Cindy Fundahn asked for, and received, Divine intervention during the birth of her child. Cindy, 32 weeks pregnant and seriously ill, was rushed by ambulance to a hospital in Sioux Falls, South Dakota. The admitting doctor immediately diagnosed her unborn son as being in serious trouble. Only one artery was supplying blood to the baby, which severely restricted his growth and left Cindy critically ill. The doctors rushed her into emergency surgery.

On the operating table, Cindy prayed that God would save her and her baby. She asked that angels guard her and her son, as well as the doctors and nurses involved in the procedure. Cindy realized the gravity of the situation and suddenly understood why, on the previous evening, she'd asked her sister to take care of important matters . . . just in case. *Was this it?* Cindy worried. She said some prayers and then happily realized that there was Christian music playing over the hospital sound system, which reflected her personal religious faith.

Moments later, Cindy's baby boy, Joseph Michael, cried at the top of his lungs at only 2 pounds, 14 ounces! Joseph was rushed to the intensive-care nursery while the doctor stitched Cindy's incision.

Later that night in her hospital bed, Cindy drifted in and out of sleep. She was very ill, in considerable pain, and had complications from the pregnancy. Through it all, Cindy whispered prayers. Then she heard low, soft voices in her room. She opened her eyes and saw little balls of twinkling lights and an elderly lady with red hair, glasses, and a flowered print blouse. The woman told Cindy, "It will be all right, dear. It will be all right."

Cindy was confused, as she was in a private room with the doors shut and the lights switched off. Yet, despite the paranormal happenings, she still felt comfortable and at peace enough to fall back asleep. The next day she checked to see if the chaplain or other visitors had stopped by, only to find out that no one had been in her room.

Cindy says, "Our baby, Joseph, beat all the odds. He only needed oxygen for a few hours after birth. He breathed wonderfully on his own and had no complications whatsoever, although he had to stay in the nursery for a month. He's healthy and normal today! I also recovered wonderfully. Thank You, God."

Prayers for a Pet

As mentioned earlier, animals and children don't have their defenses up where healings are concerned, so prayers on their behalf are especially effective.

Cody is a 13-year-old Australian cattle dog belonging to Sylvia Allen and her family. One November day in 2002, Cody disappeared. Since Sylvia's home is on 40 country acres complete with cougars, coyotes, and bears, her family naturally worried about Cody's safety. The Allen family searched for hours, with no sign of their dog.

Eight days passed, and Sylvia was distraught. Then she remembered having just purchased my book *Healing with the Angels* the previous week. Sylvia opened the book to a section about asking the angels to retrieve and protect lost pets. She said the suggested prayer, then put the book away and gave it no more thought.

The next evening, the Allens came home from dinner and went inside the house for the night. An hour later, Sylvia's husband noticed a dark object on the front lawn that hadn't been there when they'd come home earlier. He walked outside and discovered that it was Cody, badly injured and so weak that he could barely stand.

Cody had been in a fight with a coyote and was near death from his wounds. Sylvia says, "There was no way Cody could've walked to where we found him, at the edge of the large lawn area surrounded by very steep hillsides. He hadn't been there when we'd gotten home earlier. I knew immediately that his angels had delivered him to us, gently laying him near our front door."

Cody's wounds were gangrenous and infected, and he'd been without food or water for over eight days. Sylvia reports, "Within a week, Cody's wounds had healed, and you'd never know he'd been wounded. It was truly a miracle that the angels brought him back to us and healed his wounds." As a result of this brush with the miraculous, Sylvia and her family now ask the angels for help on a daily basis.

THE ANGELIC SURGEON

The following story shows Heaven's sense of humor, and also reveals how a very spiritually minded woman was able to translate her faith in the angels into help for her father and her client.

Nicole Pigeault is an Angel Therapy Practitioner who works closely with Archangel Raphael in her healing work. When her father was scheduled to have a pacemaker put in his heart, Nicole prayed to Raphael to please handle all aspects of her father's healing. Nicole's mother called her after the surgery and said it had gone well and that her father had the nicest doctor . . . whose name was Dr. Raphael! Nicole said, "The angels never cease to amaze me with their added touches of love and humor."

A few months later, Nicole was giving an angel-therapy session. Her client, Susan, was distressed because she was scheduled for additional surgery on her colon. Susan had already endured two previous operations, with very long and challenging recovery periods.

Nicole said, "This time we'll ask Archangel Raphael to do the surgery." When Susan looked confused, Nicole explained that they'd invoke Raphael to work with the surgeon.

Nicole and Susan worked together for two weeks prior to the surgery. On the day of the operation, Nicole and Susan called upon Raphael and his healing angels to please assist Susan and her surgeon with every step of the procedure. They also asked Raphael to work through the surgeon.

Susan called Nicole the next day with the good news. "All I remember," Susan said, "was being taken into the operating room, and then waking up thinking that it was time to go into surgery."

The nurse told Susan, "No, your surgery is already completed. What's more, your surgery was expected to last five hours but was completed in under four! The doctor was amazed, but during the surgery he had an insight as to how to operate differently, which saved one and a half hours."

Susan recovered so quickly from her surgery that she astonished her family and friends. She knew beyond a doubt that it was because of Raphael.

ANGEL VISIONS

People who pray hard, coupled with crystal-clear intentions, often receive angel visitations to assure them that their prayers have been heard and are being answered.

L. Dardano was frightened when her mother called to say that she was undergoing medical tests for possible breast cancer. L. prayed very hard to God, Mary, and the angels to intercede on behalf of her mother.

That night, L. awoke to find the presence of someone in her room. She saw a silhouette of a woman wearing a skirt and a gauzy white shirt, and she had light-colored hair pulled back from her face. The woman stood and stared at L. while holding a white, yellow, and golden flower with four petals on it. The woman rotated the flower like a pinwheel as L. looked over to see if her sleeping husband was noticing the visitor.

The next day, L. called her mother and told her about the angelic encounter, saying, "I know without a doubt that you'll be okay and that the medical tests will come back negative." They did.

A few days later, L. was flipping through a calendar of angel paintings when she was struck by a portrait of Archangel Gabriel with Mary. In the painting, Gabriel was carrying the exact same flower that L. had seen in her visitation.

L. says, "I knew that the person in my room that night was the Archangel Gabriel. I know that this happened. It was all too real!"

The presence of the angel comforted L., and also probably brought in healing energy that supported her mother's health. The next story is another example of someone's strong prayers resulting in an angelic vision.

When Bronwyn Trillo's husband left her and their two children, she was devastated and thought that it was the end of her world. She then lost her job and felt that she couldn't manage to go on. Within two weeks, she had a serious emotional breakdown and became so ill that she couldn't get out of bed or eat. Finally, Brownwyn was hospitalized, and when she was released, she was put on sedatives.

She prayed continually. (With humor, Bronwyn says that she was too incapacitated to do anything else *but* pray!) She clung to faith that she'd recuperate.

Then one night, something woke Bronwyn up. She looked to her left and saw a beautiful glowing angel with very large wings. The glow prevented Bronwyn from seeing the angel's face, although she could see that the angel's head was cocked to one side and was looking at her.

Bronwyn says, "The angel was so serene and peaceful. This was the most beautiful experience I'd ever had. I lay there looking at her for some time until she finally disappeared."

The experience healed Bronwyn, and she recovered her strength. She feels renewed and continues to see sharp flashes of light that let her know that the angels are still with her. Since the day she saw the angel, Bronwyn says, "There has not been one single day when I don't communicate with my angels and watch for all their blessings in my life. I am very happy and peaceful, knowing that I'm always guided."

POWER IN NUMBERS

Several scientific studies suggest that the more people who pray for a situation, the better the results. With regard to prayer, there seems to be real power in numbers. When a situation needs healing, it's a good idea to enlist prayers from friends and prayer ministries, as the next story illustrates.

Jennifer Fountain of New Zealand relates that when her sister turned 39, she became pregnant. Her sister and her new husband were thrilled, until an ultrasound revealed that the baby had a rare and serious condition called a sacrococcygeal teratoma. This condition only occurs in one of 40,000 infants, and can result in prenatal or early childhood death.

The word *teratoma* is Latin for "monster," and it describes the size and ferocity of the growth. It consumes the bladder, bowel, reproductive organs and also grows outside the body, sometimes including the spine. On some babies the growth is as large as the baby itself.

Since Jennifer's sister lived in Florida, all she could offer as support were prayers and affirmations. Jennifer asked everyone she knew to pray, too, and to surround her sister and the baby with healing angels.

Jennifer recalls what happened next: "My sister passed the riskiest period of her pregnancy, yet the tumor continued to grow aggressively. The doctors scheduled a time for the birth and immediate surgical removal of the life-threatening tumor. Again, I asked everyone I knew to send prayers and healing angels to my sister, her husband, the baby, the doctors, and the caregivers.

"I spoke with my sister just after the baby was born, just prior to surgery for the tumor removal. She was tearful because the doctors had twice warned her that her baby's death was very likely because the surgery was so invasive, complicated, and risky. I told her that my friends were sending millions of healing angels to her side for the operation.

"My sister said she was happy to receive the help of angels, but her husband really wasn't into that stuff so she didn't tell him that we were sending them. Yet, when he visited the hospital gift shop, he felt absolutely compelled to buy a small, stuffed angel. He gave it to my sister in a state of bewilderment, not really understanding why he'd bought it. But she said she knew clearly that he had caught an angel sent by all of us in New Zealand and Australia who were praying for her baby.

"The surgeons did a miraculous job (by their own admission) on the baby, although they reported that it was the largest tumor they'd ever removed. They expected the baby to be hospitalized for three *weeks* while recovering from the massive surgery. Three *days* later she was home with her mother, her stuffed angel at her side.

"Now, at two months, the doctors say they don't expect to ever see my sister's baby again. The risks are completely gone. This Crystal Child has an angel made manifest in the form of a stuffed toy angel at her side."

HEALTH-CARE GUIDANCE

Sometimes our prayers are answered when the angels give us guidance that sends us to just the right physician. Some people may wonder why Heaven would introduce a "middle person" instead of directly intervening into a healing—but didn't God create the physicians?

Many medical specialists are extremely intuitive individuals who undoubtedly follow Divine guidance as they care for their patients. The next story shows how a doctor's willingness to listen to his inner guidance was the answer to his patient's prayer to have her arm saved from possible amputation.

Mandi Gabler and her friends were Rollerblading in a London suburb. Her friends wanted to Rollerblade one more time before going home. Mandi's guidance told her not to go, but she didn't listen. She fell hard on her right arm and completely shattered her elbow joint. A physician on vacation from Spain saw the accident and assisted her before the ambulance arrived. The hospital doctor told Mandi that her arm was so badly damaged that she might lose it completely. Terrified of an amputation, Mandi asked her friends to join her in a prayer to save her arm.

Mandi was filled with faith, and she felt peaceful knowing that she was in the arms of angels and that God was in charge. The doctor wanted to wait two days to make a plan for the operation. Although family and friends thought this delay was unhealthy, Mandi wanted her doctor to take his time and really think about the best way to operate on her arm. Mandi still felt peaceful, and just knew that it would all turn out well.

After the operation, the doctor stated that he'd been completely guided during the procedure, and that he too knew that Mandi's arm was going to be perfect. Mandi says, "I was smiling and completely grateful to my angels for the help they'd given the doctor and me. I now have 95 percent use of my arm, and can even play golf! There's no doubt in my mind that angels were watching over me, healing me, and helping the doctor."

The injury also led Mandi deeper into the spiritual path. Mandi decided that she'd spent too much time in the past not following her guidance. She became an Angel Therapy Practitioner who listens to her angels and helps others do the same.

The next story is a perfect example of someone who prayed for help in finding the right physician for her health challenge.

When Ariel Wolfe was diagnosed with breast cancer, she knew that choosing the right physician was of the utmost importance, so she decided to interview doctors, and in a meditation-and-prayer session, she implored her guardian angels to guide her to the right doctor.

She intuitively chose a doctor from a list of specialists. Before visiting this physician, Ariel asked her angels
to give her a crystal-clear sign that she'd chosen the right
one. As Ariel and her daughter, Liz, walked into the doctor's office, she noticed a display of Native American artifacts. Since Ariel has a strong connection to Native
American spirituality, she thought, *Okay, so far, so good
. . . but still not enough.*

When Ariel met the doctor, she was pleased to find
that the physician was warm, candid, appeared very capable, and answered all her questions. Yet, Ariel was still
looking for that clear sign.

The doctor mentioned that she'd studied to be a classical pianist, but when she found performing in front of
an audience difficult, she turned to medicine instead.
This impressed Ariel, who had performed as a classical
pianist herself for most of her teen and adult years. Ariel
thought, *Okay, so we're getting closer, but it's still not a
sure sign.*

Sitting in the doctor's office after the examination,
Liz mentioned that Ariel and the surgery would be surrounded by healing angels. The doctor looked up and
said, "You know, my patron saint is Archangel Michael."

Ariel thought, *Well, I don't have to be hit by a two-by-
four to know when I'm in the right place!*

During the biopsy, Ariel called all her angels and
archangels to be present during the procedure, and the
doctor explained the discomfort that Ariel might feel. As
Ariel looked at the doctor, she saw Archangel Michael
and Raphael guiding the physician's hands. Ariel says that
she never felt a thing, since she was guided and protected by the powerful angels. Her blood count is now down
to normal, and Ariel feels wonderful.

KEEP THE FAITH

Undoubtedly, our faith in the efficacy of prayer is our greatest aid when we ask God and the angels and archangels to help us. With faith, we're more likely to hold fast to our convictions and trust our Divine guidance. The next story shows how a couple stuck to their decision to go through with a pregnancy even when doctors advised them not to.

When doctors told Maria Perez that her unborn baby had a life-threatening condition, she and her husband were horrified. Doctors explained that the fetus had an occipital encephalocele (also known as Knobloch Syndrome) on the back of her head, and that brain tissue was protruding from the hole in her skull. The diagnosis was grave: The baby would either die at birth or live as a vegetable (the doctor's exact words) who would have to be institutionalized for life.

A woman of great faith, Maria prayed for a sign as she sat outside in her yard. She looked up to see a loving face in the clouds smiling down at her. Maria knew that this was a positive confirmation from God and the angels, telling her that the baby would be fine.

Contrary to doctors' recommendations, Maria and her husband decided to go through with the pregnancy. Every night, Maria prayed to God and asked the angels for help, guidance, strength, and faith. One night she watched an episode of the television show *Touched by an Angel*. In the episode, Monica (the angel played by Roma Downey) called for additional angels to help her with a drug-addicted woman. The angels circled around the woman and Monica, and sang angelic songs to heal and support the situation. That night, Maria asked the angels to sing to her as a sign that her daughter would be okay.

On the day that Maria gave birth, the doctors and nurses gathered around her labor bed, expecting the worst. But little Angela Perez would show them that miracles do happen. The baby girl was born strong and healthy!

Although the little girl still required surgery to repair the hole on the back of her head, one-day-old Angela recovered from the surgery beautifully. The next evening, Maria awoke at 3 A.M. to the sound of singing in her bedroom. She thought it was her imagination, or the after-effects from her C-section, but Maria woke up her husband, and he too heard the angels. He also saw three of them standing in front of their bed. The angels sang the Spanish song, "Let's Sing to Maria." Next to her baby's cry at birth, it was the most beautiful sound that Maria had ever heard.

Today, Angela is a beautiful four-year-old girl, and Maria knows that her daughter was sent from Heaven to help her connect with God and the angels and to grow spiritually. Maria says, "I see Angela reach out to her angels and smile at them every time she sees them. She is a beautiful child of God."

It's been said that prayer is when we talk to Heaven, and meditation is when we listen. Our team of angels is constantly on alert for our prayers. When we "pray without ceasing" by continually communicating with our angels (through our thoughts or aloud), we work together with them like a well-organized sports team. Together, in perfect harmony with our angels, we can heal our health and manifest our needs.

CHAPTER 18

Angels of Light and Love

Calling upon angels is a powerful way to bring light and love into any situation. Anyone can call upon the angels; you needn't belong to a certain religion or "earn" the right to do so. Angelic help is the Divine right and privilege of everyone. Since angels are our gift from our Creator, we're showing gratitude to God by enjoying this gift.

You can call upon angels by doing the following:

- Thinking the thought, *Angels, please help me!*

- Mentally telling your troubles to the angels.

- Asking God to send you angels.

- Visualizing angels surrounding you, your loved ones, or the situation.

- Visualizing white or colored lights surrounding a person, object, or situation.

- Making your request to God or the angels out loud.

- Writing a letter to the angels.

- Singing or chanting your request.

- Using angel oracle cards.

- Lighting a candle.

It's not so important *how* you contact the angels, but that you *do* contact them. Remember: The Creator and the angels aren't allowed to intervene in your life without your permission. The only exception is when you're in imminent danger before it's your time to go.

Since angels are extensions and messengers of God, whether you ask them directly or send your request to the Creator, the results are the same. Think of angels as Divine mail carriers, bringing messages of love and light from the Creator to the created.

Angels illuminate our minds and hearts with a big infusion of light. They help us see the Divine truth of situations through the fog of fearful illusion. They remind us that, despite all appearances to the contrary, everything really is okay in the end.

The intense unconditional love of an angel's presence is often enough to effect an immediate healing, as the next story shows.

When Sandra Clark of Queensland, Australia, developed kidney stones and was scheduled for inpatient surgery to have them removed, she was understandably upset. Her friend Kerrie Field, who does energy healing work, offered to do a session on Sandra.

As Sandra was lying on a massage table, Kerrie called in angels to assist. In her mind's eye, Kerrie could see the room filled with angels who were working on Sandra. Kerrie says, "They must have been the 'giggling' angels, since Sandra and I just started laughing until we curled up and could barely breathe! It was the most we'd laughed in a long time—and we normally laugh a lot."

When Sandra went in for her surgery a few days later, there was no sign of any kidney stones. The doctors were stunned, as the stones had been quite large and had been causing a lot of bleeding and pain. They asked Sandra how much it had hurt her to pass the stones.

When Sandra said she'd had no pain whatsoever, the doctors said that she surely must have felt *something*. After all, the doctors said, the stones were so huge it would have been like passing a watermelon through the eye of a needle. Sandra and Kerrie credit the angels with painlessly removing the stones, and for the fact that Sandra has never been bothered with stones since that day.

THE ANGELS HEAL INANIMATE OBJECTS— AND FINANCES, TOO

We aren't limited to using angel medicine to heal physical bodies. Since the entire Universe is comprised of love and light, *anything* can be healed. I have many childhood memories of my mother praying that an appliance or our family automobile would be fixed, since we didn't have the money to take these things to a repair shop. Her prayers were always answered very quickly!

This next story is a beautiful example of how the angels can help us heal *anything*.

Annette Hinton knows how to type on a computer, but she doesn't consider herself computer-literate in terms of knowing how to fix, troubleshoot, or program them, so she was horrified when her boss gave her his Palm Pilot handheld computer and asked her to call their technical support division. He explained that the Palm Pilot wasn't synchronizing to his desk computer, and that their own in-house computer expert couldn't fix the situation. Since the boss needed to leave for an all-day meeting, he expected Annette to resolve the situation.

Annette spoke with five different technical-support people, who each talked her through a procedure without success. The Palm Pilot was dead, and removing the battery and replacing it did nothing. All the technical-support people told Annette that the item was corrupt and should be sent in for repair or replacement.

But Annette was determined to fulfill her boss's request to fix the computer. It was then that she remembered to ask her angels for help. After all, she'd had success in enlisting angels' assistance in the past.

Her hands were resting on the keyboard as she spoke to her angels. Suddenly, her fingers dropped onto the keys, and the computer screen started flashing and reacting. Annette was unsure what was happening, but when the words "Continue: Yes or No" came up, she pressed "Yes" and hoped for the best. After doing this several times, the words "Synchronization Complete" flashed on the screen.

Amazing! Annette's request for angelic help had been answered! She says that there was no other explanation for the computer working, as she hadn't a clue what she was doing. When her boss returned, he insisted on knowing how Annette had fixed the computer, so Annette told him that she'd asked her angels. Even though he didn't believe her, the computer worked for months afterward with no further problems.

The angels say that we don't need to struggle with anything in life, including material objects or our finances. As I wrote earlier in this book, the angels are here to bring us peace. While we can grow through struggles, we can grow faster through peacefulness. That's why, when we ask them to help us with issues such as finances, they're very happy to assist.

Jacky Dalton had experienced a miracle when she'd asked the angels to help her daughter recover from chronic depression, and her daughter was subsequently healed. After that, Jacky's faith in asking the angels for help was strong. So when she and her family needed enough money to get through Christmas, Jacky felt certain that the angels would assist her.

On one particular Monday, Jacky asked the angels to somehow provide her with enough money to cover her business and Christmas expenses without worrying. The next day, Jacky's husband withdrew money from an ATM and the receipt showed a balance of more than $4,000. Jacky and her husband assumed that the bank had erred. Jacky added, though, that if the balance was legitimate, it was definitely the doing of the angels!

Jacky and her husband verified that the bank had deposited $3,200 into their account on Monday night, right after Jacky's request to the angels. It was a payment for a family allowance that they didn't know was coming to them!

Jacky says, "It's a tragedy that there are so many people who don't know you can ask your angels for help, or who refuse to believe in angels. I'm so grateful, and I always ask my angels what I can do to repay them. They always tell me the same answer: *'Keep listening'*—and that's what I intend to do."

THE HEALING POWER OF LOVE AND PURPOSE

Love can come into our lives in many ways, including through romantic partnerships. This was the doorway that the angels used to heal an Australian woman's body, mind, and heart.

Annette Doyle sat in the back of a Sydney, Australia, taxi, and like many passengers, she didn't put on her seat belt. Moments later, a stolen vehicle being chased by a police car collided with her cab. Annette remembers being thrown around the backseat like a rag doll before losing consciousness. She broke ribs and fractured three vertebrae in the crash, and she spent the next 14 months taking medication, including morphine, and visiting various doctors for relief from her chronic pain. Annette relegated herself to a lifetime of misery, and she became clinically depressed. This led her to lose her job and many of her friends.

However, a new boyfriend came into her life who helped her start thinking positively about her health. This lifted her depression and led to Annette receiving Divine guidance. She says that the angels told her that she was here on Earth to perform a very important purpose, just like everyone else, and that she couldn't waste her life in a haze of morphine dependency. The angels told Annette that she was a healer, and that she needed to heal herself so that she could help other people. That message hit a chord with Annette on a soul level, and gave her the courage to wean herself off of pain medication.

Annette says, "I'm very happy to report that I'm 98 percent free of physical and emotional pain now. I feel strong and happy. I'll always remember that Monday morning when I received the majestic message from my angels, reminding me on a deep level of what I chose to do in this lifetime, and helping me heal my body to be able to do just that. I believe I experienced this healing in order to be able to heal others. I also *know* that my acceptance of receiving the message allowed the healing to occur. I feel so blessed and honored, and I'll always look to this experience as proof that it can be done. In my case, it can even be done when you're not consciously asking for it. After all, isn't it in the angels' job description to help keep us on track?"

Annette has a new job working for a company where most employees have angel oracle cards on their desk. She also works part-time for motivational speaker Anthony Robbins. Annette says that her new life is loving, supportive, and highly motivational—definitely part of her life's mission.

Ultimately, what healed Annette was having a sense of purpose. We all need to know that our lives are meaningful and that we're needed in this world. Sometimes, we're so afraid of knowing what our purpose is that we go into a type of amnesia as to its existence. Or, we may fear failing at our purpose so we avoid taking steps toward its fulfillment.

The *Manual for Teachers,* which is part of the three-book compilation known as *A Course in Miracles,* says that "all forms of sickness, even unto death, are physical expressions of the fear of awakening."

The *Course* says that we become ill as a delay mechanism because we're afraid of either success or failure if we work on our life's mission. The mission for all of us is the same, even though its form may vary widely: It always involves teaching and learning about love through our passions and natural interests. If we delay our heart's desire, then we also postpone the possibility of feeling emotional pain if we don't succeed. We also avoid the emotional pressures that come with success.

This isn't blaming the victim or saying that someone's pain is imaginary. Pain can be a very real experience. It's just that it stems from an unreal premise of believing that we're victims of pain. Overcoming pain involves moving to a proactive stance of surrendering to a Higher Power; staying positive that healing will occur; and focusing on the question "How may I serve?"

When we maintain our focus on helping others, we stop concentrating on ourselves. This automatically reduces the awareness of pain by projecting our awareness toward compassion to others.

SWEET DREAMS

The angels help us with our daily lives so that we'll be healthier and happier each day. This includes helping us get a good night's sleep.

Michelle of Australia was struggling with some life stress, which included parenting two small, active children. Exhausted, Michelle was in need of sleep, yet her children were waking her up every night. Finally, in desperation, Michelle called upon the angels for help. She recalls, "I saw this beautiful angel bending over my little girl's bed. She immediately went back to sleep."

The angels also love to heal us while we're sleeping because we're more open-minded in this state while asleep.

Rebecca D'Amato of Manchester, England, went to bed one night crying and feeling so wretched and miserable that she thought she'd never smile again. She asked Archangel Michael for his help and then fell asleep.

The next morning, Rebecca woke up feeling refreshed and happy. She had a spring in her step that hadn't been with her for years. She says, "All the things I'd felt miserable about didn't seem important to me anymore. Things made sense; and I felt calmer, wiser, stronger, more capable, and in control. I even managed to laugh at myself about what had made me feel so bad in the first place."

You can call upon any of the angels or archangels to come into your dreams and clear away emotional or physical distress. You may not recall the dream interactions with the angels the next morning, but you'll know that you were visited. And, like Rebecca, you'll see an improvement in how you feel.

SIGNS FROM THE ANGELS

When we call upon the angels, it's nice to receive physical confirmation of their proximity. The next three stories show the diverse ways in which angels let us know they're with us in order to boost our faith and confidence in their loving presence.

Nine-year-old Brittany Ryan asked her angels to visit her one Wednesday evening. The next morning, she woke up and saw a feather next to her chest. Brittany ran to show her parents, and her mother believed it was an angel feather, too. Brittany has collected two more feathers since then.

✳   ✳   ✳

Wendy Luke wanted a clear sign from her angels showing that they were real and that they truly heard her prayers. One night, Wendy lay in bed asking for a clear sign from her angels. She heard a wry voice say, "What do you want, fireworks?" And Wendy laughed out loud and said silently, "Yes, I want fireworks!"

Wendy fell asleep with a smile, and no expectations about what might happen. At 3:45 A.M., she was awakened by loud noises that sounded like fireworks. She was about to roll over and ignore the noise when she realized that her angels might be sending her a sign. As Wendy peered out her window, she saw the big, beautiful lights of a firecracker in the sky. Wendy looked toward the nearby sports complex to see if someone was setting off fireworks there, but it was dark and empty. She then woke up her husband, who also saw the display.

Wendy says, "I learned three things that night: First, ask and you really will receive; second, our angels can be very clever and resourceful when they want to show us love; and last, those who insist on believing in coincidences are missing out on miracles."

✳   ✳   ✳

Suzanne Vigliotti was feeling depressed and alone one evening. As she sat in front of the TV, flipping through the channels, Suzanne asked Archangel Michael to give her a sign as reassurance that he was with her.

Just then, she switched the channel to a station where an operatic tenor was singing "In the Arms of an Angel." Suzanne remembered how much she loved that song, and she felt very reassured as she settled into a very peaceful night's sleep.

HELPING AND HEALING OTHERS

Sometimes our prayers are made on behalf of a loved one. These prayers are just as powerful for another as they are for ourselves—provided the other person is willing to be healed. In the next story, you'll notice how a daughter had to listen carefully to messages from her angels in order for her mother to be healed.

Debbie Clarkson had struggled with alcoholism for much of her adult life. Her 18-year-old daughter, Jaimie, remembers Debbie having months-long drinking binges. When Debbie drank, she often became violent, hostile, and angry—in contrast to her sober persona, which is loving, kind, and gentle. Jaimie believes that her mother is an Earth angel who uses alcohol to numb awareness of her life purpose and fears.

Growing up, Jaimie felt confused and guilty because she couldn't stop her mother's drinking, so she did the only thing she could: love her mom. Somehow, Jaimie knew intuitively that love was the answer. However, she also felt despair because the drinking was affecting Debbie's liver, kidneys, and heart. When Jaimie's stepfather died, she thought that her mother would drink herself to death from the grief.

So, Jaimie prayed for a healing for her mother. She received the answer to her prayer in the form of guidance, which told Jaimie, *"Just affirm that your mother is healed."*

She says, "So I did! With blind faith and trust, I began regularly telling myself: 'Yes, Mum is completely healed.'

That's all I did! Well, it was a miracle right before our eyes. Immediately, my mother lost the compulsion to drink! Now she feels an aversion toward alcohol. Not only that, but she's facing her grief fully and honestly. She's no longer hurting herself and is now on a path of incredible spiritual growth."

Jaimie's mother now realizes her own spiritual gifts, including clairvoyance, and she's asking her angels for help in her everyday life. Both Debbie and Jaimie are constantly amazed by the pure magic that the angels weave for her. They both see that Debbie's healing has been a deep healing for the entire family.

Part of doing angel medicine with children is the opportunity it affords us to teach our kids about working with angels. Children are naturally attracted to these Divine beings, and they find great comfort in calling upon Heaven for help.

Stephanie Watkeys was driving her nine-year-old son, Oliver, to school. He complained of severe pain in his upper right arm, and winced when he lifted it. Oliver wondered if he'd be able to write in school that day. So, as they drove along, Stephanie asked Oliver to get very quiet, close his eyes, and communicate directly with Archangel Raphael. Stephanie instructed her son to ask Raphael to heal the pain so that he could go to school and be able to write and play that day. Oliver did so, and they arrived at school a few minutes later. Stephanie could tell that Oliver was still in pain and she told him, "Please be patient while Raphael works on you."

When Stephanie picked up Oliver at the end of the school day, he came rushing up to her, very excited. Oliver exclaimed that only a couple of minutes after getting out of the car that morning, he realized to his amazement that he no longer felt any pain in his arm. He smiled to himself and thanked Raphael.

Stephanie now frequently works with Raphael to help her two sons. When her two-year-old son, Bryn, had a high fever, accompanied by other symptoms of illness, she put him to bed and gave him some homeopathic medication. But Bryn's fever continued to climb.

In desperation, Stephanie pleaded with Archangel Raphael to please bring Bryn's temperature down. Five minutes later, Bryn was sound asleep. And a half-hour after he awakened, his temperature was back to normal! Bryn began playing and walking, with no sign of illness.

Should you work on someone without their permission or knowledge? This is a controversial topic with no one correct answer. On the one hand, it's said that healing without someone's permission is a karmic violation, and that it's akin to putting a small bandage on a severed artery—in other words, it's not dealing with the deeper issues. Yet another point of view is that if you see someone drowning, you're going to jump in and rescue that person, regardless of whether you've been asked to do so. Each parent and healer needs to make this personal decision alone.

Ron, who lives in Australia, has worked with angels and spiritual healing for many years. While his wife shares Ron's views, their 25-year-old son, Steve, remains skeptical.

Steve is a member of the Royal Australian Air Force. He worked very hard to earn a position in a class where he'd train to be a fire and rescue officer, so he was devastated when he dislocated his elbow playing basketball. The doctors said that it was the worst case they'd ever seen, and that he'd be off his normal duties for several months.

Steve told his father that he was very upset, because this would prevent him from starting the fire and rescue officer course! That's when Ron decided to ask for angelic intervention, without telling Steve. Ron knew that the angels would only offer healing love, and that they wouldn't interfere with Steve's free will.

So, Ron visualized angels surrounding Steve and his arm. Ron, who's also a Reiki practitioner, also sent his son healing energy.

Two days later, Steve phoned and said, "Dad, you're not going to believe this, but a couple of days ago, my arm started feeling better. The doctors are amazed!" Very soon, Steve returned to his normal weight-lifting and exercise routines. He also resumed his duties and completed his course, and Steve is now a proud member of the fire and rescue service.

Ron says, "I know the healing was sent to him from God via the angels, who so often help me in my work."

When we invoke angels for others, we often receive signs—as discussed earlier—as validation that the angels have appeared. This confirmation may come as a physical sign, as an inner knowing, or as a feeling. Another concrete validation is when the person we've prayed for miraculously heals.

In the next two stories, the women who invoked angels on behalf of other people received amazing validation of their invocations. In both cases, the person for whom they invoked the angels reported *seeing* the angels . . . even though they weren't told about the angelic invocation!

Bernadette Mercer of Queensland, Australia, is a graduate of my Angel Intuitive course. She was performing an angelic healing session on a woman who had been experiencing profound emotional pain. The woman lay prone on a massage table while Bernadette held her hands on the woman's head.

Bernadette closed her eyes and called upon Archangel Raphael to help the woman. Bernadette says, "I felt a difference in the energy of the room, so I opened my eyes. There, standing at the end of the massage table, was a tall, beautiful, golden angel!" Raphael's hands were on the woman's feet.

Bernadette mentally said, "Thank you, Archangel Raphael. I'm honored that one as great and powerful as you would come to help me."

She heard Raphael reply, *"Child of God, I am no more powerful than you are."*

Bernadette says, "He stayed until the end of the session. It was such a profound and beautiful experience that it's etched indelibly in my memory."

At the end of the healing session, the woman said that she'd had a beautiful dream of Archangel Rapahel holding her feet and healing her! She said that she felt much better as a result.

You might say that Laura V. Phillips of Houston, Texas, is an Earth angel, working as a counseling intern at a hospice where most people only check in for a few days before crossing over. A man named John in an advanced stage of cancer checked in to the hospice, and Laura noticed that he was very kind and polite. John touched Laura's heart so much that she made a point of spending time with him daily, even though he was unconscious much of the time.

On his fourth day in the hospice, Laura found John staring toward the foot of his bed, looking frightened and perspiring. Laura asked what was wrong, and he replied, "There's a devil right there, and his tail is on fire!" John put a pillow over his head to shield himself from the horrible sight, while Laura reassured him that he was safe. Although she doesn't believe in devils, per se, Laura realized that our fears can materialize according to our beliefs.

While a nurse ran in and attended to John's vital signs, Laura silently called for Archangel Michael and his band of mercy angels to surround John and protect him from whatever was frightening him. Suddenly, John exclaimed, "I see angels!" Laura's heart leapt, and joyful tears filled her eyes, as John had no way of knowing about her invocation of angels.

"What do they look like, John?" Laura asked.

"Beautiful . . . beautiful . . . beautiful!" he replied. John then fell asleep peacefully. He never woke up again, and he crossed over the next day with a wonderful, calm expression on his face.

Invoking angels is one of the most powerful and profoundly healing activities you can perform in the face of seeming illness or injury. Even if you're unsure or disbelieving, the act of calling on angels has immediate benefits for those who are ill—as well as their loved ones.

CHAPTER 19

In Summary

The time is ripe for us to remember, and return to, ancient wisdom about natural healing practices. After centuries of being brainwashed by fearful messages given to us by religious and political figures who wanted to ensure that they had all the power, we're once again taking charge of our spiritual and healing practices.

Science supports this ancient wisdom, with studies showing the health benefits of sunlight, crystals, prayer, energy healing, and colors. Mainstream hospitals and medical centers are now employing "complementary health-care practices," which is a term they use for energetic and spiritual healers. Doctors use instruments employing crystals, UV, and color-based treatments, with powerful results. Physicians regularly prescribe exercise, meditation, and stress-reduction courses as part of their treatment programs. Psychologists now refer their patients to hypnotherapists, psychics, and astrologers for supplementary insights.

It's a new world, based upon very ancient wisdom. We're recovering the healing wisdom that we employed in Atlantis, and perhaps from civilizations that existed before then.

If this book has triggered your memories of past lives, using healing methods, I urge you to explore this realm. You may want to consult a past-life regressionist or a certified hypnotherapist, or use an audiotape with past-life regression guidance such as my

Past-Life Regression with the Angels program or Brian Weiss's book-with-CD *Mirrors of Time* (both available from Hay House).

Working with the angels and employing the love-and-light treatment works in conjunction with traditional mainstream healing practices. Pray and meditate for additional guidance about your health. If you're getting messages to improve your lifestyle through healthful eating, sleeping, and exercising, this is very real angel communication that is worth following.

I wish you much love and light!

PART III

HEALING WITH ANGEL MEDICINE

CHAPTER 20

Angel Medicine
Healing Methods

In this final chapter, you'll read about healing methods used in the practice of angel medicine. Feel free to add to or change the steps, as your own inner guidance and angels advise. The exact words and steps behind a particular technique aren't as important as the intentions related to each one. It's best to hold an attitude of faith and optimism as you practice each method.

CHAKRA CLEARING

Clearing and balancing the chakras helps us enjoy a greater amount of energy, enhanced psychic abilities, and better health. The intention is to enlarge all of the chakras equally, and to ensure their cleanliness inside and out. Think of chakras as porous jewels that need regular internal and external polishing. There are many methods to clear and balance your chakras. Here are two that are fast and effective:

Deep Foam Cleaning

Imagine pouring a pitcher of white, foaming liquid cleanser into the body through the crown chakra opening at the top of the head. See and feel this foam pouring over and into each chakra. The foam quickly deep-cleans all grime, grease, and debris from the inside and outside of each chakra. Then ask Archangel Raphael to pour liquid green light inside of you to wash away all of the foam and debris—until your chakras are sparkling clean.

White Light

See or feel a beam of bright white light entering through the top of your head and extending deep into your body. See the white light first clean, polish, and enlarge your ruby-red root chakra at the base of your spine. Next, see or feel the white light clear and enlarge the bright orange chakra midway between your navel and your root chakra. Then, the white light cleanses and increases the yellow solar-plexus chakra, directly behind your navel.

After that, the white light warms your chest and increases the size and clarity of your emerald-green heart chakra. The white light then opens, clears, and enlarges your light blue throat chakra in your Adam's-apple area. Next, the white light awakens, cleanses, and increases your indigo blue third-eye chakra, located between your two physical eyes. After that, the white light opens up and clears your ear chakras, which are above each eyebrow. Finally, the white light passes back through your royal purple crown chakra at the top of your head. All your chakras are equally large in size, and are all glowing with white light from the inside.

ETHERIC CORD CUTTING

When we have fear-based attachments to a person or an object, we form spiritual leashes to keep the person or object from leaving or changing. These leashes look like surgical tubing, and they grow larger as a function of the length and intensity of the relationship. So, the largest cords are to parents, siblings, and other longtime, intense relationships.

The cords are hollow tubes, and energy runs back and forth between the attached persons. These are fear-based cords, which are always unhealthy and based upon dysfunction. They have nothing to do with the love or the healthy part of the relationship. Cutting cords isn't abandoning or divorcing a person; it's releasing the unhealthy part of the relationship. Etheric cords are also unrelated to the silver cord, which attaches the soul to the body. The love and silver cord can't be accidentally severed.

Let's say that you have a cord attached to a friend or relative who's feeling depressed or needy. That person will begin draining energy from you, like siphoning fuel at a gas station. You'll feel tired without knowing why. No amount of caffeine, exercise, or sleep will be able to revive your energy if the source is etheric-cord draining. I firmly believe that chronic fatigue syndrome stems from people being drained of energy through etheric cords. Many people I've worked with have regained their energy levels just through using this simple method of cutting cords.

If the person you're etherically attached to becomes angry, their anger energy will come tumbling through the etheric cords, straight into your body and chakras. This can result in physical pain that seems to have no cause, and which is unresponsive to treatment.

People who are professional helpers, such as teachers, counselors, and healers, often have a lot of cords attached to their students and patients. (The same is true with individuals who are always helping needy friends and relatives.)

So it's important to cut cords after every session of helping someone, or whenever you feel physical pain or lethargy without any apparent reason. Cords can grow back if the relationship resumes with fear mingled in it. New cords are thinner, though, so less energy can be drained from you or tossed at you.

Cord Cutting with Archangel Michael

Michael carries a sword that cuts all attachments to negativity. Simply think the thought, *Archangel Michael, I call upon you now.*

Please cut the cords of fear that are draining my energy and vitality.
Sit quietly while he cuts your cords. He'll send healing energy
through the severed cords to both you and the other person.

Sensitive people will feel bodily and air-pressure changes
as Michael cuts the cords, followed by increased energy and a
reduction or cessation of pain.

Cutting Stubborn Cords

Michael can only cut cords if you're willing to let go of old
resentments that are associated with the person to whom you're
attached. If you're holding on to anger or unforgiveness, the
cord won't cut. In these cases, as you use the method described
above where you call upon Michael, also add the following as you
think about the person: *I am willing to trade all pain for peace. I
ask for peace to replace any pain now.*

Cutting Specific Cords

In addition to the two methods above, I recommend going
through this step. Think of these specific individuals one by one
and hold the intention of cutting cords of fear associated with
them: mother; father; siblings; and past or present lovers. These
are the specific relationships that most often yield cords associated with physical pain.

Brissy Anti-Icky Sticky Foam

While in Brisbane (which is affectionately called "Brissy"—
pronounced *Brizzy*—in Australia), I noticed that new attachments are similar to spiderwebs, in that they're thin and sticky.
Michael's sword stuck to these cords like a knife going through a
web. I asked Archangel Raphael for help, and he gave me this
method:

"See or feel Archangel Raphael approaching you with a can of cleansing foam, which he sprays all over your body. This foam, similar to oven cleaner, instantly dissolves fear-based cords attached to new or short-term relationships. Once the foam has completely dissolved the cords, Raphael spray-cleans the foam away with a hose of green healing liquid. You're now free of all small cords and should notice an increase in your energy level."

Addiction Cord Cutting

In a seated position, think about any addictive behaviors or situations that you'd like to release. Be sure that you really want to release them, because this method is very powerful. After you perform this technique, you'll either quit cold turkey, or you'll have one last binge that will result in your quitting.

Next, imagine that the addictive items or situations are sitting on your lap. Then, see or feel them floating about one foot in front of your belly. Notice the web of cords extending from your belly to the addictive items. The cords look like the roots of a tree. Mentally ask Archangel Raphael to cut those cords completely. As the cords are cut, notice the items falling away easily from you.

Afterward, Raphael will surround your belly with emerald-green light to heal any old wounds completely. As you breathe deeply, he'll send healing green energy into your body through the severed cords. As you inhale, any former emptiness or anxiety is now filled, healed, and balanced by Raphael's powerful healing energy. We thank Raphael for this healing!

Cutting Cords to Material Objects

A telltale sign that you're etherically corded to a material object is when it won't sell at any price. Many people with whom I've worked have cords to their homes or automobiles, because a part of them doesn't want to sell the item. Consequently, no amount of advertising or price-slashing works.

Cords to objects generally grow from the bottom of the person's feet and are attached to the part of the item (or the room of the house) where one is most attached. If you truly want to sell the item, ask Archangel Michael to cut the cords from the bottom of your feet, and be assured that something better will replace the item. Know that the next person who owns it will benefit from your generous "releasement."

VACUUMING WITH ARCHANGEL MICHAEL

This is a method I've discussed in other books, but it bears repeating since it's so effective for healing. With this method, you and Archangel Michael are vacuuming away lower energies such as psychic debris, fearful energy, and entities.

You can use this technique on yourself or on other people who give you permission to spiritually heal them (you can ask for this permission silently, by mentally contacting the other person's higher self). This method is especially effective for calming hyperactivity, lessening aggressive behavior, decreasing addictive cravings, and smoothing out mood swings.

Think of the person whom you wish to vacuum (yourself or another person). Mentally ask Archangel Michael to join you, along with his band of mercy angels. Notice that Michael is carrying a vacuum tube. Decide whether to turn the vacuum's suction speed on low, medium, high, or extra-high. Work with Michael to place the vacuum tube in through the crown chakra, and into the person's head. Vacuum all around the inside of the head, suctioning away any areas of darkness. Pay attention to the areas around the jaw and around the brain.

Vacuum down into the throat, and then move the vacuum tube into the chest cavity. Notice any areas of darkness, and work with Michael to direct the vacuum tube to these areas to suction the lower energies away. If you notice any areas of redness, which indicates physical pain, send loving energy from your heart or hands to that area. Vacuum all of the organs, including the ovaries on a female and the prostate on a male.

Send the vacuum tube down along the spinal column and through the arms, into the fingers. Be sure to vacuum the tips of the fingers, where darkness sometimes hides. After the upper body is cleared, vacuum down into the lower body, the legs, kneecaps, lower legs, ankles, feet, and toes.

Once the body is completely cleared, Michael will reverse the switch on the vacuum. Now, toothpaste-like liquid white light emerges from the vacuum tube, sparkling like diamond-white caulking material. It fills up the entire body, and heals and balances any former areas of distress. We thank Archangel Michael and his band of mercy angels for this healing and clearing.

CURSE AND DAGGER LIFTING

You can use this method on yourself or another. Make sure that your back isn't touching anything, such as a chair. Lean forward or lie on your side or front.

Call upon Archangels Raphael and Michael to surround you, and then breathe in and out very deeply. Sometimes when people are angry at themselves or someone else, they send anger energy that can harden into a form that imbeds itself inside of bodies. At times, we curse ourselves or another, unconsciously or consciously.

Be willing to let go of and lift any anger energy from your body. Release any daggers, arrows, swords, or other sharp or painful objects from your back or other areas. As these daggers and other objects now lift from your body, you may be surprised to learn who sent them to you. Be willing to send those people your forgiveness, to the best of your ability, as a way to heal yourself even further. Keep lifting the objects out of your entire body, letting go of them completely. All curses will now be lifted completely, in all directions of time.

Raphael will now cover you in a liquid green healing gel, which immediately heals away any former incisions. As you heal, Michael covers you in a shield of purple rubber, which ensures that any further attacks bounce away from you. As they do so, they're transmuted into love and returned to the sender, in order to heal that person.

You're now completely cleared and protected. Thank Raphael and Michael for your healing.

SHIELDING AND PSYCHIC PROTECTION

It's important to energetically shield yourself whenever you're going to be in a situation with lower energies, such as a public place, or when you're around ailing or angry people. This is especially important for sensitive individuals who tend to absorb others' energy.

To shield yourself, just imagine, think, or see yourself completely enveloped in whatever color light you choose. You can also shield others, or objects such as vehicles or homes, with light. Shields wear off, so you'll need to reapply them approximately every 12 hours or so.

Here are some colors you may choose from, depending upon the situation you're in:

- **White light:** Good for protection against crime or physical attack. Invokes additional angels around you.

- **Pink light:** The pink shield protects against negativity. Helpful in situations where you're around negative-minded, complaining, or gossipy people, as only love can permeate a pink shield.

- **Green light:** A physical healing shield. Use the green shield for someone who's injured or ill.

- **Purple light:** Psychic protection. Shields against psychic attack and entities.

- **Mirrored ball:** When you're feeling vulnerable, or when your chakras are open and clean, and you're about to go into harsh energy (such as crowds of strangers or an intense business meeting, for instance), see or feel yourself stepping inside of a mirrored ball. All negative energy bounces away from the ball.

- **Lead shield:** The ultimate shield against negativity whenever a battle is anticipated, or you're feeling extra vulnerable or open. See or feel yourself completely surrounded by lightweight lead metal, which nothing can penetrate.

- **Triple shield:** Pick three or more of the colors and layer them on top of yourself for complete protection.

ENTITY AND EARTHBOUND SPIRIT REMOVAL

Sensitive people sometimes unknowingly pick up hitchhiking spirits. This isn't possession, as the entity hasn't taken over control of you and your body. However, these spirits can interfere with your health and happiness.

Entities are thought-forms of fear, which have a life-form. They're products of the ego, not of love, so they don't really exist in truth. However, if we're in a period of time where we're really afraid, we can be affected by entity attachment.

Earthbound spirits are deceased humans who haven't gone to the light in the afterlife plane. Most of them don't realize they're dead. They're attached to Earth because of the addictions they had when they died; and they often hang around pubs, bars, and places where drugs are used to secure a vicarious high from living addicts.

Sometimes earthbound spirits are afraid to go to the afterlife plane because of hellfire and damnation beliefs. Other earthbound spirits are so attached to their homes that they don't want to leave. This is where ghosts come from. Earthbound spirits listen to living people instead of angels or ascended masters because these spirits think that they're alive.

Signs of having an entity or earthbound attachment include: manifesting a strong addiction, depression that doesn't respond to treatment, becoming accident-prone, an inability to focus or concentrate, and sudden changes in lifestyle or personality. Anyone can manifest an entity or earthbound attachment, and it's nothing to be afraid or ashamed of. It's just something that needs addressing.

There are many ways to release these entities:

— **Call for help.** Mentally or aloud, ask that any deceased people who love and care for the earthbound spirit come to help you. Ask these deceased people to come for the earthbound spirit and take him or her to the light. Usually, the earthbound's grandmother or grandfather will respond to this call and immediately take the spirit to the afterlife plane so that the spirit can evolve, heal, and grow.

— **Ask Archangel Michael.** Request that Archangel Michael remove the entities and earthbound from you, your loved ones, clients, and home. Then ask Archangel Michael to permanently stay by your side to act like a "bouncer" who ensures that no one gets near you unless they're supposed to, and that if they *are* near you, they come from a place of love. Remember that Michael, like all the archangels, has no time or space restrictions, so he's able to simultaneously and individually be with everyone who calls on him.

— **Cutting cords.** When an earthbound spirit is a deceased loved one, the living person may have cords to the spirit. The cord actually keeps the spirit leashed to the living person. An example would be a living woman whose abusive, alcoholic, deceased father hasn't yet gone to the light and is still attached to her. He may wish to make up for his previous behavior; however, he's not in a position to help her because he's unhealed. His presence is unconsciously depressing her. In these cases, call upon Archangel Michael to cut the cords to the spirit, while simultaneously being willing to release old anger, or a desire for revenge against the spirit.

— **Pulling and extracting entities.** This is a method to use on another person. First, shield yourself in a mirrored ball, and ask Michael and his band of mercy angels to accompany you. Then, pull the entity through the top of the crown chakra, like pulling a long, dark scarf. Give the entity to Archangel Michael, who will remove it from the room. Keep pulling out dark entities until the person is clear. Sometimes the entities will be difficult to pull out, like pulling a stubborn weed with a big root. Clear yourself and your hands afterward, and shield yourself with purple light and Archangel Michael's presence.

— **Chakra clearing.** My audiotape and CD called *Chakra Clearing* has an entity- and earthbound-clearing effect, since Archangel Michael was invoked by both myself and the musician, Randall Leonard. So, Michael's energy is doubly invoked on the soundtrack. Many people use *Chakra Clearing* like a bug bomb, leaving it to continuously play in a room with dark energy.

SEVERING VOWS

Sometimes vows that we've taken in past lives follow us into this life. Old vows of poverty can create financial troubles, celibacy vows can lead to sexual and relationship difficulties, and vows of self-denial can create self-sabotage tendencies. When we sever these vows, their negative effects are lifted and healed.

Here's how to sever old vows:

> *Get centered and quiet, breathing deeply. Mentally or verbally say, "I hereby sever any vows of poverty that I may have made in any lifetime. I ask that all effects of those vows of poverty be lifted and undone in all directions of time.*
>
> *"I hereby sever any vows of celibacy that I may have made in any lifetime. I ask that all effects of those vows of celibacy be lifted and undone in all directions of time.*
>
> *"I hereby sever any vows of self-denial that I may have made in any lifetime. I ask that all effects of those vows of self-denial be lifted and undone in all directions of time."*

SURROUNDING YOURSELF WITH ANGELS FOR A GOOD NIGHT'S SLEEP

As you're falling asleep, mentally ask that guardian angels be posted at each of your doors and windows, guarding and protecting you all night. Visualize yourself, your home, your loved ones, any worrisome situations, and the world surrounded with a thick layer of white light for protection. Then, see or feel Archangel Raphael giving you a blanket of green healing energy. Pull this blanket of green healing light over you, and feel your body completely relax. Sleep well!

WORKING WITH CRYSTALS

Crystals focus healing energy, and are helpful for boosting the light in your healing work. You can purchase crystals at metaphysical bookstores and gift shops, at many yoga studios, at gem and mineral shows, and over the Internet. Select your crystal intuitively, according to your attraction to its color and the way it makes you feel when you hold it. Hold the crystal near your third eye, and notice any tingling to see whether the crystal is alive and has a high life-force energy. Tired crystals won't produce any tingling as you hold them.

Clear your crystal of its previous energy as soon as you can following its acquisition. The best way to clear a crystal is by putting it in direct sunlight for two to four hours. Some people recommend soaking the crystal in saltwater; however, this can have a wearing effect on crystals.

Charge your crystal in moonlight, especially on the evening prior to the full moon. Even if clouds block the moonlight, its energy will still enter and charge your crystals.

Crystals are powerful when worn as jewelry, held in the hand, placed on areas of illness or injury or over the chakras, or put in the home. Many people enjoy sleeping with crystals on their nightstand or beneath the bed, while other people find this too stimulating for restful sleep.

Crystals can also be placed in bathwater to charge the healing energy of a bath. They also bring healing light to drinking water when placed inside the bottle or glass (be careful not to swallow the crystal, of course!).

Many New Age books offer more details about healing with crystals, and I have a book called *Crystal Therapy* (Hay House, Jan. 2005) but the best source of information is your own intuition and experience. Trust your inner wisdom; and enjoy working with the magical, living members of the mineral kingdom.

ANGEL COLOR READING

If you don't feel well, lie down and imagine yourself reclining on a cloud with many angels surrounding you. See or feel the angels combing their hands through your aura, eradicating any psychic debris. A few of the angels have crystalline flashlights that shine healing colors over your body. Notice which colors they're shining on you. Enjoy and absorb these colors with your breath. Allow yourself to be totally taken care of, and perhaps drift off to sleep for a while.

Afterward, recall the colors that the angels were shining upon you. These colors show what is imbalanced or needed in your life:

- **White:** Connect with your angels, both the earthly ones in your life and your celestial ones. Talk to them about your concerns, and accept their help and love.

- **Purple:** Pray, meditate, and take quiet time for yourself, away from noise and other people. Spending some time in a beautiful outdoor location listening to the sounds of nature would be very healing for you right now.

- **Violet:** You need to be listened to, trusted, and heard without judgment.

- **Dark blue:** Trust your intuition, and don't be dissuaded by other people's arguments.

- **Light blue:** Creativity is needed in your life right now, either your own artistic projects, or adding beauty to your environment by playing music or purchasing some new artwork.

- **Turquoise:** You need other people's support and help. Make sure that you're asking for help, and are delegating when you need to.

- **Emerald green:** Rest and sleep is needed right now, along with detoxification and purification of the diet and energy that you absorb.

- **Light green:** You need to be honest with yourself about your true feelings, without rationalizing, guilt, or fear.

- **Yellow:** Take care of a situation involving employment or school, as it's taking a toll on you and needs changing right away.

- **Orange:** You need to take care of your home environment to make it more livable, healing, and comfortable.

- **Pink:** You have a desire for love, affection, and hugs.

- **Red:** Release anger and worries to Heaven, as they're creating physical imbalances when you hold them inside your mind and body.

A combination of colors shows multiple needs and concerns, so they should each be addressed.

Crystal Selection Guide

Here are suggested crystals to use for various situations, body parts, or ailments. Hold or place the crystal near the affected area:

Abrasions:	Carnelian
Abundance, creating:	Jade; cinnabar; abundance quartz
Abuse issues, healing:	Iolite; spinel; smoky quartz
Aches:	Celestite; charoite
Acne:	Smithsonite; gemmy rhodonite; nontronite
Addictions:	Aventurine; barite; zeolite
AIDS:	Diaspor; petalite; dioptase
Alcoholism:	Nissonite; thalenite; smithsonite
Allergies:	Chrysocolla; zircon
Anorexia:	Moss agate; quartz with mica inclusions; rhodocrosite
Anxiety:	Lapis lazuli; smoky quartz; citrine
Appendicitis:	Citrine; carnelian
Appetite, decreasing:	Diaboleite; chlorite; moonstone
Appetite, increasing:	Epidote; unakite
Arthritis:	Copper; chrysocolla; engraved smoky quartz
Asthma:	Green tourmaline; rhodonite; macfallite
Astral travel:	Angelite; apophyllite; green calcite
Autism:	Tektite; gold
Back:	Blue calcite; golden topaz; martite
Backache:	Chrysocolla
Bladder:	Orange jasper; bloodstone; carnelian
Blood:	Bloodstone; carnelian; hematite
Blood pressure:	Dioptase; bloodstone; turquoise
Bones:	Calcite; howlite; gold tiger's-eye
Breast:	Peridot; pink snowball amethyst; bravoite

Breathing:	Amber; morganite
Broken bones:	Calcite; hematite; dioptase
Broken heart:	Rose quartz; pink topaz; malachite
Bronchitis:	Red jasper; pyrite; rutilated quartz
Bulimia:	Quartz with mica inclusions; ocho
Burns:	Iris agate; sodalite
Business, increasing:	Citrine; cinnabar; manifestation quartz
Calm feelings:	Rose quartz; blue lace agate; clear quartz
Cancer:	Sugilite; rhodocrosite; flame aura quartz
Cardiovascular ailments:	Eastonite
Change, dealing with:	Elestial smoky quartz; pink tourmaline; garnet
Childbirth:	Moonstone; ruby; jasper
Child conception:	Garnet; crocoite; coral
Circulation:	Ruby; citrine; pyrite
Clairaudience:	Phantom quartz
Clairsentience:	Smithsonite
Clairvoyance:	Amethyst; azurite; clear quartz
Colds:	Clear or purple fluorite; jamesonite
Colic:	Malachite; jade
Colon:	Amber; malachite; laguna agate
Coma:	Moldavite; tanzanite
Confidence, increasing:	Amazonite; aventurine; gold
Constipation:	Rhodochrosite
Cramps:	Celestite; smithsonite; moonstone
Dehydration:	Hancockite; waterfall quartz; flame aura quartz
Depression:	Azurite; kunzite; topaz
Diabetes:	Amethyst; owyhee jasper; malachite
Digestion:	Red jasper; gold calcite; citrine
Dog bite:	Dioptase; carnelian; amethyst
Dreams, remembering:	Herkimer diamond; smithsonite; rutilated quartz

Ears:	Amber; sapphire; blue fluorite
Emphysema:	Rhodonite; chrysocolla
Endometriosis:	Gem silica; chrysocolla
Energy, increasing:	Peridot; jasper; amber
Entity removal:	Serpentine; onyx; obsidian
Epilepsy:	Moldavite; jet
Eyes, health of:	Chalcedony; aquamarine; rhodocrosite
Eyesight:	Fluorite; emerald; rhodocrosite
Fallopian tubes:	Moonstone; chrysocolla
Fatigue:	Smoky quartz
Feet:	Jet; aquamarine; onyx
Fever:	Chrysocolla; blue lace agate
Fibromyalgia:	Aventurine; imperial topaz
Gallbladder:	Malachite; garnet; jasper
Genitals:	Red garnet; black obsidian; smoky quartz
Grief:	Obsidian; lapis lazuli; rose quartz
Hair:	Quartz; opal; malachite
Hands:	Faden quartz crystal; oligoclase; fersmannite
Headaches:	Blue lace agate; sugilite; amethyst
Hearing:	Sodalite; sapphire; lapis lazuli
Heart:	Dioptase; peridot; gold
Heartburn:	Fluorite
Hepatitis:	Sugilite; silver
Hiccups:	Red coral
Immune system:	Malachite; blue quartz; lepidolite
Impotency:	Verdite; padparadjah; garnet
Infection:	Galena; ruby; turquoise
Infertility:	Garnet; orange tourmaline
Inflammation:	Blue lace agate; blue fluorite
Injury/accident (preventing)**:**	Yellow carnelian; spinel; kunzite
Insect bites:	Lazulite; monazite
Insomnia:	Fluorite; lapis lazuli; sodalite
Itching:	Malachite; azurite; dolomite

Joints:	Dioptase; hematite; albite
Kidneys:	Honey calcite; carnelian; jade
Legs:	Dravite; jade; bloodstone
Leukemia:	Alexandrite; bloodstone
Life purpose:	Clear quartz; luvulite; emerald
Liver:	Azurite/malachite; peridot; rhodocrosite
Lungs:	Chrysocolla; dioptase; galena
Lupus:	Pink phantom
Lymph nodes:	Lemon opal; simpsonite; lazulite
Manic depression:	Lepidolite; kunzite
Memory:	Fire agate; amber; pyrite
Menopause:	Lapis lazuli; garnet; moonstone
Menstruation:	Smoky quartz; moonstone; dolomite
Migraines:	Jet; tourmaline; dioptase
Money issues:	Jade; cinnabar; citrine
Mouth:	Sodalite; mordenite; meliphane
Muscles:	Chalcopyrite; apatite; yoderite
Nails (fingers and toes):	Calcite; pearl; opal
Nightmares:	Chalcedony; rhodonite; amethyst
Nosebleed:	Hematite
Osteoporosis:	Green calcite
Ovaries:	Periclase; tiger's-eye; moonstone
Pain:	Boji Stone; sugilite; malachite
Pancreas:	Green moss agate; alexandrite; lodestone
Past lives:	Meteorite; amethyst; obsidian
Performance anxiety:	Red tiger's-eye; moonstone; aquamarine
Pineal gland:	Clear quartz; fluorite octahedron; zircon
Pituitary gland:	Lapis lazuli; fluorite; amethyst
Pregnancy:	Pearl; moonstone
Premenstrual syndrome:	Moonstone; hematite
Prostate:	Aurora borealis stone; osarizwaite; tetrahedrite

Rashes:	Asphaltum
Shock:	Hematite; moonstone
Shoulders:	Blue lace agate
Sinuses:	Sulphur stone; fluorite; eliat stone
Skin:	Azurite/malachite; conichalcite; zircon
Smoking:	Oregon amethyst; aventurine; barite
Sore throat:	Angelite; larimar
Speech:	Blue tourmaline; blue fluorite
Spine:	Labradorite; magnetite; jasper
Spleen:	Jade; apophyllite
Stomach:	Peridot; jasper
Stomach ulcer:	Rhodochrosite
Stress:	Azurite/malachite; Boji Stone; turquoise
Swelling:	Quartz
Teeth:	Fluorite; calcite; howlite
Tension:	Calcite; selenite
Throat:	Turquoise; tourmaline; amber
Thymus:	Aquamarine; cuprite; rhodocrosite
Thyroid:	Peridot; lapis lazuli; chrysocolla
Tongue:	Mordenite; whitlockite; sodalite
Tonsillitis:	Larimar; chalcedony
Tumor:	Malachite; blue kyanite
Veins:	Aquamarine; opal; snakeskin jasper
Ulcers:	Chrysocolla; gold tiger's-eye; pyrite
Urinary tract:	Amber; jade; citrine
Weight, decreasing:	Labradorite; picasso stone; serandite
Weight, increasing:	Epidote; unakite
Worrying:	Tangerine quartz; orange calcite

This crystal healing chart was created by Judith Lukomski and Rachelle Charman:

Judith Lukomski joyfully shares the connection of Heaven on Earth, working with the wisdom of the mineral kingdom and angelic realms. An intuitive since childhood, she has developed her gifts to assist those in search of change and growth. She is a gifted teacher, energy healer, life coach, and author.

Certified as a crystology master, Angel Therapy Practitioner, medium, and clinical hypnotist, Judith acts as a guide for those interested in personal evolution and expansion. Her publications include: *Gifts from Heaven: Practical Application of Crystal Energy, Questions about Quartz: A Guide to Crystalline Configurations,* and *Crystal Therapy* by Doreen Virtue and Judith Lukomski (Hay House, January 2005). Judith's Website is: **www.crystalfriends.net.**

* * *

Rachelle Charman is well known throughout Australia for her continual research and participation in seminars and work-shops in the field of personal development. She gives workshops about her two passions, angels and crystals. Rachelle is the head of the Angel Intuitive Mentor Group in Australia, where she supports almost 2,000 of her fellow Certified Angel Intuitives.

Rachelle has spent a lifetime researching and working with crystals, and has practical hands-on experience. The crystal healing methods Rachelle has discovered have assisted her, as well as many others, in releasing lifelong destructive patterns of addiction and abuse. To learn about Rachelle's workshops or sessions, please send an e-mail to: **white_light33@hotmail.com.**

AFTERWORD

Remember that you are light and love, and you have remarkable self-healing abilities. You are made in the image and likeness of the Creator, and you exhibit all of the perfect health, abundance, wisdom, and creativity of the Creator right now. Affirm that you're healthy, abundant, wise, and creative. Call upon your inner light and love to grow and expand.

May you enjoy the light upon, around, and within this earth. May you frequently send more light into the earth's ley lines, and surround the earth with healing white light. May you see and feel the light of God and the angels. May the light warm your heart, mind, and body.

May you be unafraid to give and receive love. May you know how lovable you truly are right now. May you know that you deserve the deepest love in all of your relationships. May you treat yourself with tender, loving care.

I'm sending you love and light in all ways!

BIBLIOGRAPHY

Albino, A.P.; Juan, G.; Traganos, F.; Reinhart, L.; Connolly, J.; Rose, D. P.; Darzynkiewicz, Z. Cell cycle arrest andapoptosis of melanoma cells by docosahexaenoic acid: Association with decreased pRb phosphorylation. *Cancer Res.* Aug. 1, 2000; 60(15): 4139–45.

Baker, B. P., et al. Pesticide residues in conventional, integrated pest management (ipm)—grown and organic foods: Insights from three US data sets. *Food Additive Contam.* May 2002; 19(5): 427–46.

Barger-Lux, M.; and Heaney, R. P. Effects of above average summer sun exposure on serum 25—hydroxyvitamin D and calcium absorption. *The Journal of Clinical Endocrinology & Metabolism.* 2002; 87(11): 4952–56.

Barnes V. A.; Bauza, L. B.; Treiber, F. A. Impact of stress reduction on negative school behavior in adolescents. *Health Qual Life Outcomes.* Apr. 23, 2003; 1(1): 10.

Bhattacharjee, C., et al. Do animals bite more during a full moon? Retrospective observational analysis. *BMJ.* Dec. 23, 2000; 321(7276): 1559–61.

Braden, G. *The God Code.* Carlsbad, CA: Hay House, Inc., 2004.

Byrd, R. C. Positive therapeutic effects of intercessory prayer in coronary unit population. *Archives of Internal Medicine.* June 23, 2003; 163(12): 1405–8.

Cha, K. Y., et al. Does prayer influence the success of in vitro fertilization-embreyo transfer? Report of a masked, randomized trial. *Reproductive Medicine.* Sept. 2001; 46(9): 781–7.

Crawford, L. Light needed: sunlight improves test scores. *Silver Chips Online News.* Oct. 7, 1999.

Curl, C. L., et al. Organophosphorus pesticide exposure of urban and suburban preschool children with organic and conventional diets. *Environ Health Perspect.* March 2003; 111(3): 377–82.

Davidson R. J.; Kabat-Zinn, J.; Schumacher, J.; Rosenkranz, M.; Muller, D.; Santorelli, S. F.; Urbanowski, F.; Harrington, A.; Bonus, K.; Sheridan, J. F. Alterations in brain and immune function produced by mindfulness meditation. *Psychosom Med*. July-Aug. 2003; 65(4): 564–70.

DeLorgeril, M., et al. Mediterranean alpha-linolenic acid-rich diet in secondary prevention of coronary heart disease. *Lancet*. 1994; 343: 1454–59.

Donnelly, I. *Atlantis: The Antediluvian World*. New York: Dover Publications, Inc., 1976.

Ebbesen, F.; Agati, G.; Pratesi, R. Phototherapy with turquoise versus blue light. *Arch Dis Child Fetal Neonatal Ed*. Sept. 2003; 88(5): F430–1.

El-Hajj Fuleihan, G.; and Deeb, M. Hypovitaminosis D in a sunny country (correspondence). *The New England Journal of Medicine*. June 10, 1999; 340(23): 1840–1.

English, D. R. Sunlight and cancer. *Cancer Causes Control*. May 1997; 8(3): 271–83.

Farmer, S. D. *Sacred Ceremony: How to Create Ceremonies for Healing, Transition, and Celebrations*. Carlsbad, CA: Hay House, Inc., 2002.

Flannery, M. Guardian angels? Terminally ill boy claimed he saw them; do photos bear him out? *ABCNEWS.com*. July 19, 2003.

Freedman, D. M., et al. Sunlight and mortality from breast, ovarian, colon, prostate, and non-melanoma skin cancer: A composite death certificate based case-control study. *Occupational Environmental Medicine*. Apr. 1, 2002; 59(4): 257–62.

Freeman, K. *The Pre-Socratic Philosophers*. Oxford University Press, 1946.

Giasson, M.; and Bouchard L. Effect of therapeutic touch on the well-being of persons with terminal cancer. *Holistic Nursing*. Sept. 1998; 16(3): 383–98.

Glerup, H., et al. Commonly recommended daily intake of vitamin D is not sufficient if sunlight exposure is limited. *Journal of Internal Medicine*. Feb. 1, 2000; 247(2): 260–8.

Gloth, F. M. III, et al. Vitamin D deficiency in homebound elderly persons. *Journal of the American Medical Association*. Dec. 6, 1995: 274 (21).

Goodyear-Smith, R. Health and safety issues pertaining to genetically modified foods. *Aust N Z J Public Health*. Aug. 2001; 25(4): 371–5.

Gorham, E. D., et al. Sunlight and breast cancer incidence in the USSR. *International Journal of Epidemiology*. Dec 1, 1990; 19(4): 820–4.

Hall, J. *The Crystal Bible: A Definitive Guide to Crystals*. Hampshire, Great Britain: Godsfield Press, Ltd., 2003.

Harris, W. S., et al. A randomized, controlled trial of the effects of remote, intercessory prayer on outcomes in patients admitted to the coronary care unit. *Archives of Internal Medicine*. June 26, 2000; 160(12): 1878.

Heraclides of Pontus [fr. 89 Wehrli] in Diogenes Laertius. *Lives of Eminent Philosophers* 8.4–5.

Hirsch, R. J.; Shalita, A. R. Lasers, light, and acne. *Cutis.* May 2003; 71(5): 353–4.

Hobday, R. *The Healing Sun.* Forres, Scotland: Findhorn Press, 1999.

Hu, F. B., The Mediterranean diet and mortality—olive oil and beyond. *The New England Journal of Medicine.* June 26, 2003; 348(26): 2595–96.

Iwao, M.; Kajiyama, S.; Mori, H.; Oogaki, K. Effects of qigong walking on diabetic patients: A pilot study. *J Altern Complement Med.* Aug. 1999; 5(4): 353–8.

Jones, G.; and Dwyer, T. Bone mass in prepubertal children: Gender differences and the role of physical activity and sunlight exposure. *Journal of Clinical Endocrinology Metabolism.* Dec. 1, 1998; 83(12): 4274–9.

Jowett, B. *Selected Dialogues of Plato: The Benjamin Jowett Translation.* Modern Library Classics, 2001.

Kime, Z. R. *Sunlight.* Penryn, CA: World Health Publications, 1980.

Law, S. P. The regulation of menstrual cycle and its relationship to the moon, *Acta Obstet Gynecol Scand*, January 1, 1986; 65(1): 45–8.

Lefkowitz, E. S.; and Garland, C. F. Sunlight, vitamin D, and ovarian cancer mortality rates in US women. *International Journal of Epidemiology.* Dec. 1994; 23(6): 1133–6.

Lei, X. F.; Bi, A. H.; Zhang, Z. X.; Cheng, Z. Y. The antitumor effects of qigong-emitted external qi and its influence on the immunologic functions of tumor-bearing mice. *J Tongji Med Univ.* 1991; 11(4): 253–6.

Leibovici, L. Effects of remote, retroactive intercessory prayer on outcomes in patients with bloodstream infection: randomised controlled trial. *BMJ,* Dec. 22, 2001; 323(7327): 1450–1.

Li, M.; Chen, K.; Mo, Z. Use of qigong therapy in the detoxification of heroin addicts. *Altern Ther Health Med.* Jan-Feb. 2002; 8(1): 50–4, 56–9.

Liberman, J. *Light: Medicine of the Future.* Rochester, VT: Bear & Company, 1991.

Lim, Y. A.; Boone, T.; Flarity, J. R.; Thompson, W.R. Effects of qigong on cardiorespiratory changes: a preliminary study. *Am J Chin Med.* 1993; 21(1): 1–6.

Matthews, D. A., et al. Effects of intercessory prayer on patients with rheumatoid arthritis. *Southern Medical Journal.* Dec. 2000; 93(12): 1177–86.

Mediterranean diet could help Asians. *BBC News.* Nov, 8, 2002.

Melody, A., *Love is in the Earth: A Kaleidoscope of Crystals.* 1995, Earth Love Publishing House.

Narby, L. *Cosmic Serpent: DNA and the Origins of Knowledge*. Los Angeles: J. P. Tarcher, 1999.

Nelemans, P. J., et al. An addition to the controversy on sunlight exposure and melanoma risk: A meta-analytical approach. *Journal of Clinical Epidemiology*. Nov. 1, 1995; 48(11): 1331–42.

Olson, K.; Hanson, J. Using Reiki to manage pain: a preliminary report. *Cancer Prev Control*. June 1997; 1(2): 108–13.

Pellegrino-Estrich, R. *The Power to Heal: A Concise and Comprehensive Guide to Energy Healing*. Brazil: Grafica Terra Ltda., 2003.

Podolsky, D. A new age of healing hands. *U.S. News & World Report*. Feb. 5, 1996; pp. 71, 74.

Prochaska, L. J. Effects of food processing on the thermodynamic and nutritive value of foods: Literature and database survey. *Med Hypotheses*. Feb. 2000; 54(2): 254–62.

Raphaell, K., *Crystal Healing: The Therapeutic Application of Crystals and Stones*. 1991, Aurora Press.

Salamone, L. M., et al. Contributions of vitamin D intake and seasonal sunlight exposure to plasma 25—hydroxyvitamin D concentration in elderly women. *American Journal of Clinical Nutrition*. Jan. 1, 1994; 59(1): 80–6.

Salih, F. M. Can sunlight replace phototherapy units in the treatment of neonatal jaundice? An in-vitro study. *Photodermatol Photoimmunol Photomed*. Dec. 1, 2001; 17(6): 272–7.

Schilter, B., et al. Limits for pesticide residues in infant foods: A safety-based proposal. *Regul Toxicol Pharmacol*. Oct. 1996; 24(2 Pt 1): 126–40.

Smith, D. W.; Arnstein, P.; Rosa, K. C.; Wells-Federman, C. Effects of integrating therapeutic touch into a cognitive behavioral pain treatment program. Report of a pilot clinical trial. *J Holist Nurs*. Dec. 2002; 20(4): 367–87.

Smith, H. Truly ancient Greeks! *The [London] Observer*. August 29, 1999.

Studzinski, G. P.; and Moore, D. C. Sunlight—can it prevent as well as cause cancer? *Cancer Research*. Sept. 15, 1995; 55(18): 4014–22.

Thomas, M. K., et al. Hypovitaminosis D in medical inpatients. *The New England Journal of Medicine*. March 19, 1998; 338(12): 777–783.

Tloczynski, J.; and Fritzsch, S. Intercessory prayer in psychological well-being: using a multiple-baseline across-subjects design. *Psychology Rep*. Dec. 1, 2002; 91(3 Pt 1): 731–41.

Trichopoulou, A., et al. Adherence to a Mediterranean diet and survival in a Greek population. *The New England Journal of Medicine*. June 26, 2003; 348(26): 2599–2608.

Trivedi, B. P. Can Earth be powered by energy beamed from the moon? *National Geographic Today.* Apr. 26, 2002.

Turner, J. G.; Clark, A. J.; Gauthier, D. K.; Williams, M. The effect of therapeutic touch on pain and anxiety in burn patients. *J Adv Nurs.* July 1998; 28(1): 10–20.

Waldie, K. E. The effects of pre- and post-natal sunlight exposure on human growth: Evidence from the Southern Hemisphere. *Early Human Development.* Nov. 1, 2000; 60(1): 35–42.

Wang, C. X.; and Xu, D. H. The beneficial effect of qigong on the ventricular function and microcirculation in deficiency of heart-energy hypertensive patients [Article in Chinese; translated]. *Zhong Xi Yi Jie He Za Zhi.* Nov. 1991; 11(11): 659–60, 644.

———. Influence of qigong therapy upon serum HDL-C in hypertensive patients [Article in Chinese; translated]. *Zhong Xi Yi Jie He Za Zhi.* Sept. 1989; 9(9): 543–4, 516.

Wardell, D. W; and Engebretson, J. Biological correlates of Reiki Touch[SM] healing. *J Adv Nurs.* Feb. 2001; 33(4): 439–45.

Waterfield, R. *The First Philosophers: The Presocratics and Sophists.* Oxford University Press, 2000.

Wolverton, B. C. *How to Grow Fresh Air: Fifty Houseplants That Purify Your Home or Office.* New York: Penguin Putnam, Inc., 1996.

Worthington, V. Nutritional quality of organic versus conventional fruits, vegetables, and grains. *Journal of Complementary Medicine,* April 2001; 7(2): 161–73.

Wu, W. H.; Bandilla, E.; Ciccone, D. S.; Yang, J.; Cheng, S. C.; Carner, N.; Wu, Y.; Shen, R. Effects of qigong on late-stage complex regional pain syndrome. *Altern Ther Health Med.* Jan. 1999; 5(1): 45–54.

Yu, T.; Tsai, H. L.; Hwang, M. L. Suppressing tumor progression of in vitro prostate cancer cells by emitted psychosomatic power through Zen meditation. *Am J Chin Med.* 2003; 31(3): 499–507.

ABOUT THE AUTHOR

Doreen Virtue, Ph.D., is a fourth-generation metaphysician and the daughter of a Christian Science practitioner. Growing up, she witnessed many healing miracles, as her family used prayer and visualization to heal everything from skinned knees to their family automobile.

Doreen is the author of the *Healing with the Angels* book and oracle cards; *Archangels & Ascended Masters;* and *Angel Therapy,* among other books, cards, and audio programs. Her *Messages from Your Angels Oracle Card* deck was the #1 bestselling nonfiction work in Australia in 2002.

A lifelong clairvoyant who works with the angelic, elemental, and ascended-master realms, Doreen holds Ph.D., M.A., and B.A. university degrees in counseling psychology, and is a former director of inpatient and outpatient psychiatric facilities at various hospitals.

Doreen has appeared on *Oprah*, CNN, *The View,* and other television and radio programs. For more information on Doreen and the workshops that she presents throughout the world, to subscribe to Doreen's free e-mail angel messages newsletter, to visit her message boards, or to submit your angel healing stories, please visit **www.AngelTherapy.com**.

Hay House Titles of Related Interest

Books

AFTER LIFE: *Answers from the Other Side,* by John Edward

BORN KNOWING: *A Medium's Journey—Accepting and Embracing My Spiritual Gifts,* by John Holland, with Cindy Pearlman

THE GOD CODE: *The Secret of Our Past, the Promise of Our Future,* by Gregg Braden

THE JOURNEY TO THE SACRED GARDEN: *A Guide to Traveling in the Spiritual Realms* (a book-with-CD), by Hank Wesselman, Ph.D.

MIRRORS OF TIME: *Using Regression for Physical, Emotional, and Spiritual Healing* (a book-with-CD), by Brian L. Weiss, M.D.

POWER ANIMALS: *How to Connect with Your Animal Spirit Guides* (a book-with-CD), by Steven D. Farmer, Ph.D.

SACRED CEREMONY: *How to Create Ceremonies for Healing, Transitions, and Celebrations,* by Steven D. Farmer, Ph.D.

SPIRIT MESSENGER: *The Remarkable Story of a Seventh Son of a Seventh Son,* by Gordon Smith

SYLVIA BROWNE'S BOOK OF ANGELS, by Sylvia Browne

TRUST YOUR VIBES: *Secret Tools for Six-Sensory Living,* by Sonia Choquette

Card Decks

COMFORT CARDS, by Max Lucado

HEALING CARDS, by Caroline Myss and Peter Occhiogrosso

HEALING THE MIND AND SPIRIT CARDS, by Brian L. Weiss, M.D.

HEALTHY BODY CARDS, by Louise L. Hay

THE PRAYER OF JABEZ™ CARDS, by Bruce Wilkinson

All of the above are available at your local bookstore,
or may be ordered by visiting:
Hay House USA: **www.hayhouse.com**
Hay House Australia: **www.hayhouse.com.au**
Hay House UK: **www.hayhouse.co.uk**
Hay House South Africa: **orders@psdprom.co.za**

We hope you enjoyed this Hay House book.
If you would like to receive a free catalog featuring
additional Hay House books and products,
or if you would like information about the
Hay Foundation, please contact:

Hay House, Inc.
P.O. Box 5100
Carlsbad, CA 92018-5100

(760) 431-7695 or **(800) 654-5126**
(760) 431-6948 (fax) or **(800) 650-5115 (fax)**
www.hayhouse.com

Published and distributed in Australia by:
Hay House Australia, Ltd. • 18/36 Ralph St.
Alexandria NSW 2015 • *Phone*: 612-9669-4299
Fax: 612-9669-4144 • www.hayhouse.com.au

Published and distributed in the United Kingdom by:
Hay House UK, Ltd. • Unit 62, Canalot Studios
222 Kensal Rd., London W10 5BN • *Phone*: 44-20-8962-1230
Fax: 44-020-8962-1239 • www.hayhouse.co.uk

Published and distributed in the Republic of South Africa by:
Hay House SA (Pty), Ltd., P.O. Box 990, Witkoppen 2068
Phone/Fax: 2711-7012233 • orders@psdprom.co.za

Distributed in Canada by: Raincoast,
9050 Shaughnessy St., Vancouver, B.C. V6P 6E5
Phone: (604) 323-7100 • *Fax*: (604) 323-2600

Sign up via the Hay House USA Website to receive the
Hay House online newsletter and stay informed about what's
going on with your favorite authors. You'll receive bimonthly
announcements about: Discounts and Offers, Special Events,
Product Highlights, Free Excerpts, Giveaways, and more!